6-Hour Safety Culture

How to Sustainably Reduce Human Error and Risk
(and do what training alone can't (possibly) do)

Tim Autrey

Human Performance Association, Inc.

Cheyenne, Wyoming

Published by:

Human Performance Association, Inc.

1712 Pioneer Avenue Suite 1166
Cheyenne, Wyoming 82001 USA

The author has made every effort to provide accurate contact information and Internet addresses at the time of publication. Neither the publisher nor the author assumes any responsibility for errors or for changes that occur after publication. Further the publisher does not have any control over and does not assume any responsibility for author or third-party websites or their content.

Autrey, Tim

6-Hour Safety Culture: How to Sustainably Reduce Human Error and Risk (and do what training alone can't (possibly) do)

Includes bibliographical information

ISBN: 978-0-9964098-1-0

http://www.6hoursafetyculture.com

The Human Performance Association, Inc. (HPA) is an international not-for-profit collaboration of next-level thought leaders and practitioners in the fields of human behavior, error reduction, culture transformation, safety, quality, instructional technology, and performance improvement. Its members are wholly dedicated to making the world a better, safer, and more productive place.
http://www.hpaweb.org

Contents

To my hero, Ray Autrey (my Dad), for always believing in me and daily demonstrating an exceptionally well-lived life.

To my Mom, Thelma Autrey, for continually reinforcing that we can be anything we want in life.

To my wonderful wife, partner, and very best friend, Suzette, the most amazing woman I have ever known, with whom I am so blessed to experience the incredible adventures of life.

To the magnificent members of the PPI Team, the finest most impactful culture-transforming professionals on the planet.

Introduction

In the early 19th century, mothers giving birth in hospitals averaged 25% mortality (one out of four didn't make it). This was average. At times, death rates reached 100%. Puerperal Fever was the culprit, caused by infection. You think we would have learned. In 2014, the leading cause of accidental death in the US is medical error, a large percentage of which result in infections...in hospitals. One Texas healthcare system, however, has apparently 'cracked the code' in stopping such errors. Since 2010, several of their hospitals have gone years without a single case of ventilator-assisted pneumonia or central line associated bloodstream infection.[1]

In 2009, a large 25-year-old coal-powered electrical generating station in rural Texas had (8) safety incidents reaching the OSHA Recordable level. For a station with a site population of approximately 285 bargaining unit employees, this was an abysmal safety record. In the fall of that year, the team at that station learned (and implemented) a simple process and approach for minimizing human error. In 2010 they had zero OSHA Recordable safety incidents. They went on to set station and unit operating history records in safety, reliability, and profitability.

In an era where it seems to be 'normal' for US airlines to declare bankruptcy, to re-organize, and to merge with other airlines to stay afloat, there is one company that is consistently rated at or near the top in virtually every category. From its inception, this organization had a priority focus 'upside down' from normal business philosophy. Today, the cost to take a ride on one of its planes are some of the lowest. It doesn't charge fees for checking baggage or changing your travel plans. It has the largest / most modern fleet of 737s on the planet, and is, incidentally, one of the most profitable airlines in US history.

- Zero infections when most hospitals just can't seem to make a dent in medical error

- Transformation of an entire Safety Culture within a few months
- An 'upside down' business model that sets records in virtually every category

How did they do it? Through simple focus upon the 'ultimate frontier' in performance- *human performance*.

---

[1] http://www.memorialhermann.org/about-us/quality-report-high-reliability-healthcare/

Prologue

Twenty years ago, I was speaking across North America on how rapidly *change* was accelerating. What I spoke of during those days *long* ago is now ancient history. Think about it. In 1995, how many of us even had an email account (let alone being able to "Google" something)? Today our world (including our workplaces) is transforming at a mind-numbing rate.

One thing I've said for many years is, "If you're not growing, you're dying. There is no standing still." In all things subject to the forces of nature, including human beings and the businesses we run, this has always been (and always will be) absolute truth. It's just faster now.

With the proliferation of technology and global connection, the need to learn and grow has never been as extreme as it is today, and quite honestly, it'll be even more extreme when we wake up tomorrow morning. This puts all of us in a very interesting place.

My work, the work of our company, The Practicing Perfection Institute, Inc. (PPI), and the recently formed Human Performance Association (HPA) (http://www.hpaweb.org) focus on human performance- *why* people do *what* they do the *way* they do it. Since 2005, we've worked with tens of thousands of employees around the globe, helping some of the largest organizations on the planet reduce error, improve safety, elevate overall quality and reliability, and ultimately, increase profitability. All of this while workers simultaneously acquire a greater sense of contribution, ownership, and self-fulfillment. A huge win for everyone involved.

There has never been a more results-oriented environment in the history of the planet than that in which we are working today. Transparency, integrity, simplicity, sustainability- such are the watch words of our current business environments. There's no place to run, no place to hide. You either innovate and produce, or someone else will- thereby taking your place (whether it's your personal job we're talking about or your entire organization's position in your marketplace). This environment is scary and worrisome for those who long for the "good olde days"; exciting and filled with opportunity for those of us who embrace it. As Valentine said in Tom Stoppard's play *Arcadia*, "*It's the best possible time to be alive, when almost everything you thought you knew is wrong.*"

As in virtually every field, the amount of learning and information accumulation relative to *human performance* continues to grow in both volume and complexity. As one who is either running a business, or has direct responsibility for improving some aspect of its performance, your job is to separate the "wheat from the chaff", and then, to transform science and discovery into actionable strategies and tactics that produce results.

Until now, most performance improvement efforts have been long, drawn out, tedious, expensive, and have typically produced results that leave organizations looking for the "next thing". This is why we've done our best in PPI (and I will do my best in this book) to provide you with, as Oliver Wendell Holmes put it, "simplicity on the far side of complexity."

6-Hour Safety Culture offers a journey, from understanding, to strategy, to actionable tactics, into how to sustainably take the performance of your organization to its next level.

The promises of what human performance can offer, not only to the benefit of enterprise, but to the wellbeing of all of the *humans* involved, is unlimited. As the technology of things continues its rapid march onward, so is it time to recognize and advance the potential of *human performance*. That's what this book is all about.

Welcome to the future of performance improvement.

Tim Autrey

February, 2015

Why This Book / Why Now

> *"It was the best of times, it was the worst of times, it was the age of wisdom, it was the age of foolishness..."* - Charles Dickens

The words used by Charles Dickens to describe the conditions in London and Paris amidst the turmoil of the French Revolution in his classic, <u>A Tale of Two Cities</u>, offer a perfect description of our world of business in 2015.

In truth, there has never been a more exciting time than right now to be in business, or to be working to improve performance within a business. The rapidly changing landscape poses massive turmoil and risk; however for those who recognize and seize the incessantly rising opportunities, times have never been better.

This book is about reducing human error and managing risk. It's about elevating human performance and developing a true, honest, and self-sustaining culture; a culture of safety, justice, and Viral Accountability®. While not directly about *external* business strategy, there has never been a time when the *internal strategies* we will be discussing have been more timely or more critical. Combined with intelligent external vision and marketplace action, organizations (and the people within them) who 'get it', and are successful *internally*, will not only thrive, they will dominate their respective arenas. Those who are not, will cease to exist.

To put this "survival" and "opportunity" into perspective, according to research done at the Babson School of Business, ten years from now more than 40 percent of today's top companies will no longer exist (lack of survival)[1]. By 2020, according to Yale professor Richard Foster, more than three fourths of the S&P 500 will be companies we've not yet heard of (massive opportunity).[2]

Upon which side of the threshold will you / your organization fall?

Reality is reality, or as I've heard my sister, Judy, so often say, "It is what it is."

Should You Read This Book?

I have written this book to share what we have learned over the past ten years of incorporating next-level human performance strategies and tools amongst tens of thousands of workers around the globe. What we have discovered about workers...about people...has been eye opening, truly enlightening, and filled with promise for the future. The possibilities for those who will grasp what I'm sharing in these pages, run with it, and continue to improve upon it are virtually limitless.

Specifically, if you are...

Business Leaders / Owners

A business leader or owner who is challenged/frustrated with the "human element" in your company and have come to the conclusion that there simply MUST be a better way...

Safety Professionals

A Safety Professional who is frustrated with (1) lack of tangible progress in improvement of your OSHA Recordable Rate, (2) having reached a 'plateau' in performance after implementing other programs designed to enhance safety, (3) concerned about the direction that senior leadership is taking on the concept of "Safety Culture", and/or (4) are looking for the "hidden answer" in how to get workers to not only take full responsibility for their own safety, but for that of their co-workers as well...

Human Performance / "Center for Excellence" Managers and Coordinators

A human performance / human error reduction manager or coordinator, or are involved in leading your organization's "pursuit of excellence" and have come to recognize that more prescriptiveness, more rules, more compliance, more slogans, and more databases are NOT the answer to taking your performance to its next level...

LEAN / Six Sigma Professionals

A LEAN / Six Sigma professional who is struggling with worker engagement, recognizes that the concept of "defects" goes much deeper and broader than those currently being targeted on the 'backend', and is looking for the "missing link" in your performance/quality improvement regimen...

Risk Managers

An individual charged with minimizing risk and dealing the burgeoning regulations, and recognize that it is going to take a "one team" effort to be successful into the future; that the only way to sustainably minimize risk is to have your entire team/organization aware, onboard, and committed to successful outcomes with a sense of personal ownership...

Enlightened "Leaders"

A "leader" at any level, within any position or job title, who recognizes that people come to work wanting to do a good job, that the people who do the work are the ones who have the answers, and that therein lies tremendous opportunity for your personal contribution as an influencer, as well as a leveraged opportunity for your organization...

This next-level approach to human performance is evolving as a movement; as a way to help make the world a better and safer place (through the workplace). This book, quite simply, is for those who want to, as Steve Jobs said, "...put [their own] dent in the universe."

The Back Story

Three Strikes and You're [supposed to be] Out

"I never planned on a lifelong commitment to reducing human error. It chased after me."
-Tim Autrey

Ever been fast, overconfident, and "invincible"? That was me. I grew up in California, which has a "three strikes you're out" policy. Fortunately, I was given a fourth chance. I never planned on a lifelong commitment to reducing human error. It chased after me.

At 20, I was qualifying as a Navy nuclear operator in upstate New York. Someone left the access cover to the lower level Reactor Compartment latched open, leaving a 36-inch hole in the narrow walkway. It was hot in there. I was doing my best to focus on the Steam Generator instruments across the room as my instructor pointed them out. He stepped over the hole. I did not. Though I have no memory of the falling part, I [miraculously] got my arms out to catch myself. In an instant, I was hanging 20 feet above a tangle of stainless steel piping, pumps and valves. The scars have faded. The memory has not. I was lucky. Strike One.

Seventeen months later, I was still in upstate New York. What remains crystal clear in my brain is the gut-wrenching impact sound, THUD, followed by life-in-slow-motion as my metallic green Firebird careened backward into the ditch. It wasn't supposed to snow in April. I was late for work. The guy in front of me was c-r-a-w-l-i-n-g along. It's totally NOT okay to be late for work in the military. I had to pass him.

It was head-on. Completely my fault. Fortunately, the only deaths were my brand new Firebird and her 1963 Buick. She wasn't injured because she was driving a tank. I wasn't wearing my seatbelt. My head almost went through the windshield…but it didn't. I was really lucky. Strike two.

I moved on to my shipboard assignment in 1980- the USS Ohio (SSBN-726). Construction of the boat was finishing up in Groton, Connecticut. It was the first Trident submarine; Admiral Rickover's dream and one of our country's linchpin deterrents in the Cold War. As crewmembers, we were proud to be "first of the class", proud to be important.

You'd think by now I would have learned to be safe. I'm down in the lower level in the Feedwater Bay. Standing on steel decking. Nothing but steel piping and electrical conduit all around. There was a shipyard worker grinding a weld outboard on the port (left) side. He and his fire watch (the guy stationed with the fire extinguisher in case sparks from the grinder caught something on fire) were engaging in colorful banter about the blonde waitress from last night's bender.

I had to take some quick voltage readings inside the Feedwater Control Panel before I could go home. While maneuvering the probes attached to my multi-meter, the index finger knuckle on my left hand contacted a live 450-volt terminal lug. My right hand was resting against the inside of the metal cabinet. If you know much about electrical shock, you know that this was a recipe for Tim Autrey to be dead. Fortunately, rather than seizing in position, the surge knocked my knuckle away from its contact. Because of this, I'm able to write these words. I was incredibly lucky. Strike three.

Over a Year Underwater

Two football fields long and 42-feet in diameter. That was the USS Ohio (SSBN-726). During our time in the shipyard, they had the "escape hatches" removed, leaving large openings in the top of the ship in three places. As construction came to completion, the hatches were installed. The day came for our first "fast cruise", which is where you seal the ship up like you're underway, and you "play" like you're at sea. It's a training exercise.

I'll never forget the feeling I had standing under the (now closed and sealed) escape hatch just aft of Maneuvering (the Engine Room "control room"). Yesterday there had been blue sky on the other side. Soon, I'd be standing in that same spot under hundreds of feet of very cold ocean.

A submarine on patrol is an interesting environment. You make your own oxygen, you filter your own air. You only get to see, talk to, and interact with the same 160 people for almost three months. When I was making patrols, we had no direct contact with family back home. The biggest challenge was mental. Each dealt with it in his own way. Most did okay. Some did not. There was the guy who adopted a pet rope. The guy who stopped talking (completely). Then there was the guy who decided it was time to leave the submarine from several hundred feet under water. Fortunately he was stopped before he was able to effect his exit.

I learned a ton about human behavior during my four patrols. I also learned how quickly things can head in a really bad direction, whether due to poor judgment, lack of having the "big picture" or flat out human error. Sometimes bad things happen. Other times you get lucky. There was one thing I'd figured out- once you make a choice, once you take a step, once you turn a switch, an instant of poor judgment or not paying attention, and things can go immediately drastically wrong. I knew this, but even though I was a three-time survivor, I apparently still had some learnin' to do.

This Time I "Got It"

During the Cold War, there were two crews on our submarine, the "blue" crew and the "gold" crew. This allowed the boat to be on location most of the time, fulfilling its mission of deterring the Soviets from considering use of their nuclear missiles.

Each at-sea cycle was called a "patrol". These consisted of taking the boat to a top secret location and then maneuvering in giant circles for almost three months. I did four of these.

At the end of each patrol, "Station the Maneuvering Watch" was the announcement everyone waited to hear. It meant that we were mere hours from docking alongside our home pier, where many of us had families anxiously awaiting. It took a few days to turn the boat over to the other crew, after which, we helped them get the boat ready for their turn at sea. This period was called "refit". It was during one of these refit periods that I experienced my "Fourth Strike".

I was the most senior electrician in the division. Well liked. Well respected. I had substantial experience and a good reputation. I was working with Patrick "T" Ferentz. The "T" stood for "Trash-mouth". He was our second-senior electrician. We had tons of experience between the two of us, especially at the job in which we were engaged.

On the Ohio, we had two large Ship's Service Motor-Generators (SSMGs). During normal operation they kept the ship's battery charged. If normal AC power was lost, the motor-generators automatically pulled DC power from the battery to maintain power to the ship's vital electrical loads. From a safety perspective, these were two [very] vital pieces of equipment.

It was four days before we were to get underway. Trash-mouth and I were cleaning carbon dust out of the port motor-generator. This was a job that had to be done often. We would remove the access covers, hook up a ventilation rig that Pat had designed, and blow, suck, and wipe until we had removed a sufficient amount of the carbon dust.

Just inside the access cover on the inboard side was a wire, secured with a bolt to the DC bus bars. We had to remove this bolt to get the wire out of our way every time we did the cleaning.

Because we had done this so many times, the threading in the bolt hole had become worn. Once we had completed our cleaning, it was time to put things back together. Neither Pat nor I were happy with the worn bolt hole. Just five inches above, on an [apparently] identical piece of bus work, was a threaded hole of identical size. We agreed that the worn hole would eventually become a problem. It was easy to attach the wire to the new location.

The final step of the process was to "burnish the commutator". This involved taking a tightly wrapped roll of canvas and running it back and forth across the spinning commutator as the motor-generator was started up. This roll of canvas was about 16 inches in length, tightly wrapped to about two inches in diameter, and secured with "EB Green" (our version of duct tape). As was typical in the military, we had a name for it. It started with "horse".

At the time, we had a Master Chief Electrician onboard. His nickname was "Andy". He was the "Chief of the Boat" (the most senior enlisted person onboard). He didn't do any actual electrical work anymore (or any "work" at all as best as we could tell). On this day, however, he wanted to be the one to "burnish the commutator".

When Trash-mouth and I were ready, we removed the Danger Tags and were ready to have the motor-generator restarted by the Electrical Operator in Maneuvering.

When Andy arrived in Engine Room Middle Level, we handed him the "horse----". He positioned himself into the access port on the inboard side of the machine. We called Maneuvering and told them we were ready. The motor-generator began to rotate. It accelerated, and accelerated, until the overspeed device tripped it offline. At the instant it tripped, an electrical flash shot out of the open access port. Andy jumped back. He was pissed. Fortunately, he wasn't hurt. But for the sake of the overspeed device and a tremendous amount of luck, I had been spared…again. Strike Four.

By moving the lead from one bolt hole to another, we bypassed the series field of the giant DC motor. It had no speed control. It's a miracle that Andy wasn't hurt or killed. Had the over-speed device not worked, the motor-generator would have self-destructed. Millions of dollars of damage would have occurred. The mission of the Ohio, at the time an integral player in our Cold War deterrence strategy, would have been dead in the water. This time…I got it.

I became my own poster child for safety, situational awareness, and thoughtful engagement. Because of my "people skills" I was able to influence others to do likewise. Not because they were forced to, but because they *wanted* to. In 1984 I was honored as "Sailor of the Year".

Too Much of a "Good Thing"

In 1986 I began my career in the commercial nuclear generation industry. I started in training, worked at several plants both as a contractor and as plant staff member, and filled several roles as my career progressed. At the time, productivity and effectiveness seemed to be measured by the pound (of documentation). This was before today's correctness of being "green". We printed everything. The taller the stack of paper, the higher the perceived value. It was a standing joke- one without humor.

As leaders, most of our energies were consumed battling a mind-numbing barrage of government regulation (consider the aftermaths of Three Mile Island, Chernobyl, and Davis Besse), HR lawyers, insurance requirements, and industry "guidelines" (aka rules). All of these things, of course, in the interest of being "better".

Somehow our entire industry had latched onto the idea that "more" would indeed make things...better. More regulation. More rules. More prescriptiveness. After all, we were still having to write letters to the families of injured or dead workers. Human errors continued to cause frustration, fines and embarrassment. The consequences and fallout of mistakes continued to cost us a ton of money.

Surely, if we just added another procedure, another requirement, another stop-and-check point, things would improve. Somehow we thought doing more of the same would generate different results.

"I have an idea"

The US commercial nuclear industry was several years beyond the Three Mile Island Accident when I landed my first job as a contract operations instructor. The massive ramp up of regulation and oversight was well underway.

The awareness and insight that I had honed after my Fourth Strike in the Navy proved a tremendous asset. Over the next 17 years, I moved around and up within the industry. I became a licensed Senior Reactor Operator, a Shift Technical Advisor, and held a rising sequence of management and leadership positions.

This was an exciting time to be involved in "human performance". Starting in the early nineties, the industry pumped tons of resources into the reduction of human error. With ever-increasing oversight from the regulator, and lots of thumb-screw-tightening by INPO, the industry drove human error rates to much lower levels. It wasn't a fun environment, but it had been very effective…to a point.

"Command and control", while necessary and appropriate in times of acute crisis, stifles the human spirit when continuously applied. Under such conditions, "compliance" is the best you'll ever get, and even then, typically only when the "management police" are around to monitor and enforce.

Because of the stringent industry requirements, the nuclear industry had become staffed with and lead by a lot of really smart (IQ) people. By the early 2000s however, the prescriptive controlling environment had begun to take its toll. Being a champion of human nature and human possibility, I found it increasingly hard to 'toe the line'. I survived by flying under the radar. I made the working environments within my sphere of influence as open and pleasant as possible. I offered as much latitude and recognition for creativity and contribution as I could get away with. From time to time, I and those who reported to me even had…fun.

In 2002, after years in Training, I became head of the "Technical Support Department". I know what you're probably thinking here, but we, in fact, had nothing to do with taking care of people's computers. Our department was so-named because we had responsibility for all of the "stuff" no one else wanted to deal with, and I think, in the incredibly left-brained world of nuclear power, it was about as creative a name as anyone could come up with. Our responsibilities included Document Control, Self-Assessments, Regulatory Affairs, Corrective Action, Observation and Coaching, and…Human Performance.

Our facility was blessed (at the time) with a pair of what I like to refer to as "enlightened leaders"- our Site Vice President and our Plant General Manager. In April of 2002, we had a "summit meeting" at the site. Myself and the entire senior leadership team got together to discuss Human Performance.

At this point, our "Human Error Rate", which is a standard nuclear Key Performance Indicator (KPI), was about average for the industry. We believed we could do better. The question was, how to do it. I saw an open door of opportunity; a genuine chance to stick my head up out of the foxhole and take a shot at actually making a difference.

Taking insights from my lifelong 'study' of motivation and human behavior, and combining them with the lessons learned from my Four Strikes, I offered, "I have an idea." I went on to pose my ideas on how to get employees to do the "right things" because they *want* to. I apparently did a decent job of presenting my case. By the end of the meeting, I was given permission and authority to "do it".

Approaching Human Performance from a *human* perspective resulted in an 87.5% reduction in our human error rate over the next 30 months. We went from good (average in the industry) to great (right at the top). We completed the most extensive plant modification outage in the plant's history on schedule and under budget without a single significant human error. Morale was at a peak. Union grievances reached an all-time low. INPO took notice. As the architect of the effort, I was given a nice promotion, stock options…I was being asked to speak at other plants around the industry, to enlighten them on "how we did it". Life was [very] good.

Insanity Returns

During the course of my 30-month "experiment", our station was purchased by one of the largest nuclear organizations in the country. We became the "diamond in the rough" of this company's acquisitions. They left us alone, wanting to learn how we had "achieved so much with so little"…for a while.

Our Site Vice President was transferred to another station within our new fleet to "fix" their performance problems. Twelve months later, the Plant General Manager, not quite fitting the "corporate" mold of our new owners, was put on temporary assignment at INPO. A new Plant General Manager was installed with an overriding mandate from on high: Make our plant look, feel, and act like all of the other plants in the fleet. Forget about the human side. It was all about the data, the metrics, the charts and graphs. During a 'fleet assist' visit by this same individual before we knew he was to become our new Plant Manager, he laughed at me for not being aware of an obscure trend graph on INPO's website. Apparently, appearance and data awareness was far more important than [human] performance.

I lasted two months after the new Plant Manager's arrival. Unwilling to take part in the undoing of the great things the people at that station had achieved, I turned in my resignation. This was in 2005. We had twin daughters in high school, car payments and mortgages. It didn't matter. For me, principle far outweighed convenience.

For two years after my departure (the period for which I still had inside sources to provide me with data), the human error rate at that station continued to get better and better (in spite of the turning tide of focus at the top). We had genuinely transformed organizational culture. Eventually, however, things began to revert.

Many senior leaders have a very hard time unlearning what they have learned. This was crystal clear as powerful fleet forces persisted. Corporate saw fit to sequentially "execute" players at the facility, replacing them with 'company men'. Five years ago the plant began to have major issues. Regulatory. Environmental. Security. The plant generated its last megawatt on December 31st, 2014.

The Rest of the Story

Leaving my position at that station was bitter-sweet. It was bitter because of the dismantling of what we had achieved; taking great Human Performance and reverting back to the corporate (and industry) standard of coercive command and control. It was sweet because what I had previously had only been able to implement in small teams had now been proven across an entire station in the most demanding and highly regulated work environment on the planet. There was a [much] bigger picture here. Thus was born the Practicing Perfection Institute, Inc. (PPI).

The Practicing Perfection® approach (as it has come to be called) confronts the traditional notion that prescriptiveness and command and control are the keys to successful performance. It uncovers the reality that the highest and best form of efficiency comes through the spontaneous cooperation of a free workforce. It transfers focus from policing for compliance to opening the door of personal desire. Essentially, this approach gets workers (at all levels) to do the right things for the right reasons because they *want* to.

One afternoon in 2010, as I was getting up from my desk to grab some lunch, the phone rang. It was Fran, the Senior Vice President of Operations for one of the largest electrical generating fleets in the United States. He was onsite at a two-unit 1700-Megawatt generating station in Texas, and was calling to tell me what he had discovered. "Tim," he said, "I absolutely cannot believe the positive culture change at this station. And it's happened so fast!"

Interestingly, we had ultimately been invited to implement our approach to "human performance" at this station because of the persistence of one of their bargaining unit members who had heard me speak at a safety conference. It took him more than a year to convince Gary, the Plant General Manager, to "give it a try".

Gary had gotten to a point in his career where he was so fed up with the endless string of problems and issues that he was considering early retirement. Following implementation, he found new energy, new enthusiasm, and a new outlook. The plant and its team went on to have the best safety record, highest productivity, and longest unit runs in its 26-year history. I've heard him say several times, "Practicing Perfection® changed my life."

Since the success of the nuclear plant "experiment", we've had the opportunity to positively impact tens of thousands of workers around the globe through the Practicing Perfection Institute (PPI). The PPI client list reveals a successive string of successes, including:

- A 72% sustained reduction in human error during a capital improvement project involving 23 different contract firms

- A 72.4% reduction in outage-to-outage human error rate during a heavy period of plant modification work

- A 70% reduction in union grievances during the year following implementation

Our business success has been tremendous. We've worked around the globe and currently have affiliate organizations in the US, Canada, Belgium, and South Africa. I've had the opportunity to work with "think tanks" such as the Electrical Power Research Institute (EPRI). I've been interviewed by Brian Tracy, and have been seen on NBC, ABC, CBS and FOX networks. We've helped some of the largest organizations on the planet achieve amazing results. Most important to me, however, is the positive impact we've had on people's lives: the accidents that didn't happen, the mistakes not made, the attitudes and relationships impacted.

When it comes to successes, my personal favorite brings me back to the Plant General Manager from Texas. Over the years of working together, Gary and I became friends. When it came time for him to move on to his next chapter, my wife and I travelled to College Station to attend his retirement party. As we were leaving, Gary's wife Cindy pulled me aside to say, "You have no idea how much you and your training have impacted my husband. I thank you, our daughters thank you, and our grandchildren thank you."

You can hear Gary and some of the members of his team offer their perceptions and experiences of the Practicing Perfection® process in the Telly Award-winning Documentary video, "Practicing Perfection®," at http://ppiweb.com/home-2-3/ppi-documentary/

---

[1] Babson Olin School of Business, *Fast Company*, April 2011, 121.

[2] Foster and Kaplan, *Creative Destruction*

Part I: THINK DIFFERENT

Chapter One: Human Performance (The Ultimate Frontier)

"All the forces in the world are not so powerful as an idea whose time has come."
-Victor Hugo

What is "human performance"?

According to Webster's Dictionary (including the online version), the phrase "human performance" doesn't exist. If you try dictionary.com, you'll also find no definition, only deferral links to a handful of other sites. One of these is the online home of the Human Performance Institute. Go to their site (http://www.hpinstitute.com), and you'll find a bunch of information about sports and athletic performance.

At the time of this writing, the only "reference" location having anything even related to human performance is the 'mother' of all internet look-up places, Wikipedia. There you'll find "Human Performance Technology":

> **Human performance technology (HPT)**, also known as **human performance improvement (HPI)**, is a field of study related to process improvement methodologies such as lean management, Six Sigma, lean Six Sigma, organization development, motivation, instructional technology, human factors, learning, performance support systems, knowledge management, and training. It is focused on improving performance at the societal, organizational, process, and individual performer levels.

HPT "uses a wide range of interventions that are drawn from many other disciplines, including total quality management, process improvement, behavioral psychology, instructional systems design, organizational development, and human resources management" (ISPI, 2007). It stresses a rigorous analysis of requirements at the societal, organizational process and individual levels as appropriate to identify the causes for performance gaps, provide appropriate interventions to improve and sustain performance, and finally to evaluate the results against the requirements.[1]

An Enigma

> *"Baseball is 90 percent physical. The other half is mental."* -Yogi Berra

The Wikipedia definition covers a lot of ground, which is fine if you're seeking a general awareness of "human performance technology". If on the other hand, you're looking for something tangible, something you can sink your teeth into and do something with, this definition will likely leave you asking the classic Austin Powers' question: "But what does it all mean Bazel?"

Relative to the *mental* performance part of *sports* performance, I believe Yogi had it upside down. Performance in any sport is more like 90 percent mental. Think about it. If you (or I) do not have the right *mindset*, we'll never even seek, let alone achieve, the *physical* outcome. However, the physical is tangible. It's concrete. It can be seen, it can be felt, it can be measured. Physical outcomes (results) have therefore been the predominant focus. Whether it be safety record, number of widgets per hour, cost per widget, number of defects, error rates, turnover rates, infection rates, or any of a huge variety of metrics and KPIs (Key Performance Indicators), your performance in the world today (as well as mine and everyone else's) is evaluated almost exclusively by results. I believe this is why (until now) we've found ourselves with little tangible understanding of the 'underneath' part, the "human" side of the performance equation.

The challenge of continuing to operate this way is that we've been using lagging indicators (results) by which to steer our course. To me, this is the same as trying to drive your car by looking in the rear view mirror.

BUT, you may counter, "Such metrics are all we have! How else are we to know how to proceed?" First off, don't get me wrong, metrics are important. We must know how we are doing. For example (back to the car metaphor), it's pretty darn important to know how much gas you have in your tank, your current speed relative to the limit, and that your oil pressure and engine temperature are within an acceptable range. But as far as steering your course, the windshield provides a far better perspective than the rearview mirror. Your 'windshield' of performance is *human performance*; that is, once you truly understand it.

Let's take a ride…

Human Performance: The Nuclear Road

More has been learned about neuroscience, brain physiology, behavioral psychology, and how the human mind actually works in the past 30 years than in the entire previous tenancy of mankind's existence on this planet.

In the mid-1990s, the Institute of Nuclear Power Operations (INPO) turned an acute focus upon human error reduction. This work involved consultation with many of the brightest minds in the field at the time. Of these, Dr. James Reason and Aubrey Daniels had substantial influence upon the overall approach. A small team of INPO employees was assembled. This team served as a conduit between the thought-leading experts at the time, and a small army of committed individuals working diligently in over 100 operating nuclear power plants across the US and Canada. Combining what they were learning with their own insights, the INPO team led a focused endeavor which the nuclear industry came to know as, "Human Performance."

This effort, which almost exclusively focused on the reduction of human error, produced substantial results. For example, average nuclear capacity factor (actual megawatt-hours generated compared to all plants operating at 100% for the entire year) rose from 75% in 1995 to 90.9% in 2013. During this same period, a focus on human performance drove the industry average OSHA Recordable Rate down from 0.38 in 1997 to 0.04 in 2013.[2]

The team at INPO came up with a simple formula for defining human performance. This formula looked like this:

$$HU = B + R$$

Where:

HU = Human Performance

B = Behaviors

R = Results

At the time, this was a breakthrough. For perhaps the first time ever, behaviors were considered along with results. Some 20 years later, this formula for human performance is still used within the nuclear industry. It can also now be seen amidst the evolving performance improvement efforts within many other industries. As we began to teach this formula within PPI in 2005, we developed an associated word definition for human performance: *Human Performance* is how we do (*Behaviors*) what we do (*Results*).

While behaviors are indeed considered in this initial concept of *human performance*, the nuclear industry (for the most part) missed the boat on how to influence them. Using a primary focus of rear-view-mirror tracking and trending (*Results*), the industry combined an overt emphasis on command and control, with development of overly prescriptive procedures, and demands for verbatim compliance in their efforts to drive human behavior. The result? In 2005, INPO published Significant Event Report (SER) 3-05, *"Weaknesses in Operator Fundamentals."* In September, 2010, they published Significant Operating Experience Report (SOER) 10-2, *"Engaged, Thinking Organization."* And, in June, 2011, they published INPO Event Report (IER) 11-3, *"Weaknesses in Operator Fundamentals."*[3]

Having "grown up" in this industry, and having spent a good portion of my career either in Operations Training or assisting Operations as a Shift Technical Advisor, I can tell you from personal experience that nuclear training programs and licensing requirements in the United States are some of the best, most stringent on the planet. This being the case, how could performance trends within the industry have possibly warranted INPO issuing such critical reports? INPO cites numerous reasons within these reports, followed by calls for specific responses and corrective actions.

For me, the corrective actions indicated in these reports appear to be 'more of the same', in other words, the same things the industry has been doing for the past 20 years. It is intriguing to think that taking the same actions will ultimately produce different results. A primary focus on 'command and control', combined with demands for 'verbatim compliance' is an old paradigm, which as has been proven by the very reports themselves, does not produce sustainable performance improvement. Secondly, the original formula (HU = B + R) is missing the most fundamental part of the human decision-making process.

Before we head into the next section, I want to make you aware of another downfall of this approach that the nuclear industry has discovered. In June of 2014, I was invited to provide the opening keynote address for the annual Utilities Service Alliance (USA) Executive Summit. I was honored to do so because the USA has represented up to 25% of the nuclear generators in the US. I was asked to center my comments on what was at the time the number one concern of US Chief Nuclear Officers (and the theme of the conference)- "Cumulative Impact."

As I discovered while doing research for my talk, the sustained low cost of natural gas, which currently represents over 30% of the electricity generated in the US[4], has rendered the nuclear generation of electricity barely viable from a business perspective (ability to generate at a profit). I found this very interesting, because marketing documents produced by General Electric during the early days of nuclear power offered that electricity generated through boiling water reactors would be, "too cheap to meter." What happened? A Policy Brief issued by the Nuclear Energy Institute (NEI) offered some insight: "Over the years, the amount of regulatory activity and industry-driven requirements has increased, requiring nuclear power plant operators to devote more resources to compliance efforts, some of which do little to enhance safety."[5]

So not only has the industry's approach generated a negative trend of unintended consequences (as indicated in the INPO Reports), it has also created a huge cost burden. Interestingly, as the industry (generators and regulators alike) has begun to address this issue, two areas have emerged where it is agreed that immediate cost and resource reductions can be made: human performance (over prescriptiveness and demand for verbatim compliance), and "corrective action" (tracking and trending).

As *human performance* and human error reduction continue to rise onto the radar of various industry leaders and regulators, one of my passions for writing this book is to help you and your organization avoid the downsides of the 'nuclear' road. Human Performance can be enhanced simply, sanely, and sensibly, and when done properly, produces dramatic sustainable results.

Taking Things to the Next-Level

As previously mentioned, we've had the opportunity to work with tens of thousands of workers in organizations both large and small over the past ten years. During this time, we've paid attention. We've also continued to study the developments in neuroscience and in the psychologies related to human behavior and motivation, incorporating key elements into our evolving implementation strategies in real time within real workplaces.

Based upon our learning and our experiences in the field, I have developed a new version of the 'formula' for human performance which leverages the previously missing 'critical element':

$$HP = W(R + B)$$

Where:

HP = Human Performance

W = WHY

R = Results

B = Behaviors

Putting this formula into a word definition, we now have an actionable understanding of next-level human performance:

Human Performance is WHY we do WHAT we do the WAY we do it.

The 'missing element' that has been added to the original formula is obviously the "W" (WHY). This understanding of human performance is fundamentally important to any performance improvement efforts you currently have in place, as well as to any that you might consider for future implementation.

The WHY addresses a multitude of underlying psychology, including overall motivation and intention, biases provided by supervisors and organizational culture, social dynamics, cognitive and emotional response to ongoing and acute external conditions and stimulations. The underlying dynamics of *why* an individual chooses to do (or say) what he or she does at any given moment can be very complex. I think Mark Twain summed this up brilliantly when he penned, *"Such a convenient thing it is to be a reasonable creature, for it allows us to come up with a reason for anything we're inclined to do."*

In the formula, note how both Results and Behaviors are multiplied by WHY. WHY impacts everything. Think about it this way: For you and me, our Results in life come as a consequence of our choices and our Behaviors. So then, where do our choices and

Behaviors come from? From our underlying emotions and motivations (our WHY), which generate our consequent moment-by-moment decision-making processes. You simply cannot tap into the potential of *human performance* without going directly after the WHY. The great news is, as you will learn in subsequent chapters of this book, the "heavy lifting" has been done by those who have gone before us. You do NOT have to be a psychologist to be an incredibly effective influencer of behaviors (which is how you ultimately transform your Safety Culture, enhance quality, improve efficiency and reliability, and reduce human error.

Before we move onward, I want to ensure that you are putting this next-level approach to human performance into proper context. To begin, consider the definition: *WHY we do WHAT we do the WAY we do it*. Now, consider your organization: To whom does *human performance* apply? I hope the answer is obvious-EVERYONE! This is not simply a "tool kit" or program aimed at frontline workers. It applies to every single member of your team, from the very top, to you, to brand new hires, to contractors working on your site. Second, consider all aspects of what your organization does, from leadership, to vision, to conceptualization, to design, to operations, sales, maintenance, and modification, to support services, to dealing with vendors and suppliers...to what does *human performance* apply? Again, because people are involved every step of the way, the answer should be crystal clear-to EVERYTHING.

Proper leveraging of *human performance* brings virtually unlimited potential to you and your organization.

"Human Performance" and its Impact Upon all of the Other Things You're [Likely] Already Doing

So now you're probably thinking, "Great, we've already invested a fortune in our Safety Program, LEAN, and Six Sigma. We've done 5S and STOP. We signed a contract for a [very expensive] database and have mandatory observation and coaching. We invited folks from the local college in to teach us about leadership and interpersonal skills. Now you're telling me I need to initiate yet ANOTHER program?!"

You may also be thinking, "Hey! The title of this book is *6-Hour Safety Culture* and you've yet to say much of anything about the process of safety!"

First and foremost, *human performance* is NOT a program. A "program" has a beginning, a middle, and typically (thank goodness) an end. Human Performance within your organization, *WHY people do WHAT they do the WAY they do it*, has no beginning and no end. It lies at the absolute core of everything you do. It creates and evolves your culture. It is the ultimate determinant of your success. The great news is, a proper focus upon human performance underscores, reinforces, and positively leverages every good process, program, and initiative you may already have underway.

Relative to *Safety Culture*, my experience has been that many organizations are spinning their wheels with the very best of intentions, remaining frustrated with ongoing behaviors and results. As I see it, this is because of one or more of three primary reasons:

- An overt focus on compliance, including roving safety 'police' looking to catch people not doing what they're supposed to be doing
- Implementation of point of action routines, that while successful to a point, remain on the surface, and do not get fully internalized
- The "shiny box" trap of relying upon massive quantities of observation info put into a database to identify where the 'problems' lie

To expand upon this, it has been my experience that many organizations do not have a truly effective, actionable, proactive perception of what *safety culture* actually means. This like so many other things, has tended to become a process, a program, or a set of documents on a shelf. For now, consider the second word in the phrase- *culture*. We will dive directly into the true context of Safety Culture (and Just Culture) in Chapter Seven. First, we need to continue to build a solid foundation of insight, awareness, and understanding.

As I previously indicated, every chapter of this book builds upon its predecessors. For now, my intention in this chapter has been to provide you with an understanding of the single common element to any aspect of performance improvement- human performance.

Key Insights from Chapter One

1. The formula for taking the performance of your organization to its next level is:
   $HP = W(R + B)$ [where HP = Human Performance, W = WHY, R = Results, and B = Behaviors]

2. *Human Performance* is WHY we do WHAT we do the WAY we do it

3. WHY is the critical element- it determines Behaviors, which ultimately determine Results

4. A proper focus on *human performance* underscores and reinforces every good thing your organization is already doing

What can you do with what you just learned?

A. Recognize that *human performance* is not a set of "tools", or a program designed to get workers to "do what they're told". It is the very foundation of everything you do.

B. Continue on to Chapter Two, where you will learn how to think different in preparation for doing different

[1] http://wikipedia.org

[2] http://nei.org/Knowledge-Center/Nuclear-Statistics/US-Nuclear-Power-Plants/

[3] Institute of Nuclear Power Operations (INPO); SER 3-05 *Weaknesses in Operator Fundamentals* (2005); SOER 10-2 *Engaged, Thinking Organizations* (September 7, 2010); IER 11-3 *Weaknesses in Operator Fundamentals* (June 15, 2011)

[4] http://www.eia.gov/forecasts/aeo/er/early_elecgen.cfm

[5] Nuclear Energy Institute; *Improving Accountability, Efficiency in Nuclear Energy Regulation*; NEI Policy Brief; November, 2013

Chapter Two: Third-Dimension Thinking

"Without deviation from the norm, progress is not possible."
-Frank Zappa

The dreaded alarm clock…

I served 8 years in the United States Navy, followed by little more than 20 years in the commercial nuclear power industry. The workdays in each of these arenas started gosh darn early. I had to get up when it was still dark outside. The "snooze" button was my coping mechanism. After three…or six 'snoozes', I'd drag myself out of bed. To me, it was painful. So painful in in fact, that toward the end of my nuclear career, a primary personal goal became to modify my circumstances such that alarm clocks were no longer required. And I am *very* happy to say, that except on days when I have to catch an early flight, I wake up…when I wake up.

Most people love weekends, me included. Why? Well, for one thing- no alarm clocks! Oh how I used to l-o-v-e to sleep in on Saturday and Sunday mornings! Wake up when I felt like it. Usually 10:30 or 11:00, sometimes even until noon. I remember a particular Saturday morning, however, when sleeping in was the last thing I wanted to do.

A good friend of mine, Rick Wesley, had a nice bass boat. He and I decided to enter a fishing tournament in the Spillway off of the Mississippi River. On that Saturday, I *wanted* to set my alarm clock- for 3:00AM! And interestingly, I was awake (on my own) at 2:20. No 'snoozes'. In fact, no alarm at all. I was all packed- gear, tackle, bait, and two cups of coffee, standing out by the curb when Rick pulled up with his boat in tow.

What was the difference between a workday three to six bangs on the snooze button followed by actual crawling-from-under-the-covers pain, and jumping out of bed to go fishing? The answer is simple- a completely different motivation. What does this have to do with *Third Dimension Thinking?* Everything, actually.

Before we move onward, you *must* be wondering how we did in the tournament. So, I'll tell you: Rick and I placed second. It was no doubt difficult for others to linger in our presence upon our return to work. After all, we were now bonafide *Tournament Fishermen*. Much self back-patting was indeed in order.

The Box

There is probably no more cliché term in the world of creativity, business, or organizational endeavor than, "think outside the box". It's been w-a-y overused and abused. I don't know about you, but I have extreme distaste for clichés. "Why then," you are undoubtedly wondering, "are you presenting one here?!" Because I couldn't think of a better way to introduce this topic.

A classic exercise used to demonstrate that solutions often do exist when you "think outside the box" has been the series of nine circles shown in the figure below. Perhaps you've been exposed to this once (or several times) during one or more of the training programs your company has put you through. It has been a favorite of consultants since the 70s.

The challenge of the exercise is to connect all nine dots by drawing a series of four straight lines without lifting your pen (or pencil) from the page. Can you do it?

NOTE:

If you would like to see the solution to 'The Box', go here:

http://www.6hoursafetyculture.com/resources/box-solution/

Cliché aside, this concept is exceptionally powerful. In fact, this is how virtually all breakthrough discoveries manifest. No, not by connecting nines dots on a piece of paper, but by genuinely thinking *different*. By casting off the shackles of constraint within our minds; those neural connections for each of us that have 'wired together' as a result of our past experience and conditioning.

There is an exercise we do in our Practicing Perfection® sessions to demonstrate this very point. It goes beyond the boundaries of a two-dimensional 'box' to demonstrate how most of us constrict our thought to two dimensions. In this exercise, by making a simple shift of taking thought into the third dimension, a very simple solution to an otherwise impossible task becomes obvious.

I would assert to you that by far the majority of attempts to influence human behavior in the workplace today are stranded in two dimensions. The 'human challenge' therefore seems very complex; an area in which any true and sustainable progress seems at best a long and arduous endeavor, and for many, near impossible. By simply taking the "third dimension" approach, you will find that this huge challenge cannot only dissolve (oftentimes very quickly), but that Human Nature itself offers you a huge positive leveraging opportunity.

The Death of a President[1]

On Thursday, December 12, 1799, George Washington rode out to inspect his property. The weather turned bad, with rain, hail, and snow. He stayed out longer than he should have, and apparently caught a cold. He wasn't feeling great as the evening progressed, yet he felt obliged to stay up late to complete some paperwork.

The next morning he awakened with a bad sore throat, and was generally feeling worse than he had the night before. He hadn't finished all of his inspections on Thursday however, so after some breakfast, he had his horse prepared, donned his hat and cloak, and headed out to complete the job. He continued to feel progressively worse, returning around mid-day. He remained indoors for the rest of the afternoon, and retired early on Friday evening.

His sleep was not good. As the night deepened, his breathing became more and more of a struggle. Finally, he became convinced he needed some medical help. As dawn approached, he called for Albin Rawlins, his estate overseer, to help him. The local doctors would come later in the morning. As he was having more and more trouble breathing, Washington directed Rawlins to administer the "cutting edge" medical procedure for such serious maladies- bloodletting.

Interestingly, Martha didn't think that the cutting and draining procedure was such a great idea, and begged that there not be too much blood let out; however, George was feeling quite poor. As even Mr. Rawlins grew hesitant, Washington encouraged him, "Don't be afraid. The orifice is not large enough. More, more."

Three local doctors arrived later in the morning, and in combination with plasters and other intended remedies, continued the bloodletting. By all historical records, it is estimated that somewhere between five and seven pints of blood were drained from the first president of the United States. At 10:10PM that Saturday evening, George Washington was dead. Yes, he likely had pneumonia, but administration of the "cutting edge" medical technique of the day, bloodletting, undoubtedly helped speed his demise.

Why did the brightest medical minds of the day subscribe to a technique that most of us today look upon with a sense of horror? Because of a *paradigm*. You see, the paradigm in the late eighteenth century was that disease was caused by "bad blood". And by letting the "bad blood" out, the person would [obviously] get better.

As science, and medical science, has evolved into the 21st century, how do we look at this particular paradigm today?

Managing People Like Things

How are people in *your* organization currently being 'dealt with'? I'd be willing to bet you have a "human resources department", some sort of personnel appraisal process, and perhaps even a "progressive discipline" system. In and of themselves, none of these are bad, or evil, or even of ill intent. Collectively, however, in many organizations they've generated and continue to support the accepted context that people need to be (1) compared to some arbitrary standard or graded on a 'curve', (2) managed through a set of prescriptive 'must' and 'must not' policies, and (3) are to be 'punished' should they stray from the rules or otherwise choose to 'color outside the lines'. All of these aspects have one common theme- control.

Why are these methods of dealing with the very people who are responsible for making our organizations able to function so predominant? Because of an outdated *paradigm*. And I will say with no reservation, based upon the successes we've had with tens of thousands of workers over the past ten years, combined with the ongoing learning about human motivation and discoveries about how the brain actually works, that the old-school *paradigm* of managing people like things is today as outdated (and ineffective) as bloodletting!

Having just read my last statement, I would imagine right now that you are either (1) excited about what you've heard so far and cannot wait to continue onward, or (2) think I don't have a clue about management, and are mounting your mental defenses for why all of your controls are necessary (in which case you'll likely not read much further). Either way, since you've read this far, if your organization is currently mired (or heavily biased) in *command and control*, I'd like to borrow words from Dr. Phil, and ask, "How's that workin' for ya?"

Third dimension thinking is having the mental courage to consider that maybe, just maybe, there is a different way to look at things, and ultimately, a different way to go about doing things. In what I consider to be his best work, one of my mentors, Stephen Covey, offered a brilliant alternative to control, to the tendency to manage people like things, in his book, *The Eighth Habit*[2],

"Leadership can become a *choice* (moral authority) rather than only being a position (formal authority). The key is to think in terms of *release*, not control; in terms of transformation, not just transaction. In other words, you manage things, you lead people."

Compliance versus Desire

A common theme within a control-based working culture is a predominant focus, especially by the folks 'at the top', on *compliance*. Combine this with the predominant western culture context that "more is better" when it comes to virtually everything, and in many industries today, the pendulum continues to swing toward more policies, more rules, more- control. While laws, regulations, and rules are necessary (and healthy) to a certain point, beyond this point they become stifling, expensive, and anti-productive. As the commercial nuclear industry in the United States has discovered (as discussed in Chapter One), over-prescriptiveness and over-the-top focus on verbatim compliance can have substantially negative consequences.

As it turns out, continual pushing or driving for compliance flies directly in the face of good ole Human Nature. Let's talk for a moment about a different way to think about an environment of *compliance*.

If we take a look at the root word for compliance (comply), it means to conform, submit, or adapt as required[3]. If you or I (or anyone else for that matter) are required/forced to conform, submit, or adapt, this generates a loss of sense of control. Whenever we sense a loss of control, our natural human response is to either withdraw or directly resist. Think about it. The last time someone took control away from you, how did you react?

Now take a look at the word, "compliance." It is, "the act or process of complying to a desire, demand, proposal or regimen, or to coercion[4]." Most organizations today have not yet evolved toward the *desire* or *proposal* side. Expectations for behaviors and actions tend to come across more as a *demand*s, and in some environments, even as *coercion*. If this is how you, or your organization is currently seeking to get people to "follow the rules", you are undoubtedly generating a lot of resentment and resistance. In addition, consider this: if you or I are only doing something because we're "made to", and we haven't really bought into the *why* of it, how likely are we to do it when no one else is watching?

Here's a fact: In compliance-based behavior, the average human being will usually follow the rules when someone else is watching, but even then will seek to "get away with" as much as they possibly can. Don't believe me? Let's work through a little mental scenario…

Let's say that you're on the east coast of the United States, and you've decided to take a vacation, by car, so that your kids can experience, first hand, the fun of family 'together time' during a 20+ hour drive to Orlando, Florida, and once there, the excitement of Mickey Mouse. To get there, you're likely to travel the great 'eastern corridor', Interstate 95. You've come from somewhere further north, made your way through traffic around Washington, D.C., through the state of Virginia, and have crossed the southern state line. There's no traffic, you're essentially in the middle of 'nowhere'. The kids are asleep, Lynard Skyard's *Sweet Home Alabama* is cranking on your sound system. You followed directions and "turned it up", and just happened to notice that, indeed, even though you're in North Carolina, the skies are so blue. There's not a cop in sight. You still have a long way to go. The posted speed limit is 70 mph. Now here's my question: If I were to look down at your speedometer, where would the needle be resting?

If you are like 98% of the population in the western world, its somewhere between 74 and 79 mph.

Next question: Do you realize that if the posted speed limit is 70, and you're traveling at any speed greater than 70- you're…breaking the law?! How do you justify that?

I have a lot of fun plodding through this scenario in live presentations. And boy do I get justifications! One time I even had a high ranking military official from a European country take up several minutes of my time following my presentation, doing his best to justify his lack of buy-in to his country's speed laws.

Following some fun with the justifications, I then like to ask another question, one that I'll ask you right now: If your speed was anything above the posted limit, do you consider yourself to be a person of integrity? (Again- lots of fun with this one in live venues.)

I hope you do consider yourself to be a person of integrity, after all, you're the only one who really knows for sure. I certainly consider myself to have integrity, and in the scenario just mentioned, my speedometer would have likely been reading 78 mph.

What's the point?

What you and I have just demonstrated is typical behavior in a *compliance-based* environment. And why do I limit my speed to 78mph? Because I know that (in most states) the traffic police set their radar at 10 mph *above* the posted limit. In other words, I know how much I can 'get away with'. This is classic *compliance-based behavior*.

Now, here's the real question: Why would you expect people to behave differently at work?

So if demanding compliance is not the pathway to sustainable performance improvement, what is? We're working our way toward the simple solution, but before we get there, I want to ensure that you are aware of (and hopefully avoid) a few classic sinkholes that will likely appear (or have already appeared) along your pathway to improvement.

The Sirens of Performance Improvement

"Next, where the Sirens dwell, you plough the seas;
Their song is death, and makes destruction please."
-Homer (The Odyssey)

Have you ever left port on a ship and traveled into the open sea? Casting off, you head outward, slicing smoothly yet deliberately through the calm emerald green harbor waters. If it's your first time, you think, "This is great! This is calm, this is smooth. Why was I worried about getting sick?" Such is similar sailing for most during initial performance improvement efforts. You decide to cast off, it all seems very simple. You navigate toward the harbor entrance. Life is good.

"Such a smooth journey!" you say to yourself. "Why do people think that improving performance is so hard?" Of course you know, you must depart the harbor calm and head into the open sea. It is there that your "next level" awaits! As the harbor opens to the sea, the question becomes, "Heading, Mam (or Sir)?" Bolstered by the ease of your initial movement, you answer as James Kirk after regaining command of the Enterprise, "Out there...that a way![5]"

Safe harbor behind, your wave of initial enthusiasm now turns to the hard work of chasing the horizon. The seas have gotten rough. What is your best course? Day-to-day demands consume your energy. Weariness sets in. Making your way to the stern of the ship, you look backward. Seeing the now distant shores where you once docked, you recognize that you have indeed made progress. This offers only momentary comfort, however, because your travels thus far certainly aren't 'good enough'. There are targets to be chased, trends to be analyzed, metrics to be calculated, KPIs to be reported. Racing back forward, to the bow, your gaze is again upon the horizon. How can you ever possibly get there?

In truth, performance improvement is like the horizon- an ongoing journey into the sunrise. You never actually "arrive". There must always be a "next-level". The secret is to be crystal clear about your current target. This is the only way to intelligently plot your course to get there. Then, just prior to arriving at what *was* your target, you precisely calculate your next one, take what you have learned from your journey thus far, and plot your ongoing course. No matter your industry, or the size of your team, department, or enterprise, this *is* your pathway to a successful future. This is, as Tony Robbins calls it, Constant And Never-ending Improvement (CANI).

Unfortunately, there are many "sirens" along such a journey, doing their best to lure you off course. In Homer's Odyssey, listening to the Sirens' song could not be resisted. *"Firm to the mast with chains thyself be bound,"* was the sole means offered for averting the otherwise ultimate doom. From my experience, the lure of analysts, consultants, and salespeople hawking everything from "tool kits", to prescriptive processes, to expensive software and databases has become irresistible to many in their ongoing search for the "next step". Unfortunately, the thrust of most offerings, in spite of their bells, whistles, and alluring song, offer (at best) surface-level behavioral influence, while many are merely different forms of attempting to manage people like things. Such are the crags, and rocks, and shoals of doom for many tasked with performance improvement. As described in The Odyssey (just because I cannot resist),

> *"In verdant meads they sport; and wide around*
> *Lie human bones that whiten all the ground"*

The two predominant Sirens of Human Performance are, *analoculitis,* and the *Shiny Box,* presented here lest ye be tempted to wander toward and be captivated by their alluring songs... In other words (getting back to 'normal speak'), these are the two predominant traps that will tend to pull you off course if you let them. As you read the descriptions that follow, should you find that you are already within their grasp, awareness and admission provide your first step to recovery.

Analoculitis

Analoculitis: (1) An acute focus upon the accumulation of massive amounts of data with the intent of extracting insight about obvious behaviors (which could otherwise be immediately reinforced or addressed through direct interaction), thereby drawing conclusions regarding the need, at some point in the future, for corrective action; (2) cranial rectal inversion[6]

Human Performance is not complicated. Let me re-phrase that: achieving next-level performance, whether your focus be upon *Safety Culture*, *Quality*, or *High Reliability* is not complicated...with a proper focus upon and leveraging of *human performance*. You simply do NOT need more Six Sigma studies, more matrices, more databases, or more multi-colored graphs and bar charts to move things in a positive direction.

Yes, measurement is important, but as we discussed previously, measurement is a means, a gage of progress, not the end result. It's like the oil pressure gage in your car. While that meter and the information it provides are indeed important, you need the engine to propel you to where you want to go. And that engine, no matter what type of business you're in, is *human performance*.

A huge example of the stagnation and lack of progress caused by *analoculitis* can be seen within the US medical industry. This is an industry currently responsible for the leading cause of accidental death in the United States. In the book published in 2000, *To Err is Human*, the Institute of Medicine (IOM) reported, "as many as 98,000 people die in any given year from medical errors that occur in hospitals[7]." In 2013, an article in the Journal of Patient Safety, elevated this estimation to between 210,000 and 440,000 hospital patients per year who suffer some type of preventable harm that contributes to their death[8].

For the life of me, I cannot figure out why there is not more outrage about this. Either the means of 'estimation' have shifted dramatically, or things are getting much worse in the medical industry. I like to believe it's the former; but either way, there appears to be very slow (if any) industry-wide resolution to the problem of medical error. This being said, wonderful rays of hope have emerged, such as the Texas medical system indicated in the Introduction. But even here, you have to ask an obvious question: If someone within the industry has 'cracked the code' on solving a significant area of medical error (infections), why in the heck hasn't their 'discovery' been immediately adopted across the industry?

From my experience and my observation, the answer is...*analoculitis*. To be fair, errors in the medical industry tend to be cloaked in clandestine secrecy for fear of being sued. This is often the case internally within hospitals, let alone sharing outside the organization so that the rest of the industry can learn. But in the case of this incredibly effective (and simple) solution to a huge problem that has been 'discovered' in Texas, the response by most within the industry appears to be a continued desire for more studies, more data, another survey. This is insanity!

Before I go further, I must say that my experiences with the medical industry have witnessed no lack of desire by those who work within it to make things better. This industry is filled with hard-working staff members who truly want to help people. But for some reason, the "system" grinds along, seemingly resistant to external input and lessons learned, whether such lessons come from outside the industry or simply from another company or institution within the medical community. The predominant focus seems to be upon a need to overhaul the *system*, which of course requires lots of money, lots of time, more Six Sigma studies, etc. This is totally *not* necessary to begin dramatically improving performance. Want proof? The 'miracle' in Texas that has led to essentially zero infections is...the simple act of doctors, nurses, and technicians washing their hands before touching a patient. A simple [committed] shift in behaviors, and one of the leading causes of patient harm in hospitals has been essentially eradicated. Achieving amazing results through focus on *human performance* is not complicated.

Here's another example of *analoculitis* from my nuclear days as head of the Technical Support Department. One of our areas of responsibility was management of the "Observation & Coaching" program. The program consisted of two major components: First off, eight hours of documented "observation time" was required of those in the positions of Frontline Supervisor (FLS) and above. Of itself, this was a great concept. Proper and frequent interaction between those who do the work and those who oversee and manage is a critical component to achieving and sustaining next-level performance.

But the second element of the 'program' was where it got all screwed up- the focus upon acquiring megabytes of data. During the observation time, each FLS/manager was armed with a "Coaching Card", providing a checklist of things to look for and grade. "What's wrong with that?" you ask. Nothing, in and of itself. However, when you pair very busy people (which most employees in defined positions of leadership are) with rote requirements, left-brain bias, and checklists, it becomes an exercise to complete the checklist rather than maximizing the opportunity for quality interaction with the people being observed. It becomes about data accumulation rather than relationships. A great idea gone bad, again falling into the pit of analoculitis. By the way, I'll be showing you how to turn this entire 'observation & coaching' concept on its head to promote alignment, relationship, and CANI in Chapter Nine (and here's an interesting point- no database required).

The "Shiny Box"

In addition to the ever-present pit of analoculitis, we are all susceptible to the luring song of the *Shiny Box*. There are four primary reasons for this:

- Our lizard brains[9] (the part of our brains that gets 'first shot' at processing incoming information and is tasked with our survival) are acutely attracted to anything that appears to be new, novel, and pleasant (this is a fact of Human Nature), AND

- Our lizard brains seek to conserve energy- we tend to look for simple concrete solutions (such as databases) to solve complex [seemingly] abstract challenges (also a fact of Human Nature), AND

- We take our focus off of (aka get bored with) the fundamentals of *human performance*, getting sidetracked by an apparent *quick fix*, something *new and revolutionary*, or the *charisma* of a speaker, consultant, or company seemingly having the cure for whatever is ailing us at the moment, AND/OR

- We have not taken the time to clearly visualize and articulate our current target (precisely what we're seeking to achieve), allowing us to be easily diverted from our course

How can you defend against these tendencies that make you vulnerable to getting "sucked in"? Relative to the Human Nature of your *lizard brain*, which is attracted to pleasant novelties and wants to conserve energy by minimizing logical thought, simply be aware of it. This is your first defense.

If you find yourself getting bored with an incessant focus on the fundamentals, patience young grasshopper. If patience is not one of your virtues (it certainly isn't one of mine), and you're tempted to dive head first into something you just saw on the internet, re-read the story of Vince Lombardi in Chapter Three before you make any decisions.

Finally, if you've never truly dug into the underlying *why* of what you're doing, which is absolutely necessary if you are to have a clear visualization and articulation of where you're headed, stop right now and complete the following exercise. Do this now, before you read any further.

This exercise involves completing what we refer to as the Transformation Conversation, developed in its original form by another one of my mentors, Dan Sullivan. When you take the time to thoughtfully have this Conversation with yourself, it will help you get to your core. If you are part of a team that is making recommendations and providing direction (especially if "excellence" is in your team's title), every member of the team should complete this exercise, first individually, and then collectively. Watch the short video first, then download the worksheets and complete them:

http://ppiweb.com/future-performance-improvement/pursuing-excellence/

All of us must continually guard against *Shiny Box* temptation. This is true in virtually all areas of life. When it comes to performance improvement, however, you can be a very easy target if you are…

a. A very busy senior leader or business owner who feels an acute sense of pressure to improve performance, whether self-induced, because of a client, competitor, or regulator, or because something really bad just happened, OR

b. One tasked with performance improvement, and you're under the gun to recommend solutions or provide results because of perceived negative trends, client/competitor/regulator demands, or the need to respond to something really bad that just happened

As humans, we make choices based upon one of two primal motivations: To eliminate pain, or to acquire pleasure. If you find yourself in either the (a) or (b) category described above, you are likely searching in earnest for some means by which to reduce your pain. This is a very strong motivation. It may very well be the reason you're reading this book. Be patient. Allow past decisions and experiences, combined with whatever it is you're currently facing, to provide you with wisdom and resolve, not reaction and temptation.

Doing the 'Right Thing' at Three O'clock in the Morning

Earlier in this Chapter (providing you played along), you demonstrated what *compliance-based behavior* looks like (remember your trip to Disney World?). It's now time to discuss the alternative, which forms the core of *third-dimension thinking*.

What is your answer to the following question?

How do you get a worker to do the 'right thing' at 3:00AM when no one else is watching?

There is truly only one answer, and it's drop-dead simple: A person is only going to do the 'right thing' at 3:00AM when no one else is watching if he or she *WANTS* to. Before we go any further, let's do some direct relating to your current area of focus:

Safety Culture

How do you get workers to take full responsibility for their own safety, as well as for that of their co-workers?

Six Sigma / Quality / Productivity / Mistake Proofing

How can you get workers to be more engaged while performing their tasks?

Human Error Reduction

How can you get people to actually *use* the tools (e.g., STAR)?

Risk Reduction

In addition to using behavioral tools, how can you get workers to take ownership of their surroundings; to actively identify and eliminate *landmines* (set ups for catastrophe)?

The answer to every one of these questions is identical:

Workers are only going to do these things if they *WANT* to.

It doesn't get any more *third-dimension* than this- moving from a culture of demanding compliance to one of nurturing desire. And before you go thinking, "Oh, here we go. We're heading into airy-fairy land." I will tell you than when done properly, this is the most hard-core approach to accountability on the planet. In this environment, you essentially eliminate the opportunity for people to ignore, to blame, to be victims. There's no place to run and no place to hide.

Level of Effort

Let's return for just a moment to the Interstate-95 (trip to Disney World) speeding example. When I run that little scenario in live audiences, there is virtually always a person (or few) who keep their speed at or below the posted limit. The rest of us (the speedsters) typically have a good laugh because of how I respond to this, but then I also take the time to ask those individuals why they drive at (or below) the limit. While there are a handful of typical reasons, all of them come back to: this is how they *want* to drive. There is an internal sense of accountability to do things this way. If we were to look at this from the organization's perspective (in this case, the government's), these individuals are doing the 'right thing'. And they're doing so because they *want* to. With these folks, without any police officers whatsoever, they'd still 'follow the rules.'

The *third-dimension* approach of moving from a culture of *compliance* to a culture of *desire* generates benefits far beyond simply getting people to 'follow the rules'.

Let's return once again to where you were exceeding the speed limit on I-95. What was your speed? Chances are pretty good it was somewhere between four and nine mph above the posted limit. Why? Because you know just how much you can typically get away with without getting nailed by police radar.

Here's the next question- what do virtually all cars do when a police officer is spotted up ahead? Brake lights come on as everyone slows down. You're forced to slow down along with the others while wondering what's going on. A bit further down the road, there he is, just sitting there, waiting to catch you. But he doesn't! Ha ha! You've gotten away with it- once again! Of course, once you're past the police car, and you've checked your rearview mirror to ensure he's still sitting on the shoulder, your speed (and the speed of those around you) moves back to where it was before. Who ever thought that a bunch of families on their way to Disney World could teach us so much about human performance?

This is where we learn about *expectations* and *level of effort*.

In our roadway example, we could say that the 'rule' is the posted speed limit. Because we have laws, it is clearly an *expectation* to drive a rate of speed at or below the limit. But what do we see? Because this is a *compliance based* environment, the *expectation* is only met when the police are around. No police? We ignore the rule and motivate ourselves down the road at essentially whatever speed feels comfortable.

On the other hand, let's consider performance in a *desire based* environment. If I'm doing the right thing because I *want* to, for example if the posted speed limit is 65 mph and I maintain 64-65 mph because this is my *desire*, it doesn't matter whether there are cops around or not. I am meeting or exceeding *expectations* all of the time. My motivation for doing so is *internal*.

Remember what happened at 2:20AM in my fishing tournament story?

Key Points:

- In a *compliance-based environment*, whatever level of expectation you put forth is typically the *best* level of performance you'll ever get out of an average worker, and you'll typically only get this when the safety-, quality-, or management-police are in the area

- In a *desire-based environment*, whatever level of expectation you put forth is typically the *minimum* level of performance you'll get out of an average worker, and you'll get this whether oversight is present or not

Viral Accountability®

Third-Dimension Thinking is the key with which to unlock the doorway of your future. Viral Accountability® is how you integrate, coordinate, and leverage the energies of others to actually push the door open, keep it open, and maintain self-sustaining positive momentum. It is essentially the multiplication of individual effort.

As defined, Viral Accountability® is: *synergy of momentum and outcome propagated through ownership and spontaneous reinforcement of team member actions and interactions*. In other words, it's a positive force, which achieves strong and sustainable positive momentum through the combined proactive behaviors and actions of team members. I am introducing it to you here because it is the overriding [essentially spontaneous] behavioral mechanism for achieving virtually anything you are seeking to accomplish within your organization- from better OSHA numbers, to higher reliability, to less waste, to better management-worker relationships. True *Third-Dimension Thinking* in action.

In practice, Viral Accountability® is the product of three distinct cultural elements, which when approached properly, are easily integrated into the fabric of organizational behavior. The three elements and how they fit together are shown in the formula below:

$$PA * PL * VC = VA$$

Where:

PA=   Proactive Accountability®

PL=   Peer Leadership

VC=   Viral Change

VA=   Viral Accountability®

I will be introducing each of these elements to you in detail in subsequent chapters. Together we'll explore HOW to initiate and activate each one. For now, I hope you will consider these elements by what their name implies, and recognize how each compounds with the others. This should give you a sense of the performance-improving power available to you through Viral Accountability®. It is your ticket to achieving and sustaining next-level performance, and should become the cultural goal of your improvement efforts.

In Conclusion

I hope you're starting to put some pieces together; that you're beginning to sense how powerful Third-Dimension Thinking can be, especially when leveraging the energies and intentions of others through Viral Accountability®.

The gazillion dollar question at this point is of course, "HOW do you go about *doing* this?" In the next chapter, I am going to develop the philosophical foundation for your implementation plan. It consists of two "key elements" (a 10,000-foot view), and four simple precepts. In Part II (Hearts, Minds, and Souls (and How to Influence Them), we'll be diving internally, first into the individual, then translating this to impact team/organizational culture. As we move into Part III (Do Different), I'll then begin to guide you, step-by-step (including an actual blueprint you can download), through precisely *how* to initiate, implement, and sustain next-level performance within your organization. Hang with me here. You'll be glad you did.

Key Insights from Chapter Two

1. Paradigms from bygone eras must be recognized as such and discarded (remember bloodletting).

2. Managing people like things is an old paradigm.

3. Third-Dimension Thinking involves moving from a culture of *compliance* to a culture of *desire.*

4. There are two Sirens of Performance Improvement: *Analoculitis* and the *Shiny Box.*

5. In a *compliance*-based environment, people will 'follow the rules' when being watched, and will otherwise tend to 'get away with' whatever they can. Expectations become the 'ceiling' (typically the best level of effort you'll get out of the average worker).

6. In a *desire*-based environment, people 'follow the rules' because they *want* to, whether they are being watched or not. Expectations become the 'floor' (typically the minimum level of effort you'll get out of the average worker).

7. Viral Accountability® is the means through which you will engage the energies and intentions of your organization members to leverage *Third-*

8. *Dimension Thinking* and *Third-Dimension Doing*.

What can you do with what you just learned?

A. Complete your Transformation Conversation, digging into the *why* of your core (or that of your team), to crystalize your current/next target (specifically where you want to get to). Watch the video and download the worksheets here: http://ppiweb.com/future-performance-improvement/pursuing-excellence/

B. Utilize your new lens of awareness regarding *compliance-based behaviors* and *desire-based behaviors*, observing the distinct differences in motivations and levels of effort between the two.

C. Find something you feel strongly about, and arrange with a friend (someone you can trust) to engage in a conversation where you defend the view you normally oppose. Observe how difficult this is. Doing this exercise will help you to begin to analyze your current paradigms, and will help loosen your mind for considering options that may lie in the third dimension.

D. Recognize if you're currently in a position of increased vulnerability to the Sirens of Performance Improvement. If so, do not make any decisions to buy or contract for anything with anyone until you have finished reading this book!

[1] Vibul V Vadakan, MD, FAAP; *The Asphyxiating and Exsanguinating Death of President George Washington*; Presented at the Annual Miranda Lecture Series of Kaiser Permanente Bakersfield 2002

[2] *The Eight Habit: From Effectiveness to Greatness*; Stephen R. Covey; Simon & Schuster; January, 2103

[3] Merriam Webster's Collegiate Dictionary, Eleventh Edition

[4] Merriam Webster's Collegiate Dictionary, Eleventh Edition

[5] *Star Trek: The Motion Picture*; Paramount Pictures; 1979; https://www.youtube.com/watch?v=to9HVz793Kc

[6] Practicing Perfection Institute, Inc.; *Glossary of Terms*; 2015

[7] To Err is Human: Building a Safer Health System; Institute of Medicine; National Academy Press; 2000

[8] Journal of Patient Safety: September 2013 - Volume 9 - Issue 3 - p 122–128

[9] Phrase attributed to one of my mentors, Seth Godin

Chapter Three: The Practicing Perfection® Approach

*"I wouldn't give a fig for simplicity on the near side
of complexity. But I'd give my right arm for
simplicity on the far side of complexity"*
-Oliver Wendell Holmes

In this chapter, I will begin the move from *conceptualization* (Think Different) toward *implementation*. We will be diving into "Practicing Perfection®"- what it is, what it is not, and how it lays what should be the foundation for all of your performance improvement efforts going forward, irrespective of whether your primary focus is upon safety, quality, or reliability.

You should now have an understanding of *human performance* (WHY we do WHAT we do the WAY we do it), and how it lies at the core of all efforts to improve performance. You should also have a good feel for how to get people to sustainably do the 'right thing' (by getting them to *want* to) through engagement (and employment) of *Third-Dimension Thinking*. These are fundamental to your ability to influence behaviors and transform outcomes. If you're still unclear on either of these, it will serve you to go back and re-read the first two chapters before you continue onward.

Practicing Perfection®- What it's NOT

In 2010, I began to do work in Europe with my friend and colleague in Belgium, Dierik Rotsaert. We held a series of Leadership Training sessions and Certification Courses, which were attended by representatives from some of the largest organizations in the EU. In the initial stages, Dierik was catching resistance from a handful of senior company leaders. "I do not like the word 'perfection'," one manager protested, "We all know that 'perfection' isn't possible." This was the first time I had heard this voiced as a direct 'objection'.

While on one hand it is indeed true that there are no perfect human beings (at least I sure as heck have never met one), on the other hand, this represented a classic example of limited two-dimension context. When Dierik relayed this story to me, we agreed that if we could get these senior leaders to suspend disbelief just enough to get them to attend, their perspectives would undoubtedly be altered. Dierik agreed, and managed to get them into the classroom.

By mid-morning on the first day of the Leadership Training, their perspectives began to shift. As they came to understand what "Practicing Perfection®" was all about, their context expanded. Their thinking moved into the third dimension. They 'got it'. One of these leaders, from a company in Belgium, had been particularly outspoken in his opposition to 'perfection'. After completing the two-day Leadership Training, he returned six months later to participate in our Certification Course. As we were celebrating graduation with cake and champagne (something we don't do until *after* hours in the US), he pulled me aside. With gratitude in his eyes, he told me, "Tim, I just want you to know. This training has changed my life." Comments like these make everything we do worthwhile.

"Practicing Perfection®" has nothing whatsoever to do with you, or me, or anyone else becoming 'perfect', 'cause it flat out ain't gonna happen! So why the name then? The answer to this should become obvious as you read onward.

What it IS

Practicing Perfection® is a *systematic approach* for capitalizing upon Human Nature. By leveraging the positive stuff going on inside of individuals, building a *one team* environment, and then aligning and synergizing efforts, [near-miraculous] organizational improvement is achieved. It spawns engagement, engenders ownership, and aligns individual motivations with those of the organization. Collectively, this generates possibilities for performance far beyond those otherwise possible. Furthermore, improvements are sustainable because they come from 'the inside out'.

With respect to human error, Practicing Perfection® acknowledges human fallibility, while also recognizing that organizational factors contribute to the majority of errors that do occur. This awareness, coupled with proper implementation, crafts an environment where the *team* can virtually eliminate consequential human error while systematically removing organizational setups (aka *landmines*). As a result, the incidence of human error is driven to the lowest possible levels of frequency and severity, while *events* (errors having significant consequence), are eliminated.

The simplistic brilliance of this approach lies (1) within the underlying built-in psychology, and (2) the completeness of the "system". Upon completing his participation in our Certification Course, Mike Blevins, retired COO of Luminant, put it this way:

"The PPI material laces human behavior and psychology together with human performance improvement processes and human error reduction techniques, and wraps them all up as one package."

The 10,000 FT View

The Practicing Perfection® approach consists of two key elements:

- Focus on the Fundamentals
- Constant And Never-ending Improvement (CANI)

Hopefully, you can see by this high level overview that Practicing Perfection® is not 'rocket science'! And before we continue, I would like you to consider how the performance of your organization would be impacted if the majority of your team members bought into these two simple strategic/behavioral elements. Let's discuss each of these in a bit more detail.

Focus on the Fundamentals

I was a 49ers fan in the 80s. Having grown up in Fresno California, it was fun watching Joe Montana and Jerry Rice hardly ever lose. Into the 90s, as I moved around the United States, I wasn't much of a fan of any team, and in fact, paid less and less attention to the NFL. In the late 90s, we moved to New England. On September 23rd 2001, Drew Bledsoe, the New England Patriots' quarterback, got injured. Bill Belichick sent in young second string #12- Tom Brady. The Patriots lost against the New York Jets that day. I didn't even watch the game. As the season progressed, however, it was hard to ignore what was happening in Foxboro. My wife and I started paying attention. We became fans. Sundays were once again about football.

It's quite something to be a fan of a team that hardly ever loses. I've enjoyed being a fan of two 'football dynasties'- the 49ers and the Patriots. Today, Belichick and Brady are the most winning Coach/Quarterback paring of all time. However, when it comes to "greatest NFL coaches", it's likely that Vince Lombardi will forever hold the post that the trophy for winning the Super Bowl, implies- the best of the best.

In 1958, the Green Bay Packers had a record of 1-10-1 (one win, ten losses, and one tie). In 1959, Vince Lombardi took over as head coach. That year, with seven wins and five losses, Lombardi was named NFL "Coach of the Year". Going from 1-10-1 to 7-5 was an amazing transformation, especially considering that he achieved this with essentially the same team of players. How did he do it?

Lombardi's coaching style was pragmatic. It was methodical. It was repetitive. With a mantra of, "Perfect practice makes perfect," there were times when he would run the team through the same play 50 or more times in a row during practice- run until each team member executed his role perfectly.

In short, Vince Lombardi had a relentless *focus on the fundamentals*. His philosophy was simple:

If you can execute the fundamentals perfectly on the practice field, you'll execute them perfectly during a game. And when you execute perfect fundamentals, it doesn't matter what the competition throws at you. You're going to win football games.

And win they did. In the next eight years, the Green Bay Packers won five division championships and the first two Super Bowls, becoming the very first 'football dynasty'[1].

As I indicated before, when approached properly, improving *human performance* is not complicated. Vince Lombardi's approach to winning football games, focusing upon the fundamentals, is essential to any effort to improve performance. This is true for you and me as individuals, for sports teams, AND for business organizations.

Constant And Never-ending Improvement (CANI)

One of our Directors, Stacey Hefner, was previously involved as a safety professional in the auto industry. She likes to tell her story of an encounter she had while attending the SEMA (Specialty Equipment Manufacturing Association) Auto Show in Las Vegas. On the huge tradeshow floor, there was a central roped-off area with a silver car positioned atop a red carpet. During the show, an announcement over the PA system caused people to gather round. The crowd was prompted toward quietness as a man in a black-tailed tuxedo and white gloves emerged. Opening the driver-side door, he reached in and started the engine. The engine was idling, yet there was no perceptible sound. He then took a silver coin from his jacket pocket, and after showing it to the crowd, placed it upon the Roll's hood (bonnet). Still- no perceptible sound or vibration.

Sir Henry Royce provided the startup engineering brains behind Rolls Royce, and ultimately built the company. Charles Rolls, proprietor of a previous motor car venture, teamed with Henry in 1904 to start Rolls Royce; however, he was killed in 1910 while flying one of the Wright Brothers' planes.

A surviving story attests to a focused pursuit of the ideal. As the story goes, one day on the factory floor, Henry happened upon two engineers reviewing some specifications. He heard one engineer say to the other, "That's good enough." Nearly flying out of his pants, he passionately inserted himself into their conversation, ensuring both of these engineers were crystal clear- "It's NEVER 'good enough'!"

Sir Henry's pursuit of perfection became legendary, as exemplified by his oft-remembered quote: *"Strive for perfection in everything you do. Take the best that exists and make it better. When it does not exist, design it.[2]"*

The car upon the red carpet in the SEMA auto show was a Rolls Royce Silver Ghost. Built in 1907, the car had (at that point) been driven more than 250,000 miles. The engine had never been rebuilt. No noise. No perceptible vibration. Such is an example of what can be accomplished through the pursuit of the ideal (CANI).

The Foundation

The soundness and sustainability of any structure depends directly upon its foundation. The foundation is the base, the beginning, the first piece that must be built. There is no difference when devising and implementing an approach to improve performance. Yet, it is common to see a hodgepodge of efforts, often pieced together over time, void of a coherent philosophy and consolidated sense of purpose.

While virtually all efforts to improve performance have good intent, and many have very positive attributes, this lack of a common theme tends to promote silos of effort, inefficiency, and confusion on the frontline. Indeed, this is likely the reason for most of the "pursuit of excellence" efforts that have sprung up over the past few years- an attempt to bring things together. My issue with the "pursuit of excellence" is that, while the intent is good, it's typically undefined and abstract. Because of this, while it sounds wonderful along 'mahogany row', the messaging to the frontline simply ends up as more "corporate speak". If you haven't yet watched the short video, *"What's Wrong with Pursuing Excellence?"* you may want to stop reading for just a moment and do so now. Here's the link:

http://ppiweb.com/future-performance-improvement/pursuing-excellence/

The purpose of this foundation, which we refer to as the Precepts of Practicing Perfection®, is to provide a common core theme for all performance improvement efforts; a consistent philosophy, consistent understanding, and consistent message. If you are starting from scratch, this foundation provides an exceptional platform from which to coherently and systematically launch your strategies, campaigns, and tools. On the other hand, if you're like most organizations, you already have efforts underway such as your safety program, Six Sigma / LEAN initiatives, quality, error reduction, etc. Laying this foundation underneath everything you are already doing will (1) help weed out the unnecessary, (2) bring your other efforts together with a simple common philosophy, and (3) synergize your efforts, thereby multiplying impact and associated outcomes.

The Precepts of Practicing Perfection®

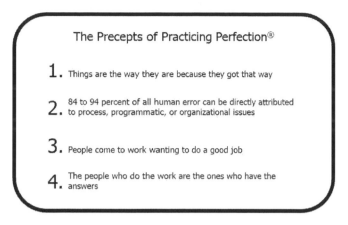

The Precepts of Practicing Perfection®

1. Things are the way they are because they got that way

2. 84 to 94 percent of all human error can be directly attributed to process, programmatic, or organizational issues

3. People come to work wanting to do a good job

4. The people who do the work are the ones who have the answers

Precept 1: Things are the way they are because they got that way

Precept number one is, in my opinion, one of the most brilliant and robust concepts anyone has ever come up with. I first came across this statement in a book titled, *The Secrets of Consulting*[3], given to me as a gift by my big brother, Larry, a couple of decades ago. I've had lots of fun with this during live presentations. Following a huge build-up of how awesome Precept #1 is, my grand 'unveiling' of the wording, is typically met with chuckles and something like, "Yea, duh!"

But when you dive into it, this precept is brilliant because of its simplistic absolute truth. It establishes a roadmap of logical thought about virtually anything. Think about it. If something (some condition, relationship, challenge, opportunity, etc.) is the way it is because it got that way, this means that there is a *reason* behind it. Understanding the *reason* (or *reasons*) why something is the way it is opens a doorway to the next level- if you don't like the way it is, or recognize that it could be better, you have the power to change it by going after its underlying *reason* (cause).

Incorporating this precept into your conscious thought does two very powerful things. First, it helps move you from *reactive* thinking to *responsive* thinking. What's the difference? Reactive thinking is essentially instantaneous. It is generated within your *lizard brain*. Remember the lizard brain? Its purpose in life is survival- your survival. Whatever condition or interaction (stimulation) has occurred, this part of your brain, your protector, will instantaneously prompt you toward one of two responses: Confront ('fight') or Run Away ('flight'). And it will do so without sending things upward to your logical brain because it wants to conserve energy. In other words, our first inclination is to *react*, and the lizard brain makes it awfully tempting. By consciously incorporating this precept into the way you conduct yourself (and yes, for many of us this takes a fair amount of effort), it causes you to slow down, and apply logical thought to whatever the stimulation happens to be. You are then able to *respond* rather than *react*.

Secondly, Precept #1 gives you the power to *choose*. Think about it- since everything in your life and in your organization is the way it is because it *got* that way, when there are things you don't like, or that are not as good as they could be, you have the power to change them! Oh, I know, you're probably now thinking, "...well, Tim just doesn't know the troubles I've seen!" You are correct. I don't know the 'troubles' you've seen. What I do know is this: while you can't do a thing to change what you have done or said (or what has been done to you) up to this point in your life, you have absolute total control of everything you say and do from this point forward. If something needs to change, you simply need to *choose* to change it! Doing anything less is surrendering your power and playing the *victim*. We'll dive into this in more detail in Chapter Five, Proactive Accountability®.

Before we move onward, I'd like to spend another couple of minutes on this topic of *choice*. All of the power, success, and happiness you currently have (or ever will have) in your life evolves from *choice*. In reality, the choices you make dictate the life that you lead. Don't believe me? Think about it this way: Consider all of the choices you have ever made in your entire life, the big ones, the little ones, the good ones, and the not-so-good ones. Put altogether, these decisions have brought you to wherever you are at this moment, reading these words. And for all of the good things you currently have going on, congratulations! These are the result of good *choices* you've made along the way. On the other hand, all of us have areas or parts of our lives that are not exactly as we would love them to be. And if such conditions in your life are ever going to change, *you* must start making different *choices.*

As I hope you've gathered, Precept #1 applies to everything you've got going on in your personal life, your relationships, your finances, your career, your role in your organization. As I've already indicated several times- this is not complicated. Things are the way they are because they got that way. Internalizing this awareness (and acting upon it) deeds to you tremendous power and opportunity to make things better.

Precept 2: 84 to 94 percent of human error can be directly attributed to process, programmatic, or organizational issues

Mistakes happen, and they are going to continue to happen. This is because human beings are *fallible*. This means that on any given day, any one of us can make a mistake. Even the best people (yes, even you and me) make mistakes. The huge problem within many organizations has been that when mistakes occur, the 'buck' often stops there. Senior leadership wants to know, "Who was responsible?!" The individual who initiated the action, or as James Reason likes to say, "*...the person on the sharp end of the stick,*" gets 'whacked', and...problem solved. After all, she screwed up, and received her punishment. She'll certainly never do it again!

Relative to that particular employee never doing "it" again, in most cases you'll be correct. You now have probably the best trained person in your organization on how to *not* do whatever she did under the specific set of conditions that existed at the time she chose to take that particular action. However, you have an entire organization of other employees, performing their assigned tasks under imperfect conditions, with imperfect processes, often less than perfect knowledge, skills and resources, in a very dynamic environment, working hard to 'get the job done'. It is highly likely (84 to 94 percent of the time[4]) that this individual, with the best of intentions, did what she thought was the right thing to do. This is a primary reason why the arena of *human error* has been such an enigma for so many for so long. With all of the HR sanctions, progressive discipline stipulations, and continually telling people, "Don't screw up!" how come errors continue to occur? How come people continue to get hurt? How come waste and inefficiency remain?

The reality is- most of the time human error occurs, some (or multiple) aspect(s) of your processes, programs, or organizational structures set the conditions in place for the mistake to have happened. Some of these contributors ("setups") are known and obvious. Some are quite subtle. Some are so obscure that they are likely not to be discovered until they dramatically reveal themselves through a daisy chain of conditions, actions, and inactions. What's important is to recognize that they exist, figure out what they are, and take action to eliminate them. This is the primary reason not to jump on the person on the 'sharp end of the stick' when an error occurs. In Chapter Seven, we'll be talking specifically about the concept of *just culture*, and how every error that does occur should be viewed as an opportunity to learn; to find out what those "setups" were and eliminate them. Take note, however- *just culture* does NOT mean "blame free" culture. Accountability is critical within a healthy highly reliable organization. We'll be delving into this in Chapter Five, Proactive Accountability®.

Within the 'science' of human error reduction, the "setups" contributing to the majority of human errors, are typically referred to as, "latent organizational weaknesses". This is an important concept for everyone in the organization to understand; however the term, *latent organizational weaknesses*, is going to lose most peoples' attention faster than a politician with a new pile of money. Remember, the lizard brain is looking for simple and tangible. In the world of Practicing Perfection®, we refer to these setups as *landmines*. Why? Everyone can relate. People know that (1) *landmines* are typically hidden, (2) you sure as heck don't want to step on one, and (3) if you do step on one, something really bad is going to happen! In other words, the average worker 'gets it'. You have their attention.

And here is something critically important for you to understand about *landmines* before we move on: your organization, right now, as you are reading this, is littered with them. Like Cambodia following the Vietnam War, they're everywhere, just waiting to be stepped on. How can I possibly know this? First, I'm going to really step out there and make a giant assumption that your organization, design, structure, and processes included, has been created by…people. And as we discussed before, human beings are *fallible*- everyone makes mistakes. Second, through my experience in this field for over 30 years, I've yet to see a business that wasn't chockfull of *landmines*. Even our organization, the Practicing Perfection Institute, Inc. harbors *landmines* (and we teach this stuff!).

This all might seem rather disheartening. People are *fallible*. *Landmines* are everywhere. What can you possibly do? Take heart. The next two precepts offer great positive hope, while Parts II and III of this book detail precisely how to put it all into play.

NOTE: We've released a short (65-second) video entitled *You're Gonna Find Whatever it is You're Lookin' For*. It offers a perfect lead-in to Precepts 3 and 4. If you've not yet seen it, go check it out now: http://ppiweb.com/human-performance-academy/the-answers/

Precept 3: People come to work wanting to do a good job

In my entire career, I've yet to meet a person who came to work wanting to make a mistake, wanting to get hurt, or wanting one of their co-workers to make a mistake or get hurt. People come to work wanting to do a good job.

Here's a question for you: Who are the most positive, most enthusiastic, most charged up members of your team? Generically speaking, the most eager 'bunch' of workers are…new people. Why? Because they (1) have been successful at achieving something they sought (their job on your team), (2) now have the means to support themselves and their families, and most importantly (3) have begun this new chapter of their lives believing (or at least hoping) that they can make a positive difference, that they can 'matter'. So why does this enthusiasm tend to wane over time? First, the sense of novelty/challenge of a 'new' job naturally diminishes over time. Second, the income derived from the job, while perhaps greatly appreciated in the beginning, becomes a 'given', no longer offering acute motivation. Both of these elements fall within the realm of what Frederick Herzberg referred to as "hygiene factors"[5], which we'll talk more about in Chapter Four. Their impact upon attitude, which we observe as enthusiasm, does not provide long term motivation.

It is the third element, a worker's believing (or at least hoping) that he or she can make a positive difference, that offers virtually unlimited win-win potential for organizations and the people who work within them. This is an intrinsic need of human nature. It is an absolute goldmine of opportunity for those who learn to leverage it. Unfortunately, through rote process, antiquated requirements, and supervisors and managers who feel the need to *control*, many organizations do a tremendous job, on a consistent basis, of stomping this enthusiasm right the heck out of many (if not most) of their workers. Let me give you an example…

A new worker, Dean, has come to work in your facility. He's thrilled to have his new job, having been out of work for four months since he left the Air Force. He was told that this was a great place to work by Juan, a friend from his tour in Iraq, who hired on as an Instrument Technician last year. Dean completed his indoctrination training, and did exceptionally well in the six weeks of classroom training required for his position. He impressed even the Operations Manager (who doesn't impress easily) with his speed of completing his OJT (On-the-Job Training). He qualified as Plant Operator in record time.

Dean has always taken a lot of pride in what he does. Like most people, he grabs personal satisfaction out of feeling that he is honestly contributing to the overall good. The further he settles into his qualified role, the more he feels ownership of 'his' equipment, the production, and the quality of his 'piece' of the overall mission of the organization.

Three months in as Plant Operator, Dean recognizes that the process for re-booting the controllers for Line A is causing excessive downtime. It is essentially 'backwards' from the way it could be done. Not only does it waste time, but it causes excessive strain on the system. Excited with his discovery, Dean takes his insights and a penciled-out 'better way' solution for re-booting the processors to his boss. His boss, Sharon, is very busy. As a supervisor, she has found herself mired in paperwork, with very little opportunity to actually 'supervise'. Sharon likes Dean; however, he's new and still 'learning the ropes'. Offering Dean but a few moments of her precious attention to listen to his ideas, she pauses, then replies, "Thanks for your input. I know you may have done things differently in the Air Force, but this is the way we've always done it here." End of discussion. Dean returns to his Operator duties.

Two weeks later, while doing his rounds, Dean identifies a *landmine* in the corner of the building where they have installed a new instrument rack in preparation for an upcoming plant modification. It's a safety hazard caused by a newly installed cable tray. To Dean, it's obvious that a slight modification could eliminate the hazard. Dean approaches Sharon. The words *safety hazard* got her attention. She listened to Dean, and appreciated his thoughts on a potential 'fix'. "It sounds like you've got a great idea, Dean," she offered. "Here's what I'd like you to do. Write all of this down, and send it to me in an email, and I'll forward it up through the system." Dean is thrilled. This is a chance to really make a difference! He spends that evening, at home, writing up his ideas. He draws a sketch of the simple fix that will eliminate the potential for head injury on the otherwise protruding cable tray. He scans his sketch into a pdf, and sends the entire electronic package to Sharon. Time passes. Sharon is busy. The 'system' for making changes is complex, convoluted, and takes a lot of time. She never gets around to submitting Dean's ideas. Construction is completed. Yellow and black caution tape is wrapped around the hazard.

Does any of this sound familiar to you? Think about this from Dean's perspective. He has gone 'above and beyond' to identify a wasteful/damaging process. He recognized a legitimate *landmine* in the making and, on his own time, prepared and submitted a simple solution. He did this because he cared; because he wanted to make a contribution beyond simply 'doing his job'. He took a risk and stepped forward...twice. And yet- nothing.

If Dean is like most, he *may* offer his insights another time or two, but at some point he'll likely figure that all he is doing is banging his head against the wall. And you know what? Banging your head against the wall hurts! At that point, if he is like the majority of people, he will make a conscious choice to stop doing it. And at that moment, both Dean and the company lose- big time. The organization has lost the creative-make-things-better energies of a bright, dedicated, and enthusiastic worker. Dean has concluded that his intrinsic need to 'make a difference' is simply not going to be met in this job within this organization.

Similar scenarios are playing out right now in organizations across the land. They are likely even occurring in *your* organization. And when an employee, no matter what their role or level in the organization, finds themselves in Dean's shoes, they'll likely make one of three choices:

- At best, the employee will become apathetic, tending toward a behavior of, "Okay, just tell me what to do." This is classic *victim* behavior. No more suggestions on how to make things better. No more working on their own time for the good of the company.

- If their level of disenchantment takes a deeper dive, and the employee chooses to hang around rather than leave and go work somewhere else, they may become disgruntled. What does this mean? The root of the word means 'to grunt' or 'to grumble'. Got the picture? You're likely thinking of an employee or two who fits such a description at this very moment. Through frustration, a disgruntled worker becomes very negative, cynical, and can actually cause problems. Such individuals often get categorized as "C Players", which we'll discuss in Chapter Four.

- The third option for the disenchanted worker is that he or she will quit. Their sense of self, and perhaps even their personal integrity will lead them to go find a place where their ideas and input are more appreciated.

In any of these three outcomes, the organization loses, big time. Are these types of scenarios playing out within your organization, in your department, on your team? If so, awareness is the first step in curing any disease.

Tapping into the intrinsic need of human beings to make a difference offers a goldmine of prospects for any organization. It's the primary mechanism through which landmines are removed, defenses are strengthened, quality is enhanced, productivity and reliability are elevated, and ultimately, profits are increased. The opportunity for your organization offered by this Precept is waiting to be tapped. *People come to work wanting to do a good job.* Isn't it time you let them?

Precept 4: The people who do the work are the ones who have the answers

As I mentioned during our discussion of Precept #2, all organizations (including yours and mine) are filled with landmines. They're everywhere, just waiting for the unaware foot, or knee, or hand, or finger, to come in contact with the detonator. So here's the question: Who do you think knows best where these *landmines* are located? Who do you think probably has the best ideas on how to 'dig them up' and get rid of them? The answer is simple- the people working closest to them.

If you were to stop for a moment, pause your reading, and think about it, I'd bet good money that you could quickly come up with at least half a dozen *landmines* that you have to deal with in your job on a regular basis. Workarounds, setups, safety hazards, potential 'holes in the deck' for you to step into. Chances are good that many of them have been there for a long time.

A critical aspect of long term sustainable performance improvement is the ongoing identification and elimination of these *landmines*. And here's where the great news comes into play. Your organization is made up of bright minds harboring potentially magnificent solutions. Further, they *want* to make things better, and when you encourage and allow them to do so, you're tapping into the 'magic' offered by Precept #3. You're giving individuals the opportunity to positively contribute (above and beyond simply 'doing their jobs'), which is more motivating than virtually anything else you can do as a boss or employer. And on top of this, you've improved safety, efficiency, reliability, morale, and/or productivity! Everybody WINs!

The 'System'

Human Performance remains as one of the most difficult areas in which to show tangible sustainable progress for most companies. A primary reason for this is that there has been a tendency to employ the same types of activities used to fix systems and equipment in an attempt to "fix" people.

The reality is...you cannot "fix" people. The good news is...most people do not need "fixing"! What's necessary is a different approach (the new paradigms we've been discussing thus far), combined with a simple doable 'system'. A 'system' containing the necessary elements to initiate, integrate, support, and sustain desired behaviors in a manner that generates continued upward momentum in performance.

Before we go any further, do you know how many ingredients there are in a loaf of French bread? (I'll bet this question caught you off guard.) There are four- flour, yeast, water, and salt. Four simple ingredients, each alone having only marginal value. BUT...when you combine these four simple ingredients together in the right proportions under the right conditions, you have something quite different. Have you ever had a hunk of French bread, still warm from the oven, slathered with *real* butter (I'm not talking about that *I Can't Believe it's Not Butter®* stuff)? That is a taste of pure Heaven! Four simple ingredients blended into magnificence. What's the point? The 'system' for achieving and sustaining next-level human performance works precisely the same way (no butter required).

As shown in the following figure, the 'system' involves four fundamental elements: Proactive Accountability®, Tools, Engagement, and Learning. Combining these elements in the right proportions under the right conditions, which graphically is where all four circles intersect, is where the 'magic' happens. This is what we refer to as the HU Factor®. The magnificent thing is, it isn't 'magic' at all.

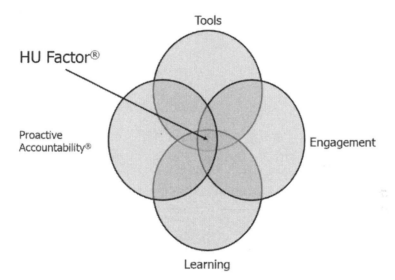

The HU Factor®

Proactive Accountability®

Within the Practicing Perfection® approach, we have created a new definition for what it means to be a *leader* within an organization. A *leader* is:

Any individual who takes full ownership of his or her actions and behaviors, and who positively influences the actions and behaviors of others.

Proactive Accountability® is essentially the internalization of being a *leader* in accordance with this new definition, and the associated behaviors that go along with it. A key word in this definition is *ownership*.

As you may recall from Chapter Two, Proactive Accountability® (PA) is the first term in the equation for achieving Viral Accountability®. This is such an important piece of next-level performance that I've devoted an entire chapter, Chapter Five, to providing you with the details for how to internally overcome the epidemic of *victimization* present in today's society, the internalization and growth of *accountability*, and how this element helps to transform your culture from being *reactive* to being *proactive*.

Tools

Beyond physical tools necessary to perform specific tasks/jobs, there are as well procedural/process/behavioral "tools" to guide and instruct your team members while they're doing their work. In order to be effective, these "tools" must:

- Be accurate, clear, and concise
- Be aligned with and promote the Core Principles of your organization
- Be easy to understand and to use
- Be appropriately robust
- Promote engaged thought during task performance
- Not conflict with other processes, policies, or procedures
- Not inappropriately impede the process of getting work done

A specific set of behavioral "tools" integrated into the Practicing Perfection® approach are the Error Elimination Tools™. These consist of (7) *fundamental* tools, which are to be used at all times while work is being conducted, and (8) *situational* tools, which are to be used when appropriate for the situation. We'll be discussing these in more detail in Chapter Eight.

The Error Elimination Tools™ have been crafted from those refined over the past 30 years within the US commercial nuclear and airline industries. At PPI, we've formatted these same tools into a fast, simple, and easy to use/understand handbook. You can grab a free copy of the Error Elimination Tools™ handbook by going here: http://www.6hoursafetyculture.com/resources/ee-tools/hb/

Engagement

In order to accelerate, maximize, and sustain improvement in human performance (and ultimately, organizational results), the operational culture of your organization (the way things actually get done on a day-to-day basis) must be *aligned* with your Core Principles. Alignment with Organizational Core Principles is critical to achieving desired sustainability. In reality, every organization (including yours) is perfectly aligned to get exactly the results it is currently getting. I'll be discussing how to help your organization define and refine your Core Principles in Chapter Four.

Engagement integrates and synergizes the other three elements of the HU Factor® on an ongoing basis. When done properly and consistently, this is the most powerful mechanism available for achieving organizational alignment.

There are three levels of Engagement:

- Focused engagement by team members upon the task at hand
- Regular engagement of members of the organization with one another

- Defined engagement between supervision/management and those doing the work (oftentimes referred to as "observation/coaching" within organizations)

We will be diving into each of these in Chapter Nine.

Learning

"Those who cannot remember the past are condemned to repeat it." -George Santayana

The truth about learning is simple:

- In a healthy organization, it is happening all the time and in all directions
- Open and honest communication is a prerequisite to learning
- Information gathering and follow-up systems must be readily accessible by all, as well as fast, simple, and easy to use
- All the learning in the world is worthless unless action is taken upon lessons learned

Learning is critical to long term sustainable performance improvement. You want to learn and take action so that you can repeat things that have gone well. You also want to learn and take action so that you do NOT repeat things that did not go well.

When melded together, the other three elements of the HU Factor® (Proactive Accountability®, Tools, and Engagement) create the platform for true Learning to take place; however, learning opportunities will not be maximized or properly leveraged unless there is a conscious and consistent intention to do so. A system should also be deployed to gather data and insights accumulated over time. Yes, this is a database. The thing to remember is that any database is simply a tool to help you identify and understand. It must never become the objective. If you don't recognize what I'm referring to, review the *Sirens of Human Performance* section in Chapter Two.

Where the 'magic' happens...

Rapid performance improvement occurs as these four elements are implemented and properly synthesized. As they become integrated into the fabric of the enterprise, long-term sustainable performance improvement results. Four simple elements. Simplicity on the far side of complexity.

Key Insights from Chapter Three

1. Practicing Perfection® is not complicated

2. A high level view of this approach reveals (2) key principles:
   - Focus on the Fundamentals (remember Vince Lombardi)
   - CANI (remember Henry Royce)

3. The Foundation for performance improvement consists of (4) simple precepts
   - Things are the way they are because they got that way
   - 84 to 94 percent of all human error can be directly attributed to process, programmatic, or organizational issues
   - People come to work wanting to do a good job
   - The people who do the work are the ones who have the answers

4. Many, many, many organizations are doing an exceptionally efficient job of stomping out new employee enthusiasm. Is yours one of them?

5. The 'System' for achieving and sustaining next-level performance is referred to as the HU Factor®. It consists of (4) elements:

   - Proactive Accountability®
   - Tools
   - Engagement
   - Learning

What can you do with what you just learned?

A. Recognize that human performance is not a mystery. By simply leveraging positive aspects of Human Nature, the culture of your organization can be transformed.

B. Take a few moments to consider what it would mean to the performance of your team/organization if the majority of members simply 'bought into' *Focusing on the Fundamentals*, and *Constant And Never-ending Improvement* (CANI).

C. Think of the two best things in your life right now (whether personally or professionally) and write them down. Now, dig down to the fundamental *reason(s)* these things exist, especially your involvement in making/allowing them to happen. Write down your reason(s). Now answer this question: What are you going to do, today, to strengthen, deepen, or further these great things in your life? Now- go do it.

D. Repeat the exercise in (C) above for the two greatest challenges you are currently facing. What are you going to do, today, to lessen, minimize, correct, or eliminate this challenge? Now- go do it.

E. Take each of the four key elements of the HU Factor® (Proactive Accountability®, Tools, Engagement, and Learning), and using the brief descriptions of each provided in this chapter, score your team/organization in each area on a scale from 1 to 10 (10 being uber super star level). This will help you know where to pay extra attention as you continue into Parts II and III.

F. Continue reading (you'll be glad you did).

[1] *When Pride Still Mattered*; <verify numbers>

[2] *Rolls Royce Motor Cars: Pursuit of Perfection*; May 2014; Hirmer Publishers

[3] *The Secrets of Consulting* (Dorset House, 1985, pg 58) by Gerald M. Weinberg

[4] 84 percent is derived from data compiled by Performance Improvement International within their work in the US nuclear generation industry; 94 percent is derived from the work of W. Edwards Deming

[5] Herzberg, Frederick; Mausner, Bernard; Snyderman, Barbara B. (1959). *The Motivation to Work* (2nd ed.). New York: John Wiley. ISBN 0471373893

Part II: Minds, Hearts, and Souls (and HOW to Influence Them)

Chapter Four: Individual and Organizational Performance

"Those who don't know how to get people to say yes
soon fall away; those who do stay and flourish."
-Robert Cialdini

On a Saturday morning in the autumn of 1976, I wandered into the base library at Naval Training Center (NTC) San Diego. No, this wasn't my idea of an ideal start to my weekend. Rather, like many young sailors, I was broke. Looking for something to do, the extremely reasonable cost of the library, aka free, sucked me in. Also, as I recall, it was about the only thing on the base that was open at that hour.

I wandered up and down the rows of books for a bit, gravitating, as I always had, toward non-fiction. About halfway down a center aisle, on the middle shelf on the right-hand side, I came upon Motivation and Personality by Abraham Maslow. I scanned the table of contents. The first three chapters sounded quite boring. What struck me was the title of Chapter Four, "A Theory of Human Motivation." I borrowed the book and headed back to the barracks. I spent the rest of my weekend inside of that book. I was hooked.

We can all look back at specific moments and circumstances in our lives that, for whatever reason, had profound impact upon us. This was one of mine- a happy 'accident' of having blown all of my money on Broadway the night before. It put me on a lifelong journey of personal study and observation of people- why we do, what we do, the way we do it.

Human motivation is fascinating. When you combine a basic understanding of how it works with insights in how to influence, you are given tremendous power- power to transform relationships, families, teams, organizations, even societies. In truth, those who have harnessed this power, both the 'good' and the 'bad', have moved the world to where it is today. Those who understand, master, and grasp this power will determine the future.

Motivation

Individually, we humans are very unique. 'En masse' however, we tend to attract, react, and respond fairly predictably. This provides you and me, those of us who want to 'make things better', with a grand opportunity. This begins with a basic understanding of *motivation*.

To begin, a look at the root word of *motivation*, "motive", yields the following definition: an emotion or desire operating on the will and causing it to act.[1] It should be clear that *emotions* and *desires* 'operating on our will' all happen inside of us. The point is- all motivation is internal. This is very important to understand when you and I are seeking to influence the behaviors of others.

Motivation 101

We previously discussed the 'gatekeeper' of the brain, the Amygdala, which I like to refer to as the *lizard brain*. Its function is your survival. All external stimulation passes through this part of the brain, and as we previously discussed, it makes very rapid *fight* or *flight* decisions. It also makes choices, whenever possible, to conserve energy by either blocking or filtering information from the 'higher' parts of the brain.

When we get to the most primal level of motivation, all of the choices we make are based upon one of two drives/desires: Either to avoid pain, or to acquire pleasure. The lizard brain has a high level of bias in the instantaneous interpretation of potential pain or pleasure. This is why we sometimes tend to *react* in a given situation without giving it much (if any) conscious thought. An example might be the 'lashing out' at another person as a defense or deflection mechanism, or the making of a stupid choice upon a moment of temptation.

What's important to understand is that while virtually all human beings make choices based upon pain and pleasure, as individuals our perceptions or interpretations of what can bring us pain or pleasure can be entirely different. For example, I like to climb to high places and look down. When we lived in the northeastern US, one of our favorite places to take visitors was to Quechee Gorge in Vermont. I loved to stand in the middle of the Quechee Gorge Bridge, hang over the rail, and look straight down at the river, 163 feet below. This brought me, as we would say in New England, a *wicked rush* (aka pleasure). On the other hand, my wife didn't even like walking across the bridge, let alone looking over the edge. To do so brought her pain.

This is where simplicity (the similarity of human beings 'en masse') is met with complexity. As individuals we can be very different. These concepts of similarity and individuality are key points to remember as we move forward to discuss how to influence behaviors. Fortunately, the Individual Performance Model™ offers a simple (and extremely impactful) approach. We'll get there shortly, but first, a bit more insight on *motivation*.

Motivation 101-601

As a human being, you make choices. Each of us makes many choices every day. Some of these choices are made instantaneously. An example would be the choice to abruptly swerve in traffic to avoid getting hit by the texting teenager drifting across the lane next to you. This, of course, is often accompanied by one or more 'colorful metaphors' gestured in her direction, also rather instantaneous. Other choices are made s-l-o-w-l-y, sometimes painfully. An example might be the decision to break up with a fiancé (or maybe to accept someone as a fiancé in the first place).

Through the entire spectrum of making decisions, the big ones, little ones, instantaneous ones, and the laborious ones- all of the choices you make are based upon your internal response to a single simple question: What's In It For Me? (WIIFM?). Whether this is a reaction processed in your lizard brain, or is made upon conclusion of a great deal of time and energy consumed by your cerebral cortex, your choice is derived from whatever you decide is the 'best' answer to this question at that point in time.

We can therefore say that all choices, whether they're yours, mine, or anyone else's, are made for selfish purposes. Even the most 'selfless' acts, careers, and aspirations are based upon an internal answer to the question- WIIFM?

As we now move forward to build your platform for becoming a powerful influencer, it will serve you well to remember these two truths regarding human motivation:

- All motivation is internal
- Every choice a person makes is in response to- WIIFM?

Maslow

Abraham Maslow is best known for constructing a 'hierarchy' of basic human needs, where human focus (*motivation*) moves upward as each 'lower level' need becomes satisfied. You've probably seen a depiction of this hierarchy in high school or college psych class, or perhaps in some leadership training that one or more of your employers has put you through. Most illustrations of the hierarchy are similar to the following figure.

Malsow's Hierarchy of Human Needs

Maslow's hierarchy may not have 'made your socks go up and down' when you were first introduced to it (mine did, but then, I'm weird like that). It likely struck you as another piece of academia that was, at best, mildly interesting. For those of us who want to influence behaviors, however, Maslow has offered us a great source of awareness and understanding into human motivation. Here are a few things to consider:

- These are *needs*, not *wants*. Needs are much more powerful than simple desires.

- Even though there are variations in relative strength, as humans we all pretty much have these same basic needs.

- The "hierarchy" implies that once a lower level need is met, an individual's focus and motivations typically move upward to the next level.

- The hierarchy also implies that if a lower level need is no longer being met, attention and motivations tend to drop down to wherever the void happens to be.

Before I give you a basic example of how this works, I want to explain *self-actualization*. The other levels are pretty obvious, but I have come across many who are not familiar with this term. Self-actualization is the sense that we are doing what we were meant to do. For example, if your sense of 'self' is that you were meant to be a writer, once your lower level needs are met, your primary motivation will be to...write. People who are self-actualized, or self-actualizing, are generally at a higher level of general satisfaction and even happiness, because they are doing (or pursuing) what they believe they were put on this planet to do. Hopefully you are such a person, and know exactly what I'm talking about.

Here's a thumbnail sketch of how Maslow's hierarchy works: Our most basic needs are physiological. We need air to breath, water to drink, food to eat. If there is lack amongst any of these needs, this essentially occupies our entire focus (and motivation). For example, if I suddenly find myself without air to breathe, nothing else much matters. Once these needs are satisfied, however, we tend to focus upon the next level- acquiring a sense of safety and security. We wear clothing. We lock our doors. We like to live in safe neighborhoods (consider the popularity of gated communities). As long as we feel 'safe', our motivations then turn toward relationships, and the need to 'belong'. We need to feel valued and respected by others. We need some sense of kinship. We need to love and feel loved. Remember, these are *needs* not *wants*. While most people resolve this need in a relatively healthy manner, unhealthy pursuits can turn into such things as joining a gang, remaining with an abusive partner, or harmful co-dependency upon others.

Some sense of being valued and respected by others, which is part of the love and belongingness need, is absolutely essential for most people to move into self-esteem. With all of the other needs satisfied, this is now where we value and respect ourselves. In most of the world today, the three lower-level needs are generally met most of the time. Self-esteem, however, is where a lot of people get stuck. This is a primary reason why "Self-Help" / "Self-Improvement" in the United States is currently a $12 Billion per year industry[2].

If you are fortunate enough to have healthy self-esteem, you can then move into self-actualization. Depending upon what you believe you have been 'put here to do', this can involve varying of levels of risk. For example, consider the level of risk involved when an artist has their first public exhibit. Or when an actor has their first audition. Providing there's no alcohol involved (I'm having visions of Karaoke bars), consider the guts it takes for a person who really believes they are meant to sing to get behind the 'open mic' for the first time. Adequate self-esteem must exist for there to ever even be a first attempt. Substantial self-esteem must be present in order to overcome/deal with the rejections that inevitably occur in the initial stages of virtually any worthwhile pursuit.

Now let's say that you're doing well in the hierarchy. You've got solid self-esteem and you generally feel that you're exercising your God-given talents and are fulfilling your life's purpose (*self-actualization*). Life is good. All of a sudden you have a very sick child, or lose your job, or your spouse tells you he wants a divorce. All of a sudden, being self-actualized and of high self-esteem are no longer so important, at least not for a while. Your focus and primary motivation will drop down to whichever need is no longer being filled.

Why are we taking the time to go through all of this 'psychology' stuff? If you want to be an effective influencer, if you want to achieve sustainable performance improvement; if you honestly want to transform the culture of your organization, a basic level of psychological awareness is critical to understanding peoples' *why*. We could go into a lot more detail, but it's not necessary. Remember, we're looking for simplicity on the far side of complexity. To move this toward practical application, let's move onto Frederick Herzberg's take on Maslow's hierarchy.

Herzberg

Frederick Herzberg was an American psychologist who became extremely well known in the field of business management. Among other things, he took Maslow's hierarchy and applied it to the workplace. Basically, what he discovered and attempted to communicate to the business world was that the things that make people satisfied and motivated on the job are different in kind from the things that make them dissatisfied.[3] I say *attempted* to communicate because, as you will see when we dive into a very simple explanation below, most organizations are still far from 'getting it'. Here's an excerpt from his 2003 Harvard Business Review article, *One More Time: How do You Motivate Employees?*

Ask workers what makes them unhappy at work, and you'll hear about an annoying boss, a low salary, an uncomfortable work space, or stupid rules. Managed badly, environmental factors make people miserable, and they can certainly be demotivating. But even if managed brilliantly, they don't motivate anybody to work much harder or smarter. People are motivated, instead, by interesting work, challenge, and increasing responsibility. These intrinsic factors answer people's deep-seated need for growth and achievement.

To keep this simple, and within the context of something you can put to immediate use, Herzberg took Maslow's hierarchy and divided it into two regions: *Hygiene Factors* and *Motivating Factors*.

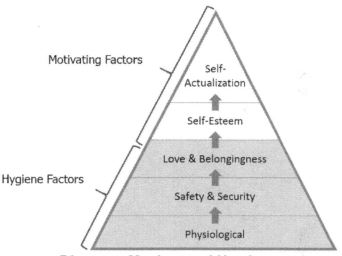

Diagram: Maslow and Herzberg

Let's return to the statement from the first paragraph on Herzberg: "the things that make people satisfied and motivated on the job are different in kind from the things that make them dissatisfied."

The things/conditions that make people *satisfied* and *motivated* on the job are what Herzberg referred to as *Motivating Factors*. When we relate this to Maslow's hierarchy, we can see that we're talking about things/conditions that help build/satisfy *self-esteem* and *self-actualization*.

Herzberg referred to the things/conditions that directly cause dissatisfaction on the job as *Hygiene Factors*. Notice where these factors reside within the hierarchy- at the bottom. Physiological (yes, people need to work to feed themselves and their families), Safety and Security (okay, a sense of job security becomes acute when it is threatened), Love & Belongingness (when respect and a sense of belongingness are not present at work, this tends to negatively impact attitudes and behaviors). Here's a key point (make sure you get this): The presence of these factors does *not* motivate workers; however, the lack of or threat to their fulfillment can (and typically does) cause acute dissatisfaction/de-motivation.

Why is this so important? Most organizations *still* have not figured this out. What types of things do most companies *still* do in an attempt to *motivate* workers? Trinkets, gift cards, pay raises, bonuses; where do all of these fall within the hierarchy? *Hygiene Factors*. And yet, senior management remains baffled: How can it possibly be, even though they've been so 'generous', that changes in behaviors do not 'stick', and workers continue to mumble and complain?

This is why the title of Herzberg's 2003 Harvard Business Review article began with, *"One More Time..."* Note a bit of frustration? He had been writing and teaching about his findings since the late 1950s / early 1960s. And today? You tell me. How is your organization attempting to *motivate* the members of your workforce?

Now for the great news! Take a look at where the *Motivating Factors* lie in Maslow's hierarchy, and consider, just for a moment, how the upper tier of *belongingness, self-esteem,* and *self-actualization* might possibly fit into an organizational scheme of promoting different behaviors, and ultimately, of transforming culture.

At this point, you either (1) totally get this and are thrilled with what you're reading, (2) kind of 'get it' but don't yet see practical application, or (3) don't have a clue. If you fall into either category (2) or (3), consider this: When was the last time you received an honest sincere compliment about something you put a lot of effort into? How did it make you feel? If the compliment was about a specific behavior, did you then repeat that behavior? Were you *motivated* to do more of the same? How much time did it take the person who complimented you to do so? If it happened at work, how much money did that compliment, that moment of positive recognition, cost the company? Are you beginning to see where this is headed?

In Chapter Two of *The Eight Habit*, Stephen Covey discusses the "Whole Person Paradigm." The basic premise of this paradigm is that Human Nature is four dimensional- body, mind, heart, and spirit. These human needs can be directly related to Maslow's *self-esteem* and *self-actualization*- to Herzberg's *Motivating Factors*. By appealing to each of the four dimensions as much as possible, an organization is filling intrinsic human needs. Employees fortunate enough to work within such organizations enjoy their jobs more, and are more committed to organizational success. Because of this, these organizations draw out greater levels of talent, creativity, and make-thing-better energies from workers. Truly WIN WIN. I am happy to say that this context is built directly into the implementation strategies and tactics of Practicing Perfection®.

PAM

Taking a final, slightly different, look at how to sustainably impact worker motivation, author Dan Pink has offered a great perspective in his book, Drive: The Surprising Truth about What Motivates Us[4].

The science shows that...typical twentieth-century carrot-and-stick motivators- which we consider somehow a "natural" part of human enterprise- can sometimes work. But they're effective in only a surprisingly narrow band of circumstances. The science shows that "if-then" rewards... are not only ineffective in many situations, but can also crush the high-level creative, conceptual abilities that are central to current future economic and social progress. The science shows that the secret to high performance isn't our biological drive (our survival needs) or our reward and punishment drive, but our third drive- our deep-seated desire to direct our own lives, to extend and expand our abilities, and to fill our life with purpose.

Pink's take on what he calls the third drive brings us to P.A.M., which stands for Purpose, Autonomy, and Mastery. Please note that I've taken a bit of literary license here. Dan presents these in the order of [APM] Autonomy, Mastery, and Purpose. I have changed the order for two reasons. First, "PAM" offers an easy (and cute) way to refer to the trilogy of the third drive, Secondly, while Dan talks about finding purpose through autonomy, which allows for the development of mastery, I prefer to look at it as when given a sense of purpose with autonomy, an individual will then develop mastery. Either way- it works. If you're a Dan Pink fan, I hope you're not upset with me, and if you Dan Pink, are reading this, I hope you see my logic.

Purpose

> *"Those who are most productive and satisfied- hitch their desires to a cause larger than themselves."*
> -Dan Pink

Why do you exist? What is your 'reason for being'? Chances are pretty good that you've thought about this a time or two. If you love your work, congratulations. You've managed to find some answers to this question (why you're here) and integrate [at least some of] them with what you do (at your job). If you don't love your work, my advice is to either figure out how to do so, which of course involves working within / doing something that satisfies your sense of purpose, or...quit and go to work somewhere else. Realize, of course, that there will likely be elements of virtually any vocation that you don't love doing. I've had the opportunity to build a business structure that I consider ideal. We have a team of unbelievably talented dedicated people. We're fulfilling our purpose by helping to make the world a better and safer place, and there are still [many of my] current responsibilities that I do not especially enjoy. Make sure that you consider the whole picture of your current situation before you decide to pull up stakes and head to different pastures.

Stephen Covey put forward his interpretation of life's journey as, to live, to love, to learn, to leave a legacy. Brenden Burchard's work asks the questions, "Did I live? Did I love? Did I matter?" Each of these culminates in... purpose. Since the first human looked up at the stars and pondered his or her existence, the question of purpose had been part of the human psyche. I've personally always looked at life as an ongoing journey of discovery and opportunity; of cause, effect, consideration and resolution. Unfortunately, because of all the 'stuff' that happens in life, many people are not consciously aware of their purpose, nor are they seeking its discovery. Nevertheless, it exists. This intrinsic aspect of Human Nature is simply lying under the surface, waiting to be discovered and embraced.

The concept of Purpose offers tremendous opportunity to organizations. Helping workers discover their purpose, and then helping them find ways to fulfill/satisfy this purpose through what they do on the job should be a corporate priority. When an individual is working with a sense of purpose, they bring forth maximum determination, resolve, commitment, and contribution of make-things-better creative energy- because they want to.

Autonomy

> *"The highest and best form of efficiency comes through the spontaneous cooperation of a free people."*
> -Bernard Baruch

In Chapter Two, we discussed the old paradigm of 'managing people like things'. If you recall, this paradigm is all about control. The opposite of control is autonomy. Autonomy is self-directed freedom. It's the opposite of micro-managing, of over-prescriptiveness, of processes and workflows mired in bureaucracy.

Unfortunately, 'command and control' is still alive and well in the corporate world. "Well, of course!" you say. "We can't simply have people running around willy-nilly doing whatever they choose! We have a business to run, regulations to meet, shareholders to make happy!" Of course you do. But as I said earlier, the old paradigm of managing people like 'things' is as outdated today as is the medical procedure of bloodletting. Here are the facts:

- *Control* leads to *compliance* (If you've forgotten what behaviors look like in a compliance-based environment, re-read *Compliance-vs-Desire* in Chapter Two.)

- Autonomy leads to engagement

So, how are we doing in "corporate America" relative to autonomy and engagement? Not too good! According to ongoing Gallup research, Less than one-third (31.5%) of U.S. workers were engaged in their jobs in 2014. Surveys revealed that a majority of employees, 51%, remain "not engaged", while 17.5% were "actively disengaged"[5]. If you're involved with LEAN / Six Sigma, you're likely familiar with the challenge of the Eighth Waste- lack of engagement / underutilized workers.

Should any of this be of direct interest to you? Wherever your particular performance improvement focus may lie, you will be directly, positively, and substantially impacted by raising worker autonomy and engagement. When you consider the following numbers, it should be obvious who [everyone] wins by affording autonomy to workers. Organizations in the top quartile of employee engagement have:

- 48% fewer safety incidents
- 41% fewer patient safety incidents
- 21% higher productivity

- 41% fewer quality defects
- 22% higher profitability[6].

Mastery

> *"The desire to do something because you find it*
> *deeply satisfying and personally challenging inspires*
> *the highest levels of creativity, whether it's in the*
> *arts, sciences, or business."* - Teresa Amabile
> Professor- Harvard University

Mastery is where the pieces of the trilogy come together and become self-reinforcing. When you combine a sense of *why* (*purpose*) with self-directed freedom to figure out the best way to perform a task, solve a problem, or create something new (*autonomy*), a worker's sense of, expertise in, and skill related to her assigned role will continually rise (*mastery*). This ongoing perception of achievement then reinforces her sense of *purpose*. The cycle continues, and builds upon itself, providing that organization leaders, managers, and supervisors do their part to initiate, allow, guide, and reinforce.

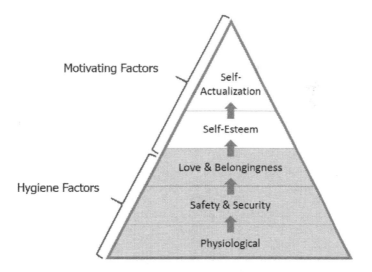

Diagram: Purpose - Autonomy - Mastery

Bringing it all Together

My first commercial nuclear power plant experience was at the River Bend Station near St. Francisville, Louisiana. Living there for six years, I developed a love for many things Cajun- Etouffee, Jambalaya, crawfish boils, Mardi Gras, King Cakes, and of course, the overall attitude of, "Laissez les bons temps roulez!" (Let the good times roll!).

River Bend was where I acquired my Senior Reactor Operator License and functioned as a Shift Technical Advisor; however, I spent most of my time there in the Training Department. My roles consisted of helping new operators pass their license examinations, as well as providing ongoing ('Requal') training to the licensed Reactor Operators (ROs) and Senior Reactor Operators (SROs).

I remember a particular student, we'll call him Jimmy, who went through training and passed his Reactor Operator license exam. I liked Jimmy. He was pretty much a 'middle-of-the-road' student, which is significant, considering the toughness of nuclear operator license regimen. He was a slight bit 'odd' in the personality department, but likeable nonetheless. After he passed his license exam, he was placed on Crew D.

Shortly after Jimmy got his license, I moved from Initial License Training to Requalification Training, which meant that I was then involved with each crew, watching them perform in the simulator, every eight weeks or so. When it was Crew D's turn, they would spend their week in the Training Center, participating in the same classroom training and simulator scenarios as the other crews. Jimmy's performance was on par with virtually all of the other licensed ROs.

As instructors, we were required once a month to spend a day in the plant. This allowed us to (1) see how training was (or was not) being utilized, (2) further our relationships with the Operators, and (3) keep abreast of what was going on in the 'real world'. My position as a Shift Technical Advisor also brought me into the plant a couple of times per month for my 24-hour shifts. During the times when I observed or interacted with Crew D, I couldn't believe how Jimmy was being treated. In the simulator, he performed as well as most of the ROs in the Operations Department, and better than some of the other Crew D ROs. Yet, on shift he was being relegated to non-licensed duties. During this and subsequent observations, it became obvious that everything he was asked to do in the plant was micro-managed by the SRO or the Shift Supervisor. I did a little digging, and discovered that the only time he was being allowed to stand watch in the Control Room was when it was necessary to keep his license current. He had become the crew's scapegoat. His fellow crew members made fun of him. He was given a nickname (which cannot be repeated here).

Needless to say, over time Jimmy became extremely discouraged. He was unhappy, resentful, and was beginning to doubt his own capabilities. None of his upper level *needs* were being met. In spite of his solid capabilities, he was being given zero *autonomy*. His self-esteem was being trashed regularly. I had to hand it to him, he hung in there a lot longer than I would have. Crew D supervision had generated a recipe for (1) a solid case of apathy (on Jimmy's part) and an accident waiting to happen, (2) Jimmy diving into 'C Player' behaviors (we'll talk about this in Chapter Nine), or (3) Jimmy finding another place to work. Fortunately, senior leadership saw fit to transfer Jimmy to another crew before he reached a point of 'no return'.

On his new crew, with a 'clean slate', Jimmy flourished. He rapidly earned the respect of his fellow crew members. His *self-esteem* rose. Because of the respect that he earned, he was given *autonomy* to do his job. His opinions mattered and were honored. He developed *mastery* within the RO ranks, and was selected for Senior Reactor Operator training. He completed his SRO exam with no problems. Last I knew, Jimmy was the Assistant Operations Manager.

Hopefully you're beginning to tie things together: Malsow's *low level needs*, Herzberg's *Hygiene Factors*, Covey's "managing people like things", and Dan Pink's *biological* and *reward and punishment drives* are saying the same thing. These do not, cannot, and will not generate the behaviors or levels of commitment required to achieve, let alone sustain, next-level performance. What's needed are fulfillment of *higher level needs* (Maslow), *Motivating Factors* (Herzberg), the *Whole Person Paradigm* (Covey), and the *third drive* (Pink).

I have presented this information to help broaden and deepen your awareness and understanding of human motivation. Fortunately, you don't need to be an expert in this stuff in order to take the performance / culture of your team or organization to the next level. As you will discover through your continued reading, the underlying psychology, *Motivating Factors*, and associated *triggers of influence* are built-in to the simple strategies and tools that I will present to you as we continue on this journey.

Influence

"The only way any transaction can be sustainable is when both parties are making a profit."
-Tim Autrey

As I hope you are now convinced, all motivation is internal. You cannot *motivate* another human being to do anything. If you want another person to do something, you have one of two choices: You can *force* them to do it, or you can *influence* them to do it.

One of my greatest blessings in life has been my parents. Not because without them I wouldn't be here (which, of course, is true), but because of how they raised me. I was not the easiest child (yes, my Mom still reminds me from time to time), but not because I was disrespectful, or got involved with the wrong crowd. Essentially, I've always been an overly-ambitious rebel. The heck with the moon, I want the stars. Tell me I can't do something and I'll do my best to prove you wrong. And one of the things I loved about my parents was, any time I was ever told 'no' (and it did happen from time to time), the reason was never, "Because I told you so!" They never lorded their parental authority over me. Whenever I was not allowed to do or have some particular thing (and yes, I hated it), they always took the time to explain *why*. Use of *force* kills relationships. I adore my parents. My Dad, Ray Autrey, passed on New Year Day 2013. He has always been, and will forever be, my hero.

Use of force is the old paradigm; of managing people like 'things'. So if *force* is out (and I hope you agree with me that it is, except in extreme cases such as worker termination), and we can't *motivate* another person to do anything, what's left? *Influence*.

Influence is the act or power of producing an effect, in our case a desired change in behavior, without the exertion of force or direct exercise of command. To make this tangible and powerful, I want you to think of your efforts to influence the behaviors of others as *transactions*. A transaction is an exchange or transfer of goods, services, or funds between two parties that reciprocally affect or influence each other. An effort to influence is a transaction- I offer you something, and I get something in return. And here's the key: the only way any transaction can be sustainable is when both parties are making a profit.

There are two ways to influence- you can either *inspire,* or you can *manipulate*. While either of these is better than *force*, only one results in true motivation- *inspiration*.

Manipulation is a 'win-lose' or 'I win more than you do' transaction. In the work environment, many are still attempting to influence behaviors using 'carrots' of promised rewards- gift cards, tee shirts, bonuses…ugly nylon jackets. To relate this back to Herzberg, all of these things fall into the category of *Hygiene Factors*

We moved recently, which involved cleaning out my closet. When doing so, I discovered that I had a bunch of tee shirts and jackets, accumulated over my years of service at nuclear power plants and with various PPI clients. I had never worn them, but until the 'clean out', had for some reason chosen not to part with them. As I was considering which of my clothes to keep and what to give away, I decided to throw all of these 'carrots' onto a separate pile. The first thing that struck me was how big the pile was (and I had never worn *any* of these things). The second thing that struck me was how *ugly* they were. Clearly, they were not going to survive the move.

As I began stuffing the tee shirts and jackets into a bag headed to the Salvation Army, I had a thought, "Had *any* of these items ever *motivated* me to do...anything?" My previous employers had spent good money on these things. They had given them to me and my co-workers in gratitude for specific achievements- schedules met, milestones reached, safety records broken. But had they in any way influenced my behaviors? My answer was a resounding- no. Such a waste!

So if 'carrots' only *manipulate,* and do not truly *motivate*, why does this remain the primary means of attempting to move worker behaviors in one direction or another? It's left-over old-school thinking. It's what's known. It's easy. And...it's what's always been done. This brings to mind the insanity of doing the same old things while hoping for different (next-level) behaviors and results.

Physical rewards are not bad things. I'm not even saying you should do away with them. Used properly, rewards can provide benefit. But the benefit comes not from the rewards themselves, but rather from the recognition that accompanies them. This is where you have a grand opportunity to move from manipulation to inspiration. Here's an example...

I previously mentioned how I had the opportunity to lead a human performance 'experiment' during my last job at a nuclear power plant. This was the effort that led to the 87.5% reduction in human error rate. About three quarters of the way through this period, the Plant Manager, Kevin, called me into his office and handed me a large envelope. The papers inside of the envelope explained that I was being awarded stock options because of my efforts and successes in elevating human performance at the plant. This was nice, and yes I appreciated it; however, my response to reading the letter was apparently not quite as enthusiastic as Kevin had anticipated. "I don't think you understand," he said, "I can count on one hand the number of people in the entire company who are receiving such a reward." And then came the important part, "I recognize, Mike [the Site VP] recognizes, and obviously the company recognizes, how hard you've worked to take our human performance to where we are now. What you have achieved is amazing."

To be honest, the stock option reward was substantial- way beyond any physical reward I had ever received before. Even still, it now being years later, I can't remember how many shares were involved or how much it was worth (I cashed it all out when I left the company). Did the stock options change my behavior? Nope. Did it make me feel better about my company? Nope. What I can tell you though, it that my meeting with the Plant Manager did have a lasting and *inspiring* impact. My motivation to move things even further was piqued. As a matter of fact, as I write this I can still feel the emotion of, and gratitude for, that particular *experience*. Not because of what was in the envelope, but because of six of Kevin's words (and how he said them), "What you have achieved is amazing."

Inspiration comes not through gifts or physical things, but through *experiences*. Any interaction you have with another human being provides each of you with an *experience*. We're going to explore this in detail during our discussion of the Individual Performance Model™. For now, remember that your direct attempts to influence are transactions, and the only way any transaction can be sustainable is when both parties are making a profit. The currency of *Inspiration* is your ticket for achieving long term sustainable performance improvement.

The Personal Screening Process

If you want to influence the behaviors of another person, you first have to make it past their *lizard* brain. Remember, the lizard brain's purpose is survival. Because of this, it functions as a gatekeeper, screening and filtering incoming information and stimulation. And it does so rapidly. As an example, let's say that you and I are having an interaction where you are wanting to influence me to do…something (it doesn't really matter what). As you begin to make your case, my 'gatekeeper' immediately asks and processes the answers to two questions. In order for any type of *transaction* to take place between us, the answers to both of these questions must be YES. This is called the *Personal Screening Process*, and is illustrated in the following figure.

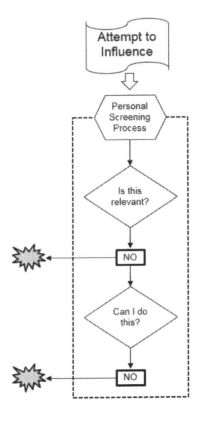

Personal Screening Process- Gatekeeper Response

If you are attempting to influence me in any way, my brain immediately asks question one: *Is this relevant?* Is this relevant to who? To me. This first hurdle, put into different words, was covered in the section, "Motivation 101-601" (WIIFM?). Remember- every decision we make is made in response to this question. In order for me to let you through the gate, I must feel that there is something in it for me; that I will somehow get something that I want out of the deal. If my answer to this question is NO, we're done. I may smile and nod, but the gate will remain closed. There will be no transaction. You will not, in this interaction, be influencing my behavior.

If I do believe this is relevant (to me), my mind immediately jumps to the second question: *Can I do this?* Do I have the ability? Am I physically and/or mentally capable? If whatever you're wanting me to do seems beyond my capabilities, my brain will perceive imminent pain should I make the attempt. As we've already discussed, our strongest primal motivation is to avoid pain. At this point, a quick balance is calculated: WIIFM versus the perception of pain involved. If pain wins, my immediate response to the question, "Can I do this?" will be NO. In this case, we're done. No transaction will be taking place. Once again, you will not be influencing my behavior.

The reason this is so important to understand is that the brain function I just covered is true for virtually all of us, all of the time. This is not a problem as long as you understand it. As you will now see, there is a simple way to deal with the gatekeeper.

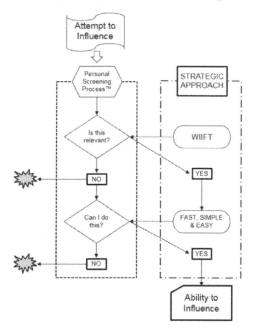

Personal Screening Process- Your Approach

As you can see in this diagram, the approach for dealing with the gatekeeper is quite simple. Once you master it, you will be amazed at how receptive others will become. And, by the way, this works every bit as well in personal relationships as it does at work. Please DO try this at home!

Step One: The very first 'gateway' you must pass through is-WIIFM? So what do you think your approach ought to be? It's obvious. You want to couch whatever it is you're wanting to promote within the context of what's in it for...THEM (WIIFT). This is where most people screw it up. Let's say you're wanting to get Mel, a 48-year old iron worker, to wear hearing protection when working in a particular area- on his own, without the safety patrol being around. The standard approach might be to point out the signs on the wall, the requirements of the safety manual, and conditions of employment. You may even use an approach such as, 'studies have shown...', or talk about how important the site safety record is. NO, NO, NO, NO, NO! Do this, and what Mel's brain will register will be nothing more than the muffled sounds of grown-ups 'preaching' in the Charlie Brown cartoons.

You want to promote the use of hearing protection from the perspective of what's in it for...Mel. You might try an approach something like, "You know, Mel, my Grandfather was an iron worker. Retired after 40 years. By the time he left the plant, he could barely hear. Back in the day, nobody wore hearing protection. As kids, we used to have fun throwing a cuss word or two into our conversation when he was the only adult in the room. He couldn't hear us. I feel badly about that now. You'll probably have grandkids soon, right? Won't it be great the first time your granddaughter looks you in the eyes with, "I love you, Granddad!" And won't it be wonderful to be able to hear her say those words?

Hopefully you get the picture. Make whatever it is about *them*, something *they* want, something *they* care about. Appeal to emotion whenever possible.

Step Two: Once you've successfully communicated that this [desired behavior] is indeed to *their* benefit, and truly is in *their* best interest, you've opened the first lock on the gate. Now it's time to turn the second tumbler by garnering a YES answer to, "Can I do this?" Once again, the strategy here is…simple. You want to make whatever it is that you want them to do to appear to be *fast, simple,* and *easy.* Break it down if necessary. As was hilariously portrayed in the Bill Murray movie, *"What About Bob?"*…take 'baby steps'. By the way, if you haven't seen this movie, and you like to laugh- I highly recommend it.

Here's an example…Think about when you taught your son to tie his shoe. You likely didn't show him once, hand him a procedure, and then say, "See, that's how you do it. Now don't screw up!" It was probably more like, "Okay- pull the strings tight, like this. See?" And you have him do it. "Now, cross the strings like this, and stick the left string under the right one. Now pull them tight." You watch as he does it. "Great!" you say, "see how easy this is?" (Positive affirmation of the desired behavior, and reinforcement that he *can* do this). "Now," you say, "use your left thumb like this," as you show him, "and your right thumb and finger like this…and you make a loop." You watch as he works at it. This one's a bit trickier, but you encourage him until he gets it. "Wonderful!" you exclaim, "now, this is the tricky part, but you're doing great! I know you'll get it! Take the loop in your right hand, then take the left string over the top like this," as you show him. "Then, pull it up through the hole to make another loop. Now…pull it tight." It'll probably take a few tries, but when he succeeds, what do you do? You celebrate! You make it a big deal; what a "Big Boy" he is! And guess what- the behavior gets repeated. Simple.

Now think about what you did there (and if you weren't the one who taught your children how to tie their shoes, I'm sorry you missed out). You took a set of actions, which if never done before, is a relatively complex set of finger and string manipulations, and in a very short period of time, helped your son learn how to master them. You did so by (1) breaking it down into a series of very simple steps, and (2) offering lots of encouragement ('you can do it') and celebration (YAY!) as each step was successfully completed. In the end- an ecstatic child and a very happy parent. [WIN WIN]

In the work environment of course, people must be treated with the respect they deserve (not like children). However, when learning anything new, the process is essentially the same. Make it fast, simple, and easy (as appropriate for the individual and whatever you're asking them to do).

Unlock both locks, "WIIFM?" and "Can I do this?" and the gate is open- you now have the *opportunity* to influence. A transaction can now take place. What comes into play now is your *ability* to influence. This is a bit more complex than simply getting through the gate; however, there is an extremely powerful and relatively simple 'model' for doing so. It's called the, "Individual Performance Model™."

Individual Performance Model™

The Individual Performance Model™ (IPM) takes the amazing complexity of human psychology and puts it into a simple workable model that gives you the insights needed to become a very effective influencer. Once you master it, you can literally get another person to do virtually anything you want them to do.

Once you understand this model, you will understand much more about yourself, as well as those around you. Understanding and implementing what you are about to learn will benefit you in dealing with (and influencing) everyone you come in contact with- all the way from a waiter in a foreign country, to the barista at Starbucks, to the people at work who report to you, your co-workers, and your bosses, to your primary relationships, and to the person looking back at you from any given mirror. This is *very* powerful stuff.

If you'd like to watch a short introductory video on the Individual Performance Model™ before you continue your reading, go here:

http://ppiweb.com/future-performance-improvement/influencing-behavior/

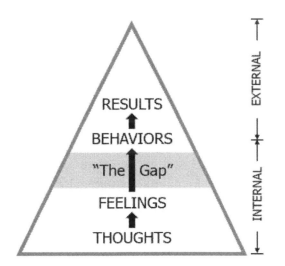

The Individual Performance Model (Part I)

I'm going to cover the IPM in two parts. The first part (as shown in the Part I figure above), provides a 'picture' of what's going on inside of us as we navigate through our day. It works like this:

- We have thoughts
- Some of those thoughts generate feelings
- Feelings pass through "The Gap" to manifest as behaviors
- Our behaviors in any given set of conditions determine our results
- Thoughts, feelings, and processing through "The Gap" are *internal*
- Our behaviors and results are *external* (and can typically be observed)

It's been generally accepted for the past decade or so that the average brain has somewhere between 50,000 and 70,000 thoughts per day. While the actual numbers are not critically important, hopefully you agree with me, as you consider all of the 'noise' and 'chatter' going on in your mind, that the number of thoughts you have on any given day is- a bunch. What's equally important to recognize, and quite fascinating when you think about it, is that

~90% of these thoughts are the same each day.[7] We are indeed, creatures of habit.

Fortunately, only a small percentage of these seemingly endless thoughts flying through our brains each day generate emotional experiences. Those that do rise to the surface, grab our focus, and often manifest as behaviors. For example, you might be working at your desk, and a thought pops into your brain, "I'm hungry". That thought leads to another, where you now consciously sense the state of your digestive system, and yes indeed, you now 'feel' empty room in your stomach. Another thought pops in- there's a bag of sugar cookies in the kitchen. Your salivary glands are now activated as you 'remember' how great those cookies taste. You've now worked yourself into an emotional state, and without exercising some means to interrupt this pattern (the opportunity for which lies in "the *gap*"), corresponding behavior will manifest- you're out of your seat and headed to the kitchen.

"The Gap"

Our brains are incredibly complex organisms. You've undoubtedly heard figures of how your brain is a gazillion times more capable than the world's most powerful supercomputer. In order to efficiently deal with what has become a very complex world, our brains develop a myriad of patterns or 'loops'. This occurs over the course of our lives, especially up until around the age of 30. Physically, when the same neurons fire in specific order, and do so over and over, they develop 'connections'. As my friend, Dr. Joe Dispenza, likes to say, "Neurons that fire together, wire together." This is one of the reasons why we can drive a car while sipping a Starbucks, and sing along to the radio at the same time. Because of these 'loops', things we do repetitively can be done with very little overt conscious thought. These connections, or 'loops' also play a predominant role in making us...us. Such is the reason why you and I may respond or react completely differently to a given person or condition. This is where *the gap* comes into play.

As shown in the IPM, the *gap* lies between emotions and behaviors. Let's say that something from your external world initiates a thought. Rather than being one of the thousands of thoughts that arise and simply dissipate, this one 'tickles' one of your mental loops. This generates an additional thought, which kicks off another loop, and now emotion starts to get involved. As this loop enters into your conscious thought, it tells you a 'story' in relation to whatever initiated it. This 'story' can then elevate your emotions, which subsequently impact your behaviors. The sugar cookie example used previously is a simple explanation of how this works. Let's now take a look at how these stories tend to bias your perceptions, relationships, reactions, and responses.

Let's say that when you were in first grade, you had an awful year. For some reason, your teacher, Miss Evans, seemed to have it in for you. As a matter of fact, as far as you were concerned, she was m-e-a-n! This is what you remember. It was traumatic. The other thing you remember about Miss Evans is that she had shoulder-length blonde hair, and always wore a red sweater. You're now 40 years old. You're walking through the parking lot at the local Target, and coming toward you is a woman in a red sweater with shoulder-length blonde hair. Your mind immediately processes the conditions, digging up and dusting off an old loop that hasn't been used in 34 years. This all happens at the speed of electricity (which is how the brain works). What 'story' is thrust into your conscious thought? This woman walking toward you is…mean! Is it true? Most likely not; however, your 'story' will evoke an emotion, and unchecked, your behaviors will be accordingly influenced. You may choose to move to the other side of the lane. You may smirk at her as she passes by you. You may simply refuse to make eye contact with her.

What's the point? Over our lifetimes, each of us has anchored in thousands and thousands of loops/stories. These form our biases, our pre-conceptions; our general 'take' on virtually everything we encounter. These loops are what make us who we are, and have tremendous impact on how we react or respond amidst the endless string of conditions and circumstances that come our way.

As a performance improvement professional, an understanding of the *gap* is important for two reasons. First, it helps you to understand yourself- your biases, your judgments, why you respond or react the way you do in certain circumstances and under certain conditions. Secondly, it helps you to understand others, their biases and judgments, and why *they* respond or react the way they do (including their responses to your efforts to influence them).

Behaviors, Choices, and Results

To complete our discussion of Part I of the IPM, the chain of thoughts, emotions, and choices that we've discussed thus far manifest as...behaviors. This is where your inner world interacts with your outer world. What you do and how you go about doing it (your *behaviors*) generates your results.

Looking at the whole picture, the choices we make and the behaviors we exhibit as we move along our individual journeys determine our results- the quantity and quality of our lives. This is true for you. It's true for me. It's true for everyone. When you consider that 90% of our thoughts tend to be the same each day, it reminds me of the scene from the Matrix, where the Agent Smith is asking Morpheus, *"Ever stood and stared at it, marveled at its beauty; it's... genius? Millions of people just living out their lives-oblivious."* No longer being 'oblivious' offers you and me tremendous opportunity. Opportunity to transform and improve our own lives, as well as to be a positive influence in the lives of others.

So now let's talk about how you and I have become who we are, and how this impacts our interactions with the world.

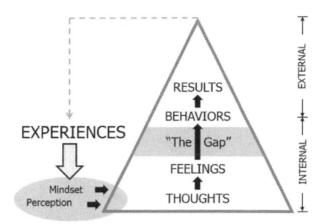

The Individual Performance Model (Part II)

Mindset and Perception

> *"If I've learned anything in life, it's that everybody has their own version of everything."* -Essie Masters

What we discussed in Part I is the progression from thoughts to emotions, to choices, actions and behaviors. It's through our choices, actions and behaviors that we interact with our world. Our interactions with our world, with people, places, and things have outcomes, which we refer to in the model as 'results'. As shown in the Part II diagram, these results generate feedback in the form of *experiences*. Over time, the experiences we have in life create and continually impact our *mindset* and our *perceptions*.

You may not have heard or thought of this before, but we do not 'see' with our eyes. Our eyes are merely lenses through which images are projected onto the photo receptors in our brains. At this point, *mindset* and *perception* process what these photo receptors have received and generate our thoughts of what we are 'seeing'. These thoughts can be strong or weak, positive or negative, definitive or ambivalent. The thing is, you and I can look at exactly the same thing, at the same point in time, under the same set of conditions, and have different thoughts. This is because of the filtering and amplifying that takes place as incoming information passes through our *mindset* and *perception*. Because thought leads to emotion, I may *feel* entirely different than you do about whatever it is that we're looking at. And because feelings (emotions) manifest as behaviors, how I respond or react may be quite different as well.

Mindset functions as our mental amplifier. Each of us has a mindset about virtually everything. We have mindsets about people, relationships, places, our jobs, the government, food, travel…life in general. And this mindset, this overall attitude, tends to amplify any incoming information regarding [whatever it is]. For example, have you ever had 'one of those days' where you woke up 'on the wrong side of the bed'? Everything seems to go wrong, doesn't it? It seems like everything and everyone is conspiring against you. In truth, they're not. It's just that when you're in such a *mindset*, everything you can find that is negative tends to be amplified, and whatever's positive tends to be ignored. A truth in life is that you're going to find whatever it is you're looking for. A negative mindset will find (and perhaps even manufacture) negatives.

Perception, on the other hand, functions as our mental filter. All incoming information, having been amplified by our mindset, then gets filtered through our perception. Let me offer a great example of perception, at least for most people living in the United States. You come home from work, and after tossing your keys on the table by the door, pick up the day's mail. Looking through it, you come to a white business-sized envelope, addressed to you. It's from…the Internal Revenue Service (IRS). What's your immediate perception- positive or negative? If you've ever had dealings with the IRS beyond simply filing your taxes and getting a refund check, there's probably an immediate unpleasant sensation in your gut, your pulse rate elevates, you may even begin to perspire, and yet at this point you have no idea what the envelope actually contains. It could be an announcement that you overpaid your taxes, and a big fat refund check is on its way. And yet, because of your perception of 'IRS', your initial perception is not likely to be a good one.

I want to keep this simple, so before we go any further, let's tie a few things together. All information from the outside world enters your brain through your mindset and perception. Your mindset and perception have developed over time, based upon your life experiences, to make you 'you'. Information being amplified and filtered is processed first by your lizard brain, which generates a 'fight', 'flight', 'ignore', or 'pass on for further processing' response. Thoughts that rise to the surface enough to generate emotion then pass through the *gap*, where you make choices. These choices manifest as actions and behaviors. Collectively, all of this can be thought of as your *personality*. And since this ongoing progression generates your results, we can say that your *personality* creates your *personal reality*.

Science has known for quite some time that for most people, our general overall mindset about 'life' is established by about the time we reach the age of six. This includes our general orientation toward whether the world is a place of lack or a place of abundance, a place of safety or a place to fear, whether people are generally good, loving, and caring, or...not. It also includes our general mindset about ourselves and our place in this world. Am I a 'good' person? Do I matter? Can I make a difference? Am I loved? Do I feel love? Does positive opportunity exist for...me? When we think about who our primary caretakers are until the age of six, this underscores the incredible opportunity and responsibility afforded to us as parents. Unfortunately, it also gives pause to consider 'the sins of the fathers' discussed in the Bible.

Science has also more recently identified interesting insights regarding the neural connections and 'loops' we discussed earlier. By the time the average person reaches thirty, the majority of 'loops' that will typically ever be generated within his brain have been created. Combine this with the awareness that 90% of our thoughts are the same, day in and day out, and it becomes clear that most people are simply repeating their past, over and over and over. Won't it be great to help ourselves (and others) develop and discover new patterns and new behaviors?

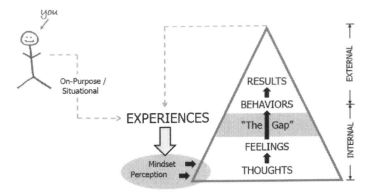

The Individual Performance Model: You as Influencer

This is where an understanding of the Individual Performance Model™ becomes very useful in your efforts to improve performance. Consider this- over time, *experiences* develop and continually impact *mindset* and *perception*. And even though mindset and perception tend to be more established as people get older, they *can* be altered when a person is exposed to new/different experiences. This is where your ability to influence behaviors comes into play.

As previously mentioned, the majority of 'loops' most people have in their brains are set by about the age of thirty. There are many reasons for this, most of which are a result of activity and habit. By this age, most people have stopped the majority of their formal learning. Without learning, you cannot make new neural connections. In addition, by this age most people have developed their 'habits' of living. Accordingly, the number of new and different experiences they have tend to diminish. Their life becomes…their life. Excitement tends to wane. Enthusiasm tends to diminish. This is what Thoreau was talking about when he wrote, *"The mass of men lead lives of quiet desperation."* I like to think of this as the majority of people are simply…asleep. Not paying attention. No longer aware of the wonders around them. It's time to wake them up!

The first thing you must recognize is that *every* interaction you have with another person generates an *experience*. Knowing this, you then consciously engage them *on-purpose*, creating an experience that will promote the mindset and/or perception that you're looking for. Here is a very simple example: We all like to feel respected. The best way to receive respect is to respect others. In a large organization, one of the best (and simplest) ways you can demonstrate on-purpose respect for another person is to take the time to remember their name. The next time you pass them in the hallway, or come across them in the plant, and you call them by name, you are overtly demonstrating that they are important to you. They will have the *experience* of feeling respected, which will make them much more inclined to be respectful (behavior) in return.

Secondly, as we've already discussed, people have different mindsets and perceptions. We all do not respond to the same things in the same ways. What works well to positively influence the behavior of one person might not work at all on another. So what you need to do is- pay attention. With a little bit of conscious effort, it's pretty easy to figure out where another person is 'coming from', their likes and dislikes, their insecurities, what's important to them, what's not important to them, and so forth. Then, based upon your awareness of *them*, create *situational* experiences intended to promote the mindset, perception, and ultimately the behaviors, that you desire. What if you don't 'nail it' the first time? Pay attention, and based upon what you learned from your prior attempt, modify your approach at your next opportunity.

A Note of Caution

There are two reasons why most people are not powerful influencers. The first is that they are 'asleep' like everyone else, not recognizing the power they have to provide positive on-purpose experiences for others. The second is our own mindsets and perceptions about things, which give us bias and prejudice. There is no way around this. You have your opinions, I have mine.

When it comes to being an influencer, however, you must develop the capability to 'rise above', otherwise you lose your ability to influence.

My *perception* of reality is my reality. Your *perception* of reality is your reality. And when it comes to influence, this is where we really tend to screw things up. It goes like this: "If my perception of reality is different than your perception of reality, I must be right, and you must be wrong." As soon as an interaction goes to this place, we've created a power struggle- the need to be 'right'. And as soon as any sense of power struggle develops, the lizard brain kicks in (it's now 'fight' or 'flight'), and the gate slams shut. No transaction will take place (at least not the type you intended). You have lost your opportunity to influence.

Into the Third Dimension

During the majority of our training courses, and in many of my talks and speeches as well, we make sure that people are aware of our PPI Vision Statement: *Event-free, world-wide; One life at a time.* We don't do this because we're really concerned with whether or not people know our vision statement. It's because it contains a couple of fundamental pieces of learning. First is the use of *event-free* (versus 'error-free'). We'll discuss why this is important in Chapter Eight. Second is the phrase, *one life at a time.*

During live presentations, I always enjoy throwing the question to the audience, "Why is [*one life at a time*] so important?" I typically get blank stares. Then I say, "Okay, let me re-phrase the question to something you're likely more familiar with: How do you change the world?" The answer then comes forward, "One person at a time." To which I respond, "Absolutely correct. Now, let's bring this a bit closer to home: How do you change the *culture* of an organization?" And of course, the answer is the same- one person at a time.

Culture is one of the most misunderstood areas within organizations today. Because of this, consultants and academics have come out of the woodwork offering formulas and recipes for how to change it. Most of these are expensive and seem to require a charismatic leader. In addition, we're being told "Look, culture change takes a long time." I am sorry. But having been involved with Practicing Perfection® for over ten years now, and having worked with tens of thousands of workers around the globe, I can say without reservation that any 'experts' telling you such things are- wrong. Organizational culture change is *not* hard, and it does *not* have to take a long time, providing you understand, latch onto, and properly implement what is being offered to you in this book.

To set the context for where I am headed, here is what Edgar Schein, considered to be one of the world's top experts on *culture*, says in Part One of his book, *Organizational Culture and Leadership*:

> Culture is both a "here and now" dynamic phenomenon and a coercive background structure that influences us in many ways. Culture is constantly reenacted and created by our interactions with others and shaped by our own behavior[8].

So what creates and sustains *culture?* Basically, it's the actions, behaviors, and interactions of the members of a given group. These actions and interactions are both tempered and instigated by beliefs, accepted 'norms' of behavior, and the results/outcomes associated with the group's interactions with its environment over time. This may sound very complex, but, let's get back to the questions I asked earlier: How do you change the culture of an organization? One person at a time.

The entire purpose of the Individual Performance Model™ is to provide a mechanism with which to understand and influence the mindset, perceptions, and behaviors of people. Now consider this: If we take the IPMs of each member of a given team, group, department, organization, or enterprise, and we stack them all together, what results is a three-dimensional model such as shown in the following figure.

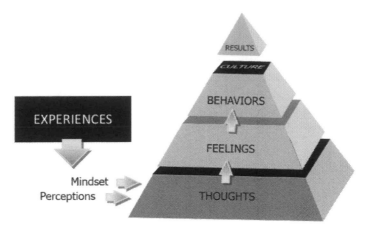

IPM → CULTURE → RESULTS

The collective mindsets, perceptions, thoughts, feelings, and behaviors of the members of the group are what generate group *culture*. And the *culture* of the group determines the *results* of the group. This is a critical point of understanding. Most people do not have a clue about *how* to transform organizational culture. If you've been paying attention, you now know precisely how to do it. Culture is transformed *one person at a time*. The IPM provides you with the insights and the strategy for directly influencing *one person at a time*.

You are probably now thinking, "Okay, I get it, but how do I actually implement this?" Excellent question. You will have your answers as you continue your reading.

Key Insights from Chapter Four

1. All motivation in internal. You can *force, manipulate,* or *inspire,* but you cannot motivate another person to do anything.

2. Factors that *motivate* workers involve self-esteem and self-actualization; purpose, autonomy, and mastery (PAM)

3. In order to have the <u>opportunity</u> to influence, you must get through the gatekeeper, the *lizard brain*, and be able to generate internal YES answers to two questions: "WIIFM?" and "Can I do this?"

4. Your <u>ability</u> to influence comes through the experiences you provide to others

5. Your personality creates your personal reality

6. The way to transform the culture of your team/organization is- one person at a time

What can you do with what you just learned?

A. For anyone you are wanting to influence, make the conscious choice to approach them from the perspective of WIIFT (What's In It For Them), and make it Fast, Simple, and Easy (baby steps if necessary)

B. Begin to observe your emotions and behaviors. Pay attention to how your mindset, biases, and perceptions are influencing your choices, your actions, and your interactions with others.

C. Become conscious of every interaction you have with others. Remember- you are providing them with an experience. Make a conscious choice to promote an emotion/behavior you would like to see. Here's a simple one- make eye contact, offer them a smile, and greet them by name. Pay attention to how they respond.

---

[1] Merriam Webster's Collegiate Dictionary; Eleventh Edition

[2] *The Paperback Quest for Joy: America's Unique Love Affair with Self-Help Books*; Laura Vanderkam (2012); Manhattan Institute for Policy Research

[3] *One More Time: How do You Motivate Employees?;* Frederick Herzberg; Harvard Business Review; January 2003

[4] *Drive: The Surprising Truth about What Motivates Us*; Dan Pink; Riverhead Books, New York; 2011

[5] Majority of U.S. Employees Not Engaged, Despite Gains in 2014; Amy Adkins; Gallup

[6] *How Employee Engagement Drives Growth;* Susan Sorenson; Gallup Business Journal; June, 2013

[7] A. Vickers, *People v. the State of Illusion;* (also) Laboratory of Neuro Imaging, UCLA

[8] *Organizational Culture and Leadership*; Edgar H. Schein; Jossey-Bass; 4th Edition, 2010

Chapter Five: Proactive Accountability®

"There's only one person on this planet who can hold me accountable for anything- me."
-Tim Autrey

On a crisp fall morning in 1983, I 'missed movement' aboard the USS Ohio. No, this doesn't mean that I missed an opportunity to use the restroom (head). It means that the boat left...and I was *not* on board. If you have any Navy experience, you know that this is just about the worst thing a sailor can ever do.

Prior to leaving for the multi-month deployment known as a 'patrol', missile submarines used to leave port for a day, and 'go to sea'. The purpose was to test primary and emergency systems in an 'at sea' environment, yet close to port so that if anything went wrong, assistance was close at hand. One such test was an 'emergency blow' of the ballast tanks, which sends you to the surface like a submerged fishing bobber let lose after the fish steals the bait. Being stationed at the time in Bangor, Washington, our tests were conducted in nearby Dabob Bay, along the western Hood Canal. We therefore referred to them as, "Bay Trials."

On this particular morning, my alarm clock didn't wake me up. I was sound asleep when the phone rang. It was Trash-mouth (remember him from the motor-generator story in the Introduction?). "Autrey," he was yelling on the other end of the phone, "where the F#*K are you?" I looked at the clock, and while exclaiming *many* 'colorful metaphors' myself, threw on my dungarees and headed to the pier.

We were living in Navy Housing, on what was known as 'Upper Base'. The piers along the Hood Canal were part of 'Lower Base' (a much more secure area). Submarine Base Bangor was so large, that as I backed out of my driveway, I was still nearly five miles from where the boat was docked. I had to pass through the Lower Base security gate, where, wouldn't you know, the Marine Private was being especially 'thorough' that particular morning. Receiving the standard, "Have a nice day," as he handed back my ID card, I headed on toward the pier. I can still recall the sickening pit I felt in my gut as I rounded the corner to see my boat, the USS Ohio... about 50 yards out into the Hood Canal.

This was one of the worst days, if not *the* worst day of my life. And it was not because of what 'happened' to me as a result of missing the day's Bay Trials. Nothing happened- no letter in my file, no reprimand. In fact, this story, as I've written it here, is the only 'official' record of it whatsoever.

Why no punishment? I think it had a lot to do with the fact that I had never had so much as a 'grey' mark in my naval career up to this point. I had worked hard, been a top performer, and had always been proactive about finding solutions and making things better. Further, I was never one to 'blame' another person or circumstance for anything that ever went less than perfect. This was obviously considered. The boat leadership at the time, from my Division Officer, up through the Engineering Officer, the Executive Officer (XO) and the Commanding Officer, had the wisdom to recognize that nothing they could possibly do to 'punish' Autrey would add any benefit to anything or anyone. And the truth was, there honestly was nothing they could have done that would have punished me as much as I punished myself.

I ended my Navy career the following year. Prior to my departure, I had been honored as 1984 'Sailor of the Year' for the Pacific Northwest. Do you think this would have happened had Ohio leadership seen fit to formally punish me for 'missing movement' that previous autumn morning? How might such a 'black' mark on my record have altered my perception of the Navy, my role, even my future possibilities? One can only speculate. Fortunately for me, and I like to think for the people I've had the opportunity to influence since, Ohio leadership looked at the 'bigger picture' when making their choices. It is also fortunate that they were allowed to use discretion; that they were not bound to some prescriptive set of HR 'rules' requiring formal (no matter what) punishment.

I won't bore you with the details of how the rest of that day played out, or with the emotional angst I suffered as I crossed the brow onto the Ohio upon its return that evening. As I have already mentioned, I punished myself *far* more than anything leadership might have done to me. This is an example of how true *accountability* works. Punishment and accountability are two completely different things. When true accountability exists, punishment is rarely (if ever) needed or appropriate. As my friend and retired COO, Mike Blevins, likes to say, "If you feel that you have to 'hold someone accountable', you've already lost."

"Accountability"

During my tenure as a member of the leadership team at the Brunswick Nuclear Plant near Southport, North Carolina, I headed up a team of volunteers known as the, "Human Performance Group" (HPG). During a refueling outage on one of the units, the HPG had been instrumental in helping to minimize human error. That particular outage was considered a huge success for the station. Following its completion, I received a handwritten thank you card from one of the Site Directors. In addition to expressing his gratitude, he also saw fit to issue our next challenge:

"Tim:

Thanks to you and the members of the HPG! Your efforts were instrumental in our very successful outage. Now that the outage is behind us, I have a new challenge for you and the HPG- find a way to help grow accountability at this station.

Thanks!

-JC"

Accountability? I had only a vague idea of where to begin. After all, my experience with 'accountability' up to that point had been basically, "He screwed up, so now we're going to 'whack' him." As a matter of fact, I had many times witnessed administration of the classic nuclear industry 'recipe' for anyone who found themselves on the 'sharp end' of the human error 'stick': (1) counsel the individual, (2) three days off without pay, (3) revise the procedure, and (4) re-train everyone not to screw up. Not exactly the *human performance* approach I was pursuing. What did he mean, "*...find a way to help grow accountability*"?

Thus began my search for and my learning about a different take on *accountability*. Though it took a lot longer than it would now with internet search capability, it didn't take me long before I discovered the book, *The Oz Principle,* which laid out a sane, positive, and proactive approach to what most (including me) had to this point considered a synonym for 'punishment'. In the Preface to the second version of the book, published in 2004, the authors offer the following:

> People who take accountability and operate Above the Line always make things happen in organizations. With a company full of accountable people, extraordinary things, even the entirely unexpected, tend to happen.

> Time and time again, we have been reminded that accountability produces results as we have added up the billions of dollars of shareholder value, increased profits, decreased costs, and productivity gains from clients and others who have successfully implemented greater accountability in their organizations. In addition to increased financial performance, we have witnessed improved morale as people come to love their jobs more, learn to cope more capably with daily obstacles, and get the results they want[1].

This edition of *The Oz Principle* was updated from the original 1994 edition, to incorporate what the authors had learned through ten additional years of experience working with and promoting *accountability*. Considering their Preface excerpt references to, "increased profits, decreased costs, and productivity gains," I hope you are seeing a direct connection to Safety Culture, quality, and the reduction of human error. Now consider their statement, "People who take accountability and operate Above the Line always make things happen in organizations." This is *engagement*. This is *proactivity*. Finally, consider, "...we have witnessed improved morale as people come to love their jobs more, learn to cope more capably with daily obstacles, and get the results they want." Does this sound like any of the elements of *motivation* we discussed in Chapter Four?

Accountability is a core element of next-level performance. Embracing it builds a foundation for bringing the individual into direct alignment with the organization.

So, what exactly is...*accountability*? First off, it is *not* punishment. It is *not* retribution. It is *not* something that anyone, any boss, or any organization can do *to* you or extract *from* you. Accountability is a willingness to accept responsibility, or to account for one's actions[2]. It is an internal [willing] *choice* each of us makes to own our behaviors, our actions, and the outcomes/consequences of the choices we make.

Think about my story at the beginning of this chapter. I could have blamed my alarm clock, the kids for disrupting my sleep during the night, that fact that the base was so frickin' huge, the overly-thorough Marine. I could have even blamed Trash-mouth for not calling me earlier! Such is a common response for many people when something [virtually anything] doesn't go exactly as planned. But I didn't *blame* anyone or anything. Fully owning my actions and behaviors was how I conducted myself. Of course, I've not been perfect at it, but it's pretty much how I've lived my life. Do you think this might have had anything to do with how my 'missed movement' story ended?

Hopefully you now 'get' that accountability is an *internal* *choice*; a choice that each team member will, or will not, choose to make. Accountability is not something that management can demand, or dictate, or push people into *compliance* with. As I mentioned before, its presence (or lack thereof) is a core element of your organization's fabric, of its culture. And it is essential to your success.

Consider relationships. For there to be any chance that a relationship will be healthy and productive, there absolutely must be *trust* between the people involved. Without trust, it's impossible for there to be openness, honest communication, generosity, empathy, or a genuine desire for WIN WIN outcomes. When you bring more than two people together, say into a family, a team, or across an entire organization, a sense of trust and 'fair play' can only be achieved through a high level of accountability at all levels- accountability as we are discussing it in this chapter.

The Great Divide

"I think the most important question facing humanity is, 'Is the universe a friendly place?'"
-Albert Einstein

Throughout history, mankind has been split on the answer to what Albert Einstein considered 'the most important question'. Some answer 'yes', some answer 'no'. On a macro scale, at times and places throughout history, political and economic tides have tended to shift overall sentiments in one direction or another. For example, consider the prevalent attitude amidst the 'geeks', the entrepreneurs, and the investors in Silicon Valley during the first week of March, 2000 (just before the stock market peak). On the other hand, consider the likely mindsets of many members of that same group during 2001, when the dot-com bubble fully burst.

We are all impacted by our surroundings and our circumstances, and yes, on a day-to-day basis, these things impact our attitudes. But at our core, our 'gut level', each of us has a prevalent mindset. Individual answers to the question of whether or not the world is a 'friendly place' form a 'great divide' amongst the members of the human race. It separates the 'optimists' from the 'pessimists', the

'I cans' from the 'I cannots'. This predominate attitude about life and our place within it has tremendous impact upon your choices and behaviors. Under virtually any set of conditions and circumstances, these choices and behaviors, in turn, determine whether you have the ability to truly make a difference (for yourself or anyone else), or whether you are merely participating as a victim.

Mindset Revisited

As we discussed in Chapter Four, *Mindset* functions as our mental amplifier. Each of us has a mindset about virtually everything, including our overall 'world view' and whether we consider our universe to be a 'friendly place' (or not). This is important to understand, because your mindset amplifies and biases all incoming information. Think about the sound of strumming the strings of an electric guitar when unplugged from the amplifier. Now, plug the guitar cord into the amplifier jack and turn on the Power Switch. Not only is the sound l-o-u-d-e-r, but it can be completely modified by adjusting the Intensity, Bass, Treble, Speed, Dwell, Reverb- each substantially altering the incoming signal to generate a different output. Your *mindset* does exactly this with every input coming into your mind from your external world. Whether it is generally negative (or positive), if you feel the world is 'out to get you' (or are trusting and open), if you consider yourself to be a victim in a given circumstance (or able to directly influence your outcomes), all incoming signals will be so modified. These *modified* output signals from your mindset have tremendous impact on your thoughts, and subsequently upon your choices and behaviors.

This reminds me of a story from ancient times. Outside the Enlil Gate leading into the city of Babylon lived a wise man. One hot dusty afternoon, a traveler from the village of Kish approached the gate, and seeing the wise man, stopped to ask him, "Please, tell me, oh wise one. I am planning on moving into this city. What kind of people will I find inside these walls?" The wise man surveyed the traveler, looked him in the eyes, and then asked, "What kind of people did you find in the village you came from?" "They were wonderful!" responded the traveler. "Kind, loving, caring...the reason I am moving here is because I have family in Babylon that I want to be near." The wise man smiled, and answered the traveler, "Well, my friend, you will find the same kind of people within these walls." Happily, the traveler passed through the gate.

It was a bit later that same afternoon, a little hotter, a bit dustier, when another traveler approached the Enlil Gate. Seeing the wise man, this traveler also approached, seeking information. "Good day, oh wise one," the traveler offered. "I am planning on moving into this city. Can you please tell me what type people inhabit these walls?" The wise man surveyed this traveler just as he had done previously. He then looked him in the eyes. "What kind of people did you find in the village you came from?" he asked. "They were awful!" cried the traveler. "Liars, cheats, thieves...I wouldn't give a plugged talent for a one of them!" Continuing his gaze into the traveler's eyes, the wise man responded, "Well, my friend, you're going to find the same type people here in Babylon."

Do you consider the world to be a 'good place' or a 'bad place'? Are people basically 'moral' or 'corrupt'? Is the 'pie' of such a size that some must have less in order for others to have more? These are variations on Einstein's question posed at the beginning of this section. And now, I'd like you to answer this question for yourself: *Do you consider the universe to be a friendly place to live?* Your answer to this question speaks volumes about how you make choices, how you approach your work, how you approach your...life. Your mindset virtually guarantees that you're going to find whatever it is you're looking for.

Scarcity

Somewhere around 15AD, a goldsmith brought an unusual dinner plate to the court of Tiberius, Emperor of Rome. It was 'different'- very light, shiny, almost as bright as silver. The goldsmith, very pleased, claimed that he had extracted the metal from clay, using a technique, "known only to himself and the gods." Tiberius was intrigued...and concerned. Surely the presence and continued production of such a metal would diminish the value of the hordes of silver and gold he had amassed through conquest and appropriation. According to the historian, Pliny the Elder, "Instead of giving the goldsmith the regard expected, he ordered him to be beheaded.[3]" The 'secret' of aluminum was subsequently lost for an additional 1,800 years. The direct result of Tiberius' scarcity mindset.

Scarcity is (1) the quality or state of being narrow, stingy, or deficient, or (2) deficient in quantity or number compared to demand[4]. It is an overall perspective where, in order for me to have more, you must have less. You likely want to take what I have, so I must hide it, guard it, protect it. It is classic *lizard brain* functioning, where the primary goal is- survival.

Now remember, your predominant mindset biases and amplifies all incoming input into your mind. Someone offers you a gift, your immediate thoughts are, "What's she going to want in return?" A man smiles as he passes you on the sidewalk, it must be a sick sexual advance. Your boss, preoccupied in thought, passes you in the hallway without saying hello, and you begin to wonder if a pink slip is in the works. Rather than gratitude, enjoyment, and realizing that everything is not about you, you are suspicious, resentful, and fearful. This is the *scarcity* mindset in full-blown production.

And as these incoming inputs are negatively biased and amplified, your thoughts will likewise tend toward the negative, as will your corresponding choices and reactions (your behaviors). Negative behaviors tend to generate negative outcomes/results, which will then feedback as negative experiences, helping to reinforce the scarcity mindset that you started with. Your feelings are justified. Your suspicions are confirmed. The cycle repeats and self-reinforces.

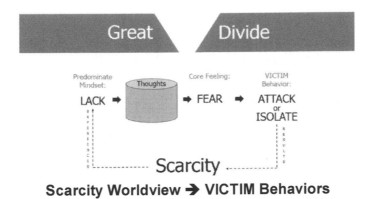

Scarcity Worldview → VICTIM Behaviors

The predominant mindset when coming from a place of *scarcity* is- LACK. There is never enough to 'go around', someone's going to miss out, why does this always happen to [you], or as our kids could sometimes be heard to say before figuring this stuff out, "It's not f-a-i-r!" When this is your predominate mindset, someone can freely (out of the goodness of their heart) hand you a $100 bill, and your likely thoughts might be, "Is that all?" or, "Who had to lose out so you could give this to me?" or, "Alright, what's the catch?"

Your predominant mindset of LACK will bias and then amplify external inputs into your thoughts. And because the bias is [generally] negative, it's likely that your mind will rapidly search for (and find) associated negative neural connections (loops). You'll pass through the gap, either very quickly in response to a perceived threat, or after much worry and angst as the negative loops and stories build one atop another, and your feelings will emerge based upon- FEAR.

A core feeling of FEAR leads your *lizard brain* with only one place to go. Remember, the primary function of your lizard brain is your survival. Therefore, your behaviors will be some form of *fight* or *flight*. These are shown in the figure as the VICTIM behaviors of either ATTACK or ISOLATE. Why would we label these as VICTIM behaviors? Because they are clearly in response to a perceived *threat.* They are in response to your perception that someone is doing something to you, taking something from you, saying something [bad] about you- whatever has popped out of your internal progression from your mindset of LACK to your feelings of FEAR.

As can be seen in the figure, this process tends to self-reinforce. Your behaviors (ATTACK or ISOLATE) generally do not have positive outcomes (RESULTS), leading to an even greater sense of *scarcity* for...you. The elevated sense of *scarcity* provides you with EXPERIENCES that justify your initial mindset and help confirm that *you* are on the correct path- the world is indeed, *not* a friendly place.

Within the work place, there are behaviors that clearly represent the *scarcity* world view. I'm going to discuss some of the common ones below. It should become clear how each behavior is ultimately the product of a mindset of LACK, and a core feeling of FEAR. As a performance improvement professional, it's important to understand where these behaviors come from. It is also important to understand that poor behaviors are expressions of the problem- not the problem itself. By doing so, you can avoid chasing symptoms when helping your team members escape the shackles of VICTIM behaviors to ultimately become proactively accountable.

Suckers' Swamp

> *"We are taught you must blame your father, your sisters, your brothers, the school, the teachers - but never blame yourself. It's never your fault. But it's always your fault, because if you wanted to change, you're the one who has to change."*
> –Katharine Hepburn

As we previously discussed, VICTIM behaviors come from a place of FEAR. What's interesting, is whenever you position yourself as a *victim*, you are essentially surrendering your personal power. You are conceding that [whatever it is] is more powerful than you. With this in mind, why then would anyone ever do such a thing? Because at the moment of making the choice (and it is a *choice*), it's often the 'easy road'. Internally, you relieve yourself of responsibility. Externally, it affords you the opportunity to shift focus on anyone or anything other than...you. Remember, your most primal motivation is the avoidance of pain. Victim behaviors tend to defer pain. Unfortunately, this is like 'kicking the can down the road'. Any relief is almost always temporary. And even if no one else ever recognizes your role in a given condition, circumstance, or sequence of events...you know. Over time, this internal 'knowing', combined with a sense of powerlessness, takes a huge toll. I believe this has a lot to do with most people's general lack of feeling 'happy'. It certainly contributes to Thoreau's observation regarding the, "mass of men leading lives of quiet desperation." Welcome to 'Suckers' Swamp'.

Suckers' Swamp

There are five 'swamp' behaviors that tend to be most common in today's environment. This is true in society every bit as much as it is in the work place. Victim behaviors are epidemic. If you doubt my word (and you can stomach it), just try objectively watching the evening news for a while. As you read through the descriptions and anecdotes associated with each of these victim behaviors, do yourself (as well as your loved ones and co-workers) a huge favor: consider how *you* (yes- *you*) have likely [recently] perched upon one or more of these. We've all done it, and as you'll see shortly, admitting this is your first step toward getting out of the Swamp.

Blame

If you live in the western world, society's been attempting to teach you for most of your life that it's okay to *blame*. Blame your parents, your siblings, your teachers, the politicians, your lousy neighbors, the guy standing on the street corner- anyone other than yourself. Blame in today's society is a disease of epidemic proportions.

Let's run through a quick example: You've been at your job for 15 years, grumbling the entire time. After all, this isn't what you thought your life would amount to. In the shower each morning, your predominant thought is how much you DREAD going to 'that place'. Some of your co-workers are 'okay', but…Sheri (your new boss)! You don't even like to be around her. And why did she get that job anyway. You've been there a lot longer than she has. Must be because she's a woman. So at work, you've done what's 'been required'. Thank goodness you can play a little Candy Crush during the day to keep your sanity! Your coffee counter conversation has, over the years, typically consisted of how unfair the manager bonuses are, how your lousy 2.5% annual raise isn't even keeping up with inflation, and/or the latest gossip about your co-workers. One Monday morning you're called into Sheri's office and given notice. She tells you that, due to the tight economy, tough choices are being made, and your job will only exist until the end of the month. Because she knows this is probably a shock to you, you can feel free to take the rest of the afternoon off. How do you react?

Well, how DARE they! After 15 years of faithful service, and giving that job everything you've had to give, they're letting *you* go?! Well, it's like you always thought- they've been out to get you- especially Sheri! You stomp out of her office in disbelief, grab your jacket and head out the door. You stop by the liquor store on the way home. Your evening is spent between gulps of Johnny Walker Black and bouts (both internal and external) of denial (perhaps you'll wake up and everything will be back to 'normal'), anger (especially toward Sheri), bargaining (maybe there's *something* you can do to save your job), and depression (the world never has treated you fairly).

So after 15 years of *hating* your job, you just cannot imagine how *they* could possibly cut you loose. It clearly can't be your fault. After all, you have been a faithful worker. You've never taken *more* than the allotted number of sick days. You've never been one to 'hog' overtime when asked to work extra hours. You've made certain to get your name attached to at least one CPI (Continuous Process Improvement) Team initiative every year (just like you're required to do to get a 'SAT' evaluation). The company, most likely Sheri, obviously had it in for you. Clearly she's biased against men with glasses and pleated pants. And that new CEO is wanting to get rid of senior workers- to hire kids at half of what they're paying you. Of course, there's also the government and their trumped up economic policies (which is, of course, is the fault of the *other* political party). Victim, victim, victim.

This is a long-term example, where 15 years of negative (scarcity) thinking and victim behaviors, combined with changing external conditions, led to a terminal conclusion that is [of course] the company's [world's] fault (he said in jest). The reality is, if you are not part of the problem, you are not part of the solution. In this example, being part of the problem over a long period of time was obvious. On a day-to-day basis however, it can become very easy to point fingers at anything or anyone other than yourself. Because this is so easy, and because it is essentially 'endorsed' by the culture in which we live, blame can become an almost automatic response when things don't go as planned. Momentary relief for sure. Unfortunately, such victim behavior leaves you powerless to make things better. And when relied upon strongly enough and long enough, this behavior can become especially harmful as you tend to also deceive yourself; to mentally remove yourself from any sense or awareness of personal responsibility.

Ignore

When you land upon this behavior, you are making a choice to bury something beneath your conscious thought processes. This is often done in the vain hope that [whatever it is] will somehow just…go away.

A classic example of this behavior is when people run up excessive levels of credit card debt. It typically begins with the 'harmless' acquisition of pleasure, made easy through a purchase of something you otherwise cannot afford. No big deal. Satisfaction with the initial pleasure can lead to more purchases, as the debt and monthly payments mount; however, you tend to *ignore* this, because you're having 'fun'. At some point, the monthly payments begin to cause pain. When this happens, you may choose to *deny* your past and current behaviors as the cause of the pain, and deflect your focus toward (*blame*) that x!$d#m amazon.com', the fact that they *had* to build that new mall (right down the street!), or those 'evil' credit card companies who make it so easy to run up balances that minimum payments will *never* pay off. The downward spiral continues until something 'breaks' or your behaviors change.

Deny

Denial typically takes a couple of different forms. One involves outright deception and/or dishonesty. This is when an individual directly involved in [whatever it is] simply denies any involvement whatsoever. The other often stems from an individual's 'fenced in' perception of where his responsibilities begin and end, resulting in some variation of, "It's not my job."

Relative to outright deception and/or dishonesty, how you respond to this is outside of the scope of what we're discussing in this chapter. One thing to consider, however, is the relative health of your organizational culture. Unhealthy cultures, with a lack of trust and accountability (as we're defining it in this chapter), and/or a punitive environment, tend to promote such behaviors. We will be touching on these issues when we directly discuss

Safety Culture and *Just Culture* in Chapter Seven, and *Culpability* in Chapter Eight.

When it comes to a behavior of, "It's not my job," (a classic denial of responsibility) this can arise from legitimate laziness on the individual's part, directly from a mindset of *lack*, where she feels that others aren't doing their 'fair share', or be prompted by an unhealthy organizational structure/culture. Such behaviors can be promoted by an organizational structure filled with 'silos'. In such environments, the members of each 'silo' (crew, department, team, line, floor, etc.) see themselves as responsible only for their 'piece of the puzzle', promoting a narrow mindset of what one's 'job' (responsibility) is. Such work cultures/structures tend to be very inefficient. The *"It's not my job"* mentality tends to become a springboard for additional victim behaviors, especially *blame* (of other teams, departments, crews, etc.).

Stacey Hefner, one of our Directors, will often share an experience she had in a well-known toy store in Austin, Texas. She was looking for a particular item for one of her young sons. Asking one of the employees on the floor of the store where she might find it, she was told, "That's not my department," and with a finger pointed toward the back of the store, was told, "You'll have to go over there." Interestingly, she had a similar experience with two additional workers. She left the store, very frustrated, without buying…anything. Apparently, the culture within this particular store had created a mindset, at least amongst these three employees, that each had a *very* narrow field of responsibility. To tread outside of this, even for the sake of serving a customer, was apparently not 'the way they did it around there'. Stacey has never since set foot in that store. While her sons are now beyond "toy store" age, they were quite young at the time. One has to wonder how much revenue that store lost because of three workers who responded to a young mother with, *"It's not my job."*

Defer

Remember Jimmy, the operator at the nuclear power plant in Louisiana? Prior to being transferred away from Crew D, he was becoming extremely discouraged. I could tell he was approaching his 'breaking point'; a level of discouragement, where he was likely to (1) become apathetic, (2) become disgruntled, or (3) quit and go work somewhere else. Fortunately for the company (and for Jimmy), he was transferred before he 'broke'. This first level of crossing the threshold away from enthusiasm and commitment is...apathy. And when a worker gives in to apathy, a common behavior is to disengage personal input, to defer responsibility, and to say, "Okay, just tell me what to do."

Whether prompted externally by the environment (an overbearing micro-managing boss, a controlling spouse, a demanding parent), by an internal lack of self-confidence, or by a combination of the two, this behavior is a common and classic means of avoiding responsibility. After all, if someone else makes the decision, if someone else tells you what to do, if/when things don't go well...it's obviously not your fault!

This behavior robs workers of any potential for having a sense of *autonomy,* let alone the opportunity to develop *mastery.* From an organizational perspective, it robs the enterprise of a critical high value asset- the creative make-things-better mindset and energies of workers.

CMA

Perhaps the most conscious, most overt victim behavior, Cover My Ass(ets), involves direct effort on an individual's part to ensure that he is not associated in any way with [whatever it is]. This may involve specific documentation (emails, database entries, etc.), public and 'hallway' conversations, ensuring that his presence (or lack thereof) is noted by key people at key points in time, etc. Interestingly, this behavior can involve more effort than might otherwise have been required to take a constructive proactive approach to 'fixing' whatever the problem/condition might be. This behavior might also involve 'throwing others under the bus', where he attempts to vindicate himself at others' expense.

From one Behavior to Another

When in the *swamp*, it's often not a single behavior or an isolated event. It tends to be more like jumping from one 'victim behavior' to another. One deflection leads to another denial, which leads you to simply wait to see what happens while you make sure everyone knows you were not involved. And the longer you stay here, the more jumping you do, the more difficult it becomes to stay afloat. It's like the classic, *"Oh, what a tangled web we weave when first we practice to deceive."* When your life is teetering upon such behaviors, simply maintaining your balance takes the majority of your energy. And if you lose it? Falling *into* the swamp can have grave consequences. Ever been there?

Fortunately, there is a cure, a way to climb out of Suckers' Swamp. Where do you go? To a mindset, emotional state, and set of behaviors entirely different than those associated with a sense of scarcity and the resulting fear-based victim behaviors.

Possibility

> *"The world is so full of a number of things, I'm sure*
> *we should all be as happy as kings."*
> -Robert Louis Stevenson

I was lucky. Being the third child, the 'baby' of the family, I was the risk taker. I never had much fear- of anything. I was raised in a very functional family. My Dad loved my Mom. She loved him. They were best friends. My Dad was my hero. My mom took great care of me. Since my sister and brother were quite a bit older (ten and eight years respectively), I had the 'luxury' of being raised pretty much as an 'only child' during a time when my middle-middle class parents were doing well financially. I was supported by my Dad in virtually every crazy scheme I came up with. While my Mom from time to time questioned my 'common sense', I can still hear her saying, "You can have anything you want in life, as long as you're willing to do what it takes."

I'm telling you all of this about my past to paint a picture of how my worldview formed from essentially the beginning of me being me. My world was a very friendly place. It was filled with opportunity. Be smart, work smart, and you can have and achieve virtually anything you want. At the same time, I was taught compassion, generosity, and accountability for my place, my actions, and my role in this world. My Dad, a very spiritual yet non-religious man, had one simple prayer. He never asked for anything. Instead, he simply said, "Thank you."

Yes, I am truly blessed. I've essentially spent my entire life on the *Possibility* side of the *Great Divide.* The absence of *fear,* and an innate desire to learn, has led me naturally to being fully accountable for my mistakes- without blaming, denying, or justifying my less than desirable behaviors (and yes, there *have* been some). This same desire to learn, coupled with my childhood gathering of compassion and sense of generosity, has also made me very aware of how conditions, circumstances, and specific life events have pushed many people to the scarcity side of the *divide.* When I consider the backgrounds and life histories of many of the people I've met, and the tens of thousands of workers we've interfaced with over the past ten years, it leaves me with two predominate feelings: (1) An ever greater sense of gratitude for how blessed I have been, and (2) an ever stronger sense of urgency and life purpose to help as many people as possible cross the *Great Divide* from lives of *scarcity* and acting like / being *victims* to *accountable* lives filled with *possibility.*

If there is one great truth I have learned in life, it is this:

The entire rest of your life lies in front of you. What it will be is entirely up to you.

Not a single one of us can do a single thing about anything that has 'happened to us' in the past. However, each of us has absolute total control of our future. Your future, whatever you choose to make of it, will be determined by *you*- by the choices you make, the actions you take, and *how* you go about making them. While this offers unlimited potential, it also pulls back the covers. No more excuses. No more blaming. No more hiding (especially from yourself). Right now, as you are reading these words, *you* have a *choice*. Remain underneath- in *scarcity*. Continue to hide behind *victim* behaviors, or...rise to *possibility* and the internal freedom of a proactively accountable life. There's a simple way to get there, but before you make your personal choice whether (or not) to take this ride, it's important for you to understand what 'life in the sunshine' truly means.

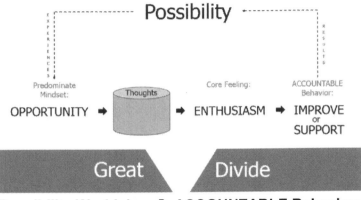

Possibility Worldview → ACCOUNTABLE Behaviors

I was going to school at Fort Miller Junior High (seventh through ninth grade) during a time that was socially pretty darn challenging for kids in Fresno, California (as well as in much of the United States). This was during the period where kids were bussed across town, whether they wanted to be or not, as part of the grand experiment of 'forced integration'. I am certainly not an expert on integration, but what I can tell you as a thirteen-year-old in the middle of it- it wasn't much fun. I didn't have to ride a bus, I walked the 1.2 miles back and forth between my house and Fort Miller. But I always felt sorry for the kids who were forced to do so. In many cases, it was pretty obvious that they really didn't want to be on the east side of town.

We were given close to an hour for our lunch period each day. Virtually everyone ate in the cafeteria. When the bell rang, we would make our way to the lunch line. It was interesting to observe that the kids from the 'other side' of town were much more aggressive about getting into this line than those of us who walked to school. This was fine, except that I and many others would have already been in line for five or six minutes, patiently waiting our turn, and groups of two or three at a time would blatantly 'cut' in ahead of us. This used to really piss me off (pardon my language, but I'm just being honest). Not because we now had to wait another whole minute or two for our lunch, but because it was a blatant lack of respect for those of us who were already in the line.

Remember- poor behaviors (such as blatantly cutting in front of others in the lunch line) are *expressions* of the problem. We could dive into a litany of *reasons* why such behaviors existed, but if we get to the core, such behaviors were generated out of a sense of scarcity, producing a mindset of *lack*. This mindset evolved underlying feelings of *fear*, which in this case came out as behaviors on the *attack* side of things, blatantly disrespecting those of us who were now further from receiving our lunches.

We could have retaliated. I was tall for my age, and hung out with kids of enough physical stature that we certainly could have 'held our turf'. Fortunately for everyone involved, we were either smart enough, or just didn't care enough, to just 'let it go'. In truth, this experience reaffirmed my worldview. Through three years of standing in that lunch line, no matter how many kids cut in front of us, there was always plenty of food to fill our trays. There was always plenty of time to eat. And this is the predominate mindset on the upper side of the *Great Divide*: There is always plenty. In order for me to have more, someone else does *not* need to have less.

As input from the external world enters through a mindset of *opportunity*, how do you think this impacts your thoughts? Are you looking for the negatives or the positives? As we already discussed, you're going to find whatever it is you're looking for. In this case, you will look for, and find, the positives, the options, the opportunities in virtually everything that comes your way. And this deserves a note of caution. This is not about putting on 'rose colored glasses', blinding yourself to the point where you deny conditions or circumstances. Rather, it is about approaching everything with your eyes wide open, recognizing that each challenge, each problem, every obstacle brings with it essentially unlimited possibility. A mindset of *opportunity* will seek out, find, and promote thoughts that will ultimately create possibilities for...you.

When my wife and I were buying rental properties, we purchased a small duplex in Brattleboro, Vermont. The previous owner was living in one side and the other was occupied with long term tenants. The previous owner was a bit of a 'pack rat', and in addition to his furniture, had filled his unit with lots of 'stuff'. He promised that it would be cleaned out by the day of closing. As part of the conditions of purchase, the previous owner had moved himself, and was in Mississippi on closing day. We did our bit at the bank and then headed over to the property. Yes, he was gone, but all of his 'junk' was still there. This was a problem, because it all had to be moved / removed so that we could refurbish the unit to get it ready as a rental.

The following Saturday morning, I was lying in bed considering our options relative to all of his 'stuff'. On one hand, I was looking at a disposal bill of several hundred dollars. Engaging in a bit of *Third-Dimension Thinking* however, I recognized that most of his furniture could be salvaged, and if we added a few pieces, we would be able to rent the unit *furnished* (which we did). In that market, at that time, we were able to get almost twice as much rent. This is a classic example of the *possibilities* that can exist when you approach conditions / circumstances with an *opportunity* mindset.

When you approach virtually any circumstance or condition with a worldview of *possibility* and a mindset of *opportunity*, your mind will root out positives. Recognition of opportunities and possibilities will generate core feelings of *enthusiasm*. Enthusiasm then opens you up to positive *behaviors*. Rather than *attack*, you want to *improve*. Rather than *isolate*, you want to *support*. The *experiences* of greater and greater *possibility* will reinforce your mindset of *opportunity*. You win. Those around you win. And ultimately, the world (the friendly place) wins as well.

Is it 'magic'? Sometimes it seems like it, but- no. Our world revolves (and evolves) upon 'cause and effect', 'stimulus and response', 'action and reaction'. One of the ways that I like to couch it is, "What goes around, comes around." Will it happen immediately? Sometimes yes, sometimes no. Will you have 'setbacks' and 'hiccups' along the way? Undoubtedly. However, with a mindset of *opportunity*, *enthusiastic* feelings, and behaviors that consistently *improve* and *support*, 'the world' cannot help but support you in return.

Crossing the Great Divide

> *"Behavior is the mirror in which everyone shows their true image."*
> -Goethe

Once the US settlers migrating westward via wagon train survived the weather, the pestilence, and the threat of Indian attack across the great plains, their toughest challenge of all was making it over/through the Rocky Mountains, the *Great Divide* separating east from west. Once they did, however, they found a whole new world- more opportunity, better weather, even silver and gold. Those choosing to cross the Sierras found some of the most fertile farmland in the world, ideal weather, more gold, and the bounty of the Pacific.

For those who have confined themselves to a worldview of scarcity, crossing the *Great Divide* into a new worldview of *possibility* can be the challenge of a lifetime. It requires overcoming your sense of lack, and the fear that whatever you have can be taken from you. It requires abandonment of victim behaviors designed to hide and protect. It requires the openness of gratitude, and the [potential] vulnerability of giving and supporting others. To get there and remain there requires openness, honesty, integrity, and true accountability. No more hiding, no more hoarding, no more denying. However, just as the settlers reaped the bounty and riches that awaited them in the west, so will you discover the gems that are literally waiting for *you* as you cross over the *Great Divide* that separates victims from those who choose to be accountable.

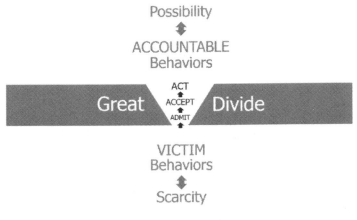

The Great Divide

The first element of crossing the *Great Divide* is to recognize that it exists; to recognize the cause/effect relationships in *your* life between a mindset of *lack* and *victim* behaviors. To focus upon *opportunity* and upon being *accountable.* Secondly you must understand that whatever your current situation in life, it is a product of the choices you have made up to this point. This gets us back to Practicing Perfection® Precept #1: Things are the way they are [in your life] because they got that way. And if you recall, the primary reason that this Precept is so powerful is because it makes it clear that if things are not the way you want them to be, *you* have the power to change them. Do you want *scarcity* in your life (scarcity of relationship, love, sense of fulfillment, self-respect, happiness), or…do you want abundant *possibility*? It is a matter of (1) *choosing* what you want and then (2) modifying your thoughts, feelings, and behaviors to get you to the 'other side'.

If you've 'had it tough'. If you were not raised under ideal conditions, nor been aware of any 'lucky breaks' that ever passed your way. If you feel like you've had to scrape and scratch for whatever you've managed to grab onto in this life; that you've been 'fit on', 'put on', or even 'spit on'. If you feel entitled- that somehow, someone, anyone, 'owes you'. You may be [right now] guffawing and harrumphing at the whole concept of *accountability*, let alone...*possibility*. If so, it's your choice- stay where you are. On the other hand, you may be in such a condition and recognize that maybe, just maybe, you don't have to remain stuck there. Yet, "modifying your thoughts, feelings, and behaviors to get you to the *other side*" seems impossible. Take heart. Just as the settlers discovered passes that made it possible to get to the other side of the Rockies and the Sierras, so too is there a *portal* to the other side of the *Great Divide*. All you need do is recognize it, and then choose to take three simple steps: *Admit*, *Accept*, and *Act*.

Admit

> *"Everyone wants to change the world- but*
> *none want to change themselves."*
> -Leo Tolstoy

On June 10, 1935, Dr. Bob Smith took his last drink of alcohol. Three years later, on August 11, he and Bill Wilson founded a fellowship in Akron, Ohio- Alcoholics Anonymous (AA)[5]. In 1939, Dr. Bob and Bill W. published, *Alcoholics Anonymous: The Story of How More Than One Hundred Men Have Recovered from Alcoholism*. It was in this book that the original *Twelve Steps* were first published[6]. Today, with chapters around the globe, AA has helped, and continues to help, millions of people overcome the disease of alcoholism.

The first step of AA's *Twelve Steps* begins, "We admitted we were powerless...[7]". Recall that when you are 'playing the victim' you are surrendering your power. This first of the twelve AA steps to recovery from alcoholism provides you with the first step to cure essentially any disease- ADMIT that you have a problem. Until you recognize and admit that you have a problem, there can be no cure. This is your entry into the portal to a whole new existence.

Admitting how much / how often you have been behaving as a victim begins with a simple, sometimes painful, yet essential personal exercise- take a good 'look in the mirror'. When was the last time *you* pointed a finger? How long has it been since *you* attributed the cause of something less than pleasing in your personal life (or at work) to someone or something else? What in your life are you currently ignoring- your relationship with your kids, that nagging sensation in your gut whenever you lie down at night, your personal or company cash flow projections? Do you tend to use the word *'they'* when describing less than stellar results, or when justifying why something didn't go as planned? If so, and be *very* honest, you have been diminishing yourself by being a *victim*. You have been surrendering your power, and therefore your ability, to make things better.

Oh sure, it's easy to rationalize or justify victim behaviors. After all, it's what [most] everyone else does. And you may be tempted to do so as you look in the mirror. But we're not talking about 'what everyone else does'. We're talking about *you* being a *leader*. And if you consider any leader who you personally admire, whether current or from the history books, you will undoubtedly recognize that this person did *not* play the victim. They took charge of themselves first, and then went on to be a positive force in the lives of others. You must do the same. It's a personal and profound choice. Admitting when and where you've been 'playing the victim' is your first step to becoming a positive force in your own life, as well as in the lives of others.

Once you've completed your 'reflective self-assessment' (aka looking in the mirror), there are a couple of specific things you can begin doing immediately to help you recognize and begin to eliminate victim behaviors. I learned the first one in the early nineties, during my tenure as a member of the turnaround team at the Brunswick Nuclear Plant. The plant had been shut down under order of the Nuclear Regulatory Commission (NRC). Carolina Power and Light, the company who owned the plant at the time, removed every 'Unit Manager' (department head) and above from the site. They then hired a new Site Vice President, Roy Anderson, and gave him the authority to build an entirely new leadership team. I had the opportunity to become part of that team.

One of the very first things that Roy did in his efforts to transform what had become a broken culture, was to issue the following edict: "From this point forward, we are eliminating the word *they* from our vocabulary." It was brilliant. You can imagine that when things had run so far downhill that the regulator shut the plant down, the culture was badly broken. Massive finger pointing, massive blame, massive justification and rationalization. By eliminating *"they"* in report outs, formal communications, and conversations, everyone was forced to use the only logical replacement- *"we"*. This was a powerful piece to the beginning of the plant turnaround, which, by the way, remains to this day as the most rapid turnaround ever in the history of the nuclear industry. In approximately 30 months, the Brunswick Nuclear Plant went from being the worst rated plant in the US, to being top decile in performance (in the top 10% of all of the nuclear plants in the country).

So try this simple exercise- pay attention (and stop yourself) anytime the word *they* is about to come out of your mouth. Figure out how to rephrase your statement. Second, pay attention to how often others use *"they"* when referring to challenges, issues, or problems currently being faced. You will likely be blown away at how often this word is used to deflect, deny, or diminish personal accountability.

The second thing you can do that will really help you recognize your role in having created your current conditions/circumstances is to consider this: *If you are not part of the problem, you are not part of the solution.*

Now, read that statement again- *If you are not part of the problem, you are not part of the solution.* Chances are pretty good that it seems 'upside down'. After all, we're all familiar with the standard, "If you're not part of the solution, you're part of the problem." So-

What does it all mean, Bazel?" This means that if you currently have a problem, no matter what it is, in order to have a prayer of making things better, the first thing you must do is acknowledge *your* role in having created it.

When discussing this in live audiences, I love to ask for a show of hands- "How many of you still have teenagers at home?" I raise this point because it has become accepted, at least in the US, that teenagers will rebel; that they will become disrespectful, belligerent, and downright ornery as they transition from puberty to young adulthood (my take is until about the age of 25). After pointing this out, I then (*without* asking for a show of hands) make the following statement: "If any of you are currently experiencing such rebellion with your kids, and ever hope to have a prayer of making things better, the first thing you need to do is to go home and take a good long look in the mirror. *You* had a role in creating *your* current circumstances." Remember- if you're not part of the problem, in other words, if you do not first *admit* your role in having helped to create [whatever it is], you cannot possibly be part of the solution.

So, to recap, there are three things you must do immediately if you want to enter the portal for crossing the Great Divide:

- Conduct a thorough reflective self-assessment (look in the mirror)
- Eliminate the word *they* from your vocabulary
- Recognize that if you refuse to admit your role in any problem you're facing, you cannot possibly be part of the solution

Accept

During my time aboard the USS Ohio, I had the opportunity to stay ashore in Pearl Harbor while the boat went out for three days of sonar and torpedo testing. It was rare that nuclear operators got such a 'break', but in this case, the testing was all forward of the

Engine Room, and I landed on the 'lucky list' of those who got to stay and play.

Along with a couple of buddies, I rented a room at the Hale Koa, which at the time was owned by the US government, and offered amazing rates to military personnel. Once we dropped our bags in our room, and stocked our ice chest, we headed off to acquire…a rental car. Looking back, it is crystal clear why rental car companies now do not rent to anyone under the age of 25. I'm not proud of it, but I must say, we had loads of *fun* with that yellow station wagon. Our mantra for the next three days was, "*Nothing goes faster than a rental car- the all-terrain vehicle!*" You can imagine. That poor car. I'm not aware of any specific damage we caused; however, I do remember using water from our ice chest to wash off the mud before we returned it. And, yes…the contract did clearly state that the car was for 'paved on-road use only'.)

What's the point? This was a car that we didn't *own*. We would simply be 'turning it back in' in three days. No 'blood'- no 'foul'. Like I said, I'm not proud of this particular story. In my current life I rent cars frequently. I care for them and treat them as if they were my own. With age, most of us gain [at least some] wisdom. And one of the things I've come to realize is that when it comes to my actions and behaviors, there's no 'turning it back in'. We make choices, we exercise our behaviors, we take actions, and all of these have consequences. In this case, the consequence is the tinge of guilt I feel as I recall my juvenile lack of sense of ownership of that poor rental car in Honolulu.

Once you've made it through the first level of the portal, and have *admitted* your influences or involvement in [whatever it is], your second step is to ACCEPT your role; to 'own' and internalize your contributions. This is pretty easy when things are going well. Let's say that you were part of a team, perhaps the leader of a team, which managed a project brilliantly- exceeded all targets and goals. It's pretty easy for most people to *accept* their role under such conditions. Recognition is far more important to some than it is to others; however, it's Human Nature to want to feel like we're part of successful efforts. This feeling is a sense of ownership. On the other hand, when things don't go well, it's often very convenient to dive into *victim* behaviors. It's easy to point fingers, to justify, to deflect attention away from us- to deny that we actually had anything to do with it, perhaps with a litany of 'could haves', 'should haves', and 'would haves' (directed at others, of course). When crossing the *Great Divide* into *Possibility* and *accountable* behaviors, ownership of your circumstances is *not* circumstantial. You must accept/own your roles and contributions at all times.

When it comes to your ability to lead and to influence, you will gain tremendous respect when you *accept* and acknowledge your role when things do *not* go as planned. As I continue to teach and write about these concepts, I more deeply understand them, and more incessantly apply them to my personal and professional life. When conditions or circumstances arise that are less than what I'd hoped for, I quickly look for my role. I recognize (*admit*) my role, and I internalize (*accept*) ownership of it. I am never afraid to admit that I've made a mistake. In fact, I make more mistakes than anyone else I know (just ask the members of our team). And I have discovered that when I *admit* I screwed up, to myself (which is *accepting* my role), as well as to others, there's a diffusion of energy and a release that takes place, leaving me free and empowered to move forward. It's also been my experience, both as a leader, and having observed and worked with many other leaders, that when a person in a position of leadership is transparent and vulnerable enough to internally *accept* (own) their mistakes, it grows respect and trust. Providing that honest learning takes place and perception of competency is not threatened, doing so actually strengthens a leader's permission to lead.

Act

Part III of this book, *Do Different*, is all about 'doing' relative to process, implementation, and sustainability of next-level performance. This section is about 'doing' and 'doing different' at the individual level. To reach this third level of the portal, you have *admitted* your engagement in *victim* behaviors. You have internally *accepted* and owned your contribution to [whatever it is]. Now- it's time to do something about it. It's time to ACT.

This is where the 'proactive' part of Proactive Accountability® comes into play. Being 'proactive' means to, "act in anticipation of." And, like every other step along your journey, you have a *choice*. I'll get right to the point: what you focus upon expands. Even though you have reached this level, you now come to a 'fork in the road'. To the left, you can choose to focus on the problem, in which case, if you've honestly *accepted* and internalized your role, you'll likely begin 'beating yourself up', OR… you can choose the path to the right, where rather than focusing on the problems, the negatives, and how you screwed up, you think, "Okay, I see where I could have done [whatever it is] differently. Now what can I do to make things better?"

I'll repeat it to ensure you 'got it': *What you focus upon expands.* This is a natural law. Focus on problems and guilt, and you'll get more. Focus on solutions, and they'll present themselves (likely in a very short period of time).

I adore my wife. She is the most incredible woman I've ever known. One of the [many] amazing things about her is that whenever an issue, obstacle, or challenge arises, her mind instinctively (and immediately) goes into solution mode. I can be smack in the middle of my *gap*, ranting and raving about whatever it is that has ticked me off, and she remains…perfectly calm. She's really quite amazing.

I was traveling back from a meeting at NRG Corporate Headquarters in Houston, where we had been laying the groundwork for fleet-wide implementation of Practicing Perfection®. It was January, and Suzette and I were staying in Pensacola for the winter. Consequently, I was connecting through Atlanta. The plane that I was on left Houston a bit late due to some administrative issues, but not late enough (or so I thought) to threaten making my connection to Pensacola. Coming off of the Jetway, I still had 15 minutes to make my flight, which was at the gate next door- plenty of time (or so I thought). A member of the airline's staff, clipboard resting on his hip, was stationed just outside of the Jetway. "Name?" he asked. "Tim Autrey," I replied. "Oh," he said as he pointed to my name at the top of his list, "You've missed your flight. You need to go over there, [pointing] to the service counter, to get your seat on a later flight."

The thing is, I could see *my* plane through the windows-right next door. The Jetway was still connected. I still had fifteen minutes! "But- the plane is still here!" I said in a slightly elevated tone as I pointed out the window. "I still have fifteen minutes!" (actually now down to fourteen). "Sorry," came his monotone reply, "you missed it. You need to go the service counter to get a new boarding pass."

Normally, I stay cool in airports, irrespective of delays, cancellations, weather problems- all of the 'delights' of the frequent traveler. You can't do anything about them. If it's a 'mechanical issue', I'm glad they found it on the ground. I do my best to have no expectations. But this was beyond reason, at least as far as I was concerned at that moment. At the service counter, they already had my boarding pass printed for a later flight- FOUR HOURS later. And the plane that I was supposed to be on- was STILL sitting there. Now...I was pissed.

I didn't cause a ruckus at the service counter. Even in my state of disbelief I maintained enough control to remember that it was not the person behind the counter's fault. I did the next 'best' thing. I grabbed a seat, whipped out my cell phone, and called...Suzette. "Hey, Babe," she answered, knowing it was me before she picked up. "You're never going to believe this!" came out of my mouth as I launched into how this 'stupid' airline was now causing me to have to sit in this airport- and for no [justifiable (from my perspective)] reason! As soon as I took a breath, she asked, "Have you looked to see if any other airlines have flights to Pensacola leaving sooner?" Well, of course, I hadn't even thought of that. "Let me call you back," she offered. We hung up. Five minutes later, my cell phone rings. "Delta has a flight to Pensacola leaving in 40 minutes. It'll cost 78 bucks. You want me to book it?" On my own, it would have taken me more than 40 minutes to get through my gap and beyond my *victim* behaviors. I would have spent the next four hours of my life sitting in the Atlanta airport. Yes, there are many things worse than sitting in an airport for an extra four hours. But thanks to Suzette's solution-based thinking, thirty minutes later I was sitting on the Delta flight, ready for the one-hour-twelve-minute flight to Pensacola. By the time the [four hours] was up, I was sitting on the couch in our living room, enjoying a cold Sam Adams Boston Ale.

Victim thinking and *victim* behavior will not get you out of Suckers' Swamp. Neither will grumbling about external conditions, or beating yourself up for whatever mistakes you've made. When you find yourself in a state of 'stinkin' thinkin' (as my mentor Zig Ziglar used to call it), you simply need to, "Suck it up, Princess!" Get over it and get over yourself, and turn your focus toward solution. Remember- *what you focus upon expands*.

So as you choose your actions and your behaviors, choose wisely. What's past is past. What you can control and influence lies in front of you. If you and/or your team members are primarily focused on 'problems' rather than 'solutions', here's a specific action you can take- consider making some signs. You may want to post one on your bathroom mirror, in your conference room(s), in the shop(s), perhaps even on your office door. We call this "The Noah Principle". Here's how your signs should read:

"No more prizes for predicting rain- prizes only for building arks."

Since you've come this far, I am going to make an assumption that you have *admitted* and *accepted* your role in creating the past, and have chosen to take solution-based action. Making such an assumption is a challenge for me, because one of the things we teach is to 'never assume anything'. But, I am going to give you the benefit of the doubt and congratulate you. I also need to prepare you- this is the toughest part of making it through the portal. But when you do, you are launching yourself into a field of virtually unlimited possibility.

The reason this part is so tough is because you now must interact with your external world. This can involve emotion, challenge to your self-esteem, dealing with unanticipated responses from others- an almost endless list of 'things that could happen.' Dwelling on 'what ifs' keeps many from taking the final step. In reality, whenever you ACT there is some level of risk involved. You must be willing to take such risk. In truth, nothing will keep you in the *victim* cycle, mired in Suckers' Swamp, more surely than a risk-avoiding attitude. If you are to be *accountable*, if you are to genuinely access *possibility*, you simply *must* ACT.

Taking action requires commitment. During our discussion of *accepting* (owning) your role in having helped create [whatever it is], I told you the story of the turnaround at the Brunswick Nuclear Plant, and how powerful it was to eliminate the word "they" from our collective vocabulary. I recommended that you do the same from yours. I'm now going to recommend that you banish another word from your lips- the word *'try'*. As our culture has sunk deeper and deeper into the swamp of *victimization*, use of this word has become rampant. The reason is because if I say I am going to *try* to do something, I have just committed to…nothing. In our training classes, we use a Star Wars clip to help drive this point home. This is the scene where Yoda is teaching Luke Skywalker to use *The Force* to move things with his mind. After losing his focus, whereupon Luke's X-wing Fighter sinks back into the swamp, Luke responds to Yoda's displeasure with, "I'm trying." To which Yoda replies, "No! Try not! Do or do not. There is no *try*!"[8] While the video is just a clip from a 35+ year-old Hollywood film, the wisdom in Yoda's simple line offers profound power in taking this final step. Do not *try*. Make a decision and, as Jean Luc Piccard would say, "Make it so."

All this being said, you can still face an internal challenge to actually taking action, due to the emotional angst of all of the 'what ifs'. Sometimes, we all just need a bit of inspiration; a little nudge. To help you with this, I want to offer you a passage from a book that has, over the years, helped me tremendously when faced with crossing the precipice of commitment- of taking action. The book, *The Scottish Himalayan Expedition*, was published in 1951 by William H. Murray[9]. Murray was a Scottish mountaineer and a writer. He survived three years in Nazi prison camps, where his physical condition from the near starvation diet was so poor that it was thought he might never climb again. In 1950, Murray was approached by Douglas Scott to join a mountaineering expedition to explore uncharted peaks in the Garwhal Himalaya. Having made his arrangements, with much unknown about what lay ahead, Murray wrote the following:

> We had definitely committed ourselves and were halfway out of our ruts. We had put down our passage money— booked a sailing to Bombay. This may sound too simple, but is great in consequence. Until one is committed, there is hesitancy, the chance to draw back, always ineffectiveness. Concerning all acts of initiative (and creation), there is one elementary truth, the ignorance of which kills countless ideas and splendid plans: that the moment one definitely commits oneself, then Providence moves too. All sorts of things occur to help one that would never otherwise have occurred. A whole stream of events issues from the decision, raising in one's favour all manner of unforeseen incidents and meetings and material assistance, which no man could have dreamt would have come his way.

As you head south from Cuenca, Ecuador on Highway 35, you pass through lush high altitude pine forests and thick native vegetation, that is, until you descend into the valley south of La Paz, where the landscape dramatically changes to rocks, sand, more rocks, wire weed, an occasional acacia tree, and…agave. Lots of blue agave. This is where the town of Oña is located. It's a small town of about 3,000 people. In the early nineties, the economy became very strained across Ecuador. There were few opportunities to make a decent living in Oña, let alone to 'get ahead'. In 1994, out of the need to feed his family, Angel Salvador Ortega made a tough choice- he would leave Oña, and hopefully make it into the United States. "I needed to make more money to take care of my family," he explained, "and the place to do that was the United States."

Angel stowed away on a banana boat out of Puerto Bolivar. Discovered by the ship's crew, he was arrested and jailed in Panama City. Following his release a few days later, while scheming on how to continue his trip northward, he met a Mexican businessman living in Panama.

As Angel tells the story, "When I told him that there was nothing for me in Oña except rocks, weeds, and agaves, the Mexican had an idea." He said, "You need to go home and use the agaves to make tequila." Angel had never seen much use for the agave plants, but he knew they were certainly everywhere in his desert valley. He had also never tasted tequila. The Mexican convinced him that he could actually do this, that it was a real opportunity.

Angel had met his 'angel'. Over the next eight months, the Mexican businessman spent hundreds of hours with Angel, teaching him the art of making tequila.

Today, Angel's distillery, Trancauaico, has become regarded as the best homegrown distillery in Ecuador. His world-class "aguardiente de agave" (you can't call it tequila unless it comes from the region around the city of Tequila in Jalisco, Mexico) has been compared to Don Julio Blanco, and is so smooth that 'no lime nor salt is required'[10].

Here was a man, leaving his family behind, in a desperate hope of being better able to provide for them- a huge commitment. Staring discouragement in the face, yet remaining open to *possibility*, then *Providence moved too*. While none being as dramatic as Angel's, looking back upon the crossroads in my life, both the large and small, I have found absolute truth in Murray's words. Once I made a decision to ACT, once I committed, *a whole stream of events occurred, raising in my favor incidents, and meetings, and assistance, the likes of which I would have never otherwise known*. Believe or believe not- like everything else in life, to ACT, or not to ACT, is your choice. But Angel's life, my life experiences, and those of countless others (even yours should you choose to recognize it) are absolute testaments to the unwavering presence of Providence and Possibility once you commit to taking action.

To cap off this discussion of the final level through the portal, remember:

- Nothing will keep you in the victim cycle, in Suckers' Swamp, more surely than a risk-avoiding attitude
- Do or do not. There is no *try*.
- Once you definitely commit to taking action, you enter the field of all possibility

Becoming Proactively Accountable

> *"Every single one of us is either coming into, in the middle of, or coming out of some form of 'crisis' at all points in our lives. And it is our attitude going in, in, and coming out that makes all the difference."*
> -Rich DeVos

Accountable behaviors are the direct opposite of *victim* behaviors. Taking ownership of your actions, as well as of your outcomes and your results, is prerequisite to having a successful life. Unfortunately, there is tremendous cultural pull toward the *victim* side. Likewise, there has been an 'externalization' of what accountability is and where it resides, leading to the misconception that we can somehow 'hold people accountable'. As a performance improvement professional, this offers you a significant challenge, as well as tremendous opportunity.

Corporate success springs from the willingness of its members to become proactively accountable

Accountable behaviors are essential to a healthy organizational culture. A fundamental piece of your efforts to improve performance must be to make the members of your organization aware of the *Great Divide*; to help them clearly see the possibilities (for them) of being accountable. When you go about this the right way, most of your team members will *want* to make their way through the portal. Since it will be their choice, you then merely need to help them understand the 'ins and outs' of making it through the three levels: ADMIT, ACCEPT, and ACT.

Within the Practicing Perfection® approach, we have chosen to use the term, "Proactive Accountability®," rather than simply using "accountability". Reasons for this include:

- Many still associate the term *accountability* with *punishment*

- Because of an externalized view of what *accountability* is, many still believe that they can "hold someone accountable"

- The general context of *accountability* is often a negative 'after the fact' perspective, where the question is asked, "Who is accountable for this?"

Use of "Proactive Accountability®" offers something new and different; a separation from what 'has been' to what 'can be'. Further, the word "proactive" implies looking forward, using the windshield rather than attempting to drive using the rearview mirror. Here is the definition of Proactive Accountability®:

Internalization of the personal responsibility to act in anticipation of future problems, needs, or changes, while fully owning one's behaviors and outcomes.

With this definition in mind, note the following: (1) *internalization* (directly interfacing with the individual's *why*; doing so because they *want* to, (2) acting *in anticipation of* (not waiting until after less than desirable outcomes to take action; actively looking for and correcting issues before things go wrong), and (3) fully *owning* one's behaviors and outcomes (internalized ownership without excuses or blame). This, my friend, is a ticket to a happy and successful life. It is also a linchpin to organizational success.

In Chapter Two, *Third-Dimension Thinking*, we discussed how individual effort is multiplied and synergized by achieving an organizational culture of Viral Accountability®. If you recall, the formula for achieving Viral Accountability® is:

$$PA * PL * VC = VA$$

Developing Proactive Accountability® (PA) is the individualized/internalized element of this formula. It is the base upon which the other elements multiply. Beyond simply 'being accountable', Proactive Accountability® directly seeks and multiplies the field of *possibility* lying above the *Great Divide*. When you consider that organizational culture is essentially the combined behaviors and interactions of its members, think about how your culture will transform when the majority of your team members make it through the portal and become proactively accountable. This taps into and positively leverages everything we have discussed thus far in the first five chapters of this book.

Backsliding

Looking at the following figure, you can see that the portal through the *Great Divide* is narrow at the bottom, and much wider at the top. It is narrow at the bottom because it is often difficult to recognize and *admit* that we have, indeed, been behaving as *victims*. In fact, people often need help. We've been amazed over the past ten years at how participants' eyes have been opened as they are made aware of what *victim* behaviors look like and where they come from. The great thing is, once their eyes are opened, most people *want Possibility*. They *want* to become *accountable*.

That 'Giant Sucking Sound'

The portal widens at the top because, quite honestly, even though you have made it through, are being *accountable*, and are living in *Possibility*, there is always a potential to get sucked back downward. In fact, as you allow yourself to drift downward, either due to losing focus, the pull of society's epidemic, or an acute situation directly tugging on your fears, the opening can act as a vortex, pulling you downward. It can become that, "...giant sucking sound," as Ross Perot became known for saying[11]. The point is, anyone (including you, me, or any one of your team members) can rise above the Divide, and for some reason, on any given day, find themselves back in Suckers' Swamp.

Talk to someone who smokes, and they'll typically tell you that the people who 'bug them' the most about smoking are- reformed smokers. I'm bringing this up, because you'll likely start looking at the world, at conditions, at circumstances, and at challenges quite differently once you've become proactively accountable. The last thing in the world you want to do is begin to act 'holier than Thou' as you become more acutely aware of the *victim* behaviors and perspectives all around you. To do so will kill your ability to influence, and can actually generate resistance to the whole idea of *Possibility* and becoming *accountable*.

Once you've arrived above the *Divide*, your role is to guide, to assist, to lend a helping hand. Help people up through their individual portals, and once they've 'tasted' life filled with *possibility*, help them (and allow them to help you) to stay there.

The Power of Synergy: Joint Accountability

Have you ever watched a perfectly executed play on the football field? Have you ever seen a triple play in baseball? Have you ever seen a brilliant press down the court or power play across the ice? It's beautiful. It's magical. It's a perfect example of *Joint Accountability*. As a society, we pay big money for (and many invest a lot of emotion into) team sports. This is an extension of our competitive nature. It gives us an opportunity, as fans, to 'belong', to feel part of something big and important. And while we may not be consciously thinking about it as we pump our fists and jump and yell, we are observing in such moments a symphony of human interaction. Each member of the team, doing their part, backing one another up- all in pursuit of a common objective.

Joint Accountability is the internalization of the personal responsibility to act and interact in a manner that best supports the overall purpose of the team.

About ten years ago we took our daughters, Becky and Evie, to a four-day 'ordeal' called, "Enlightened Warrior Training Camp." It was a great experience to share with our kids. It was also the most physically demanding four days I've ever spent. There were approximately 200 people participating in the voluntary torment. Ages ranged from ten to seventy-three, from fit and athletic, to…not at all fit and athletic. They split us into four 'tribes'. Each day each tribe had a different 'experience' designed to pull us out of our comfort zones- to challenge us physically and mentally.

Our tribe's challenge on Tuesday was what they called, "Peaks." It was basically a five-mile hike in the hilly terrain of central New York. I'm in pretty good shape, and I was looking forward to a nice leisurely walk in the woods. What they didn't tell us in advance was that, as a team, we would be carrying [full] 5-gallon Coleman water jugs, and…bricks. Yes…bricks! The goal of the day was to (1) get as many tribe members as far along the trek as possible (documented by tallying accumulated colored stamps on team members' badges), and (2) to get as many people and bricks as possible to the summit by 3:00PM. One tribe did this on each of the four days. At the end of the week, the tribe who best achieved the overall objectives (most colored stamps AND people/bricks to the summit) would be announced as the 'winner'.

As we loaded our packs with bricks, and were discussing our plan of who would be carrying the water jugs, I must've been looking like I was having too much fun, because I got 'yelled at' by one of our counselors. "Look!" she said, glaring at me, "This is not about seeing who can race to the top the quickest. You're here to help as many of your tribe members as possible get as far as they can. Got it?!" I nodded. So much for my leisurely walk in the woods.

Suzette and I started out toting one of the water jugs. This was in addition to my pack stuffed with bricks. Shortly into the trek, it became readily apparent that some of our team members were really struggling- not because they were carrying water or bricks, but simply because they were [grossly] out of shape. We clearly had to develop a strategy to maximize speed of movement (getting the maximum number of people and bricks to the summit by 3 o'clock), while helping our less capable members get as far along the path as possible. A clear sense of *Joint Accountability* evolved within our tribe. Some, Becky and Evie amongst them, were to move ahead as quickly as possible. Others, Suzette and I included, stayed back to help those who needed it. As the clock approached 2:40PM, I decided, along with one of the other tribe members who had been holding back to help, that it would be worth it to sprint the remainder of the way, in hopes that we could make it to the peak before time ran out. Suzette stayed back with the water jugs and the 'less capable' as the two of us raced onward and upward.

As we got closer, we could hear our cheering tribe members at the top. A counselor descending from the peak (the same one who yelled at me earlier that morning) demanded that we STOP. Time was up. I sat on a rock alongside the path, exhausted and disappointed. After all who made it to the top had descended, passing by us on their way down the trail, we followed them back to the initial gathering spot, and then back to the lodge. Becky and Evie told me the view was incredible. I'm sure it was…

By the way, that evening I walked 30 feet upon a bed of red hot coals- barefoot. So did Suzette, and Becky, and Evie. But this is a different story for a different time...

At the Awards Ceremony on Thursday evening, we found out that our tribe won the Peaks competition. We certainly were no more physically capable than the other tribes. We certainly had our 'weaker links'. I'd spent most of my Tuesday helping them. But my role was no more nor less important than that of those who we sent racing to the top (such as Becky and Evie), or the folks who spent most of their time carrying water (such as Suzette), or of those who really struggled to simply gather as many of the colored stamps as possible. We had somehow simply achieved the highest level of *Joint Accountability*. And we won- by a wide margin.

The workplace is certainly not about carrying water jugs and bricks and tallying how many can make it to a mountain peak by three in the afternoon. It is, however, about common objectives, backing one another up, and leveraging strengths. It [should be] every bit as much a team activity as football, baseball, or any other team sport. *Joint Accountability* is an integral part of a *one team* approach to doing whatever it is that your team, department, and organization does. It leverages team member internalization of Proactive Accountability® into a synergized force that can achieve *event-free* next-level operations and outcomes.

In geometry, the 'perfect' shape is the sphere. This is because, when passing through the center, every point on the sphere is equal distance from every other point on the sphere. I bring this up to put forth the following illustration.

Proactively Accountable Team Members

Consider a small team of three people within your organization. Once each of these team members has embraced Proactive Accountability® they can be represented as 'whole'; as solid, viable, accountable, 'looking ahead' members of the team.

When we expand beyond the internalization of individual Proactive Accountability® to where team members are actively looking for ways to assist one another, to back one another up, we enter into the realm of *Joint Accountability*.

Joint Accountability

As you can see, *Joint Accountability* develops a field of virtual invulnerability as team members look out for, assist, and spontaneously back up their co-workers. This is how you can achieve zero *events* in spite of the fact that humans are *fallible*; that individually, we *all* make mistakes.

How can you get there? Proper exposure to Proactive Accountability® taps into our intrinsic need to matter. Most will be naturally drawn to it (motivated) once they understand it, see leaders behaving differently, and come to believe that your organization truly supports it. It directly feeds the human needs of self-esteem and self-actualization. Once the concept of *one team* is properly developed, which we will be discussing in Chapter Nine, *Joint Accountability* naturally springs forward, provided it is properly modeled and supported by those who lead. The step-by-step for how all of this is developed is laid out for you in the *Human Performance Blueprint* in Chapter Ten.

Key Insights from Chapter Five

1. *Accountability* (just like *motivation*) is internal. You cannot 'hold someone accountable'

2. *Accountable* behaviors are directly opposite of *victim* behaviors

3. The culture in which we live influences the way we think and behave. Our society is in the midst of an epidemic of victimization. This needs to be countered in the workplace.

4. The mass of humanity can be divided into two basic world views: *Scarcity* and *Possibility*

5. A world view of *Scarcity* leads to a mindset of *lack*. A mindset of *lack* leads to a core emotion of *fear*, which generates basic *victim* behaviors. The five most common *victim* behaviors are:

   • Blame

- Ignore
- Deny
- Defer
- CMA

6. A world view of *Possibility* leads to a mindset of *opportunity*. A mindset of *opportunity* leads to a core emotion of *enthusiasm*, which generates *accountable* behaviors.

7. There are three steps one must take to transition from the victim behaviors of scarcity to accountability and possibility:

- ADMIT
- ACCEPT
- ACT

What can you do with what you just learned?

A. Recognize that poor behaviors are expressions of a problem, not the problem itself

B. Understand and own your role in helping to create whatever problems you're facing

C. Eliminate the word *they* from your vocabulary

D. Eliminate the word *try* from your vocabulary

E. Adopt the 'Noah Principle': No more prizes for predicting rain- prizes only for building arks

[1] *The Oz Principle: Getting Results Through Individual and Organizational Accountability*; Roger Connors, Tom Smith, and Craig Hickman; 2004

[2] Merriam Webster's Collegiate Dictionary, Eleventh Edition

[3] *Naturalis Historia*; Pliny the Elder; Book XXXV, *Earth*

[4] Merriam Webster's Collegiate Dictionary, Eleventh Edition

[5] *The Twelve Traditions*; the AA Grapevine; November, 1949; ISSN 0362-2584 OCLC 50379271

[6] *Alcoholics Anonymous* (4th Edition); Bill W.; June 2001; Alcoholics Anonymous World Services; ISBN 1-893007-16-2.OCLC 32014950

[7] *Alcoholics Anonymous* (4th Edition); Bill W.; June 2001; "Chapter 5: How it Works"; Alcoholics Anonymous World Services; ISBN 1-893007-16-2.OCLC 32014950

[8] *Star Wars*; released on May 25, 1977; 20th Century Fox

[9] *The Scottish Himalayan Expedition*; W.H. Murray; 1951; J.M. Dent & Sons, Ltd.

[10] *The tequila maker: artisanal distiller Angel Salvador Ortega produces world-class aguardiente de agave in a desert valley south of Cuenca*; David Morrill; December 30, 2014; CuencaHighLife

[11] Ross Perot comments relative to NAFTA; second Presidential Debate; October 11, 1992

Chapter Six: Transform Your Culture (One Team at a Time)

"Never doubt that a small group of thoughtful, concerned citizens can change the world. Indeed it is the only thing that ever has."
- Margaret Mead

After laying the foundation of next-level thinking in Part I, we moved on to motivation, influence, and behaviors in Chapter Four. In Chapter Five, I developed the world views of *Scarcity* and *Possibility*, and the cause/effect relationship with their associated 'bins" of *victim* and *accountable* behaviors. We also discussed the three steps anyone must take (you and I included) to get out of 'Suckers' Swamp', and rise above the *Great Divide* separating victims from those who take charge of their lives, their careers, and their futures.

Until now, we've focused on the mindset, thoughts, feelings, and behaviors of individuals. We've discussed motivation, which is internal to the individual, as well as accountability, also internal to the individual. I have wanted to help you build a foundation of awareness and understanding of the individual because (1) much of it flies in the face of what you've likely been taught about how to *manage* people, and (2) the way to change the world (including the culture within your organization) is- one person at a time. What we have been discussing thus far has been designed to help you understand, and reach, *one person at a time*.

We are now going to transition toward your team/organization. While motivation comes from within, and accountability resides within, humans are social creatures. We live together, we work together, we tend to form and belong to 'tribes' with like-minded individuals. Within organizations, we are given titles, positions, and job descriptions, we are put onto lines, placed into crews and departments, and [hopefully] given some sense of how our individual efforts fit into the overall scheme/mission of the enterprise. The social and environmental impacts of all of these offer input to each individual involved, influencing mindsets, thoughts, feelings, and ultimately (that which we can observe)-behaviors.

This is where 'rocket science' (or flat out 'mystery') often enters the picture for many seeking to improve performance. You can find libraries filled with volume upon volume of scientific studies, research, and theories relative to organizational and social psychology. These run the gamut from mechanized process-oriented prescriptive solutions, to 'airy-fairy' group hug kumbaya team building. We're not going to either one of these extremes, nor are we going to dive into complexity. The truth is, there is a very simple approach with which to leverage Human Nature (and all of the psychological principles we have discussed thus far) in the group/organizational setting.

Another of my mentors, Tony Robbins, has maintained since near the beginning of his career that the quickest way to achieve success (in virtually anything) is to find someone who has successfully achieved want you want to achieve, and then- simply do what they did. And this is where we're headed. I am now going to show you *how* to rapidly transform the culture of your organization using the same approach that we have successfully used for the past ten years.

"Culture"

Culture is essentially the accepted beliefs and behavioral 'norms' of a group. Put more than two people together for any length of time, and some form of culture will develop. For some reason, many seem to think that once we start talking "culture", it somehow becomes a mystical science, the intricacies of which only a select few can dissect. This is probably why so many 'consultants' have penned "culture change" as a service offered when hanging their proverbial shingles. I will agree that digging into the histories and nuances of how a given culture, the Irish population living in rural Chicago for example, came to acquire its symbols, and beliefs, and accepted practices when attending Sunday Mass, can indeed go very deep and get very complex. I will also concede that attempts to change such a culture would likely require significant effort and take a long time. But this is not the type of culture change we're here to talk about.

We're here to talk about the culture of your team, at your plant, within your department- the accepted beliefs and behavioral 'norms', both as a factor of influence, and as influenced by, the behaviors, actions, and interactions of your team members. You're likely reading this book because you want to change behaviors. Whether these are behaviors related to safety, quality, reliability, efficiency, error reduction, or 'all of the above', the only way to achieve sustainable performance improvement is by transforming your culture; by taking it from where it is to someplace new.

When you consider that combining the Individual Performance Models of each member of a group essentially creates its culture (see Chapter Four), *and* you consider that the way to change [the world] the culture of your organization is…one person at a time, this *should* dispel most of the mystery for you about culture change within organizations. This is why I went into such detail regarding motivation, influence, and Proactive Accountability®.

At PPI, most (if not all) of our clients hire us to help them implement next-level human performance with a common goal in mind- improvement of safety and the reduction of human error. And while their expectations regarding safety and error reduction have most always been exceeded, they ultimately achieve something much more profound- culture transformation. This is because all of the processes are structured knowing that the only way a person is going to do the 'right thing' consistently (when no one else is watching) is if they *want* to. In order to get a person to *want* to do [anything], you have to get 'inside' of them; tap into whatever motivates them. When you do so effectively, their behaviors change. Change the behaviors of a majority of a team of people, and…you transform the culture. It really is that simple.

Before you go any further, if you have not yet watched the documentary on Practicing Perfection®, it will serve you well to do so now. You can access the documentary here: http://ppiweb.com/home-2-3/ppi-documentary/

The Myth

"Culture change is *hard*, and it takes a *long* time." I cannot tell you how many times I've heard this, read this, or inferred this from so-called 'experts' in management, leadership, change management, psychology, and/or performance improvement. As I indicated in the introduction to this chapter, if you're talking about changing centuries-old customs and cultures, yes- this may be so. But when it comes to changing the culture of a team, department, or organization of workers, such is simply NOT the case. It is *not* hard, and it does *not* have to take a long time.

I say this without any reservation because, as I have previously mentioned, we (PPI) have worked with tens of thousands of workers over the past ten years, and have witnessed massive rapid culture change in organizations both small and large.

'Top Down' or 'Bottom Up'?

There are two predominant 'schools of thought' regarding *how* to go about changing the culture of an organization. The first is *Top Down*. With this approach, culture change is initiated at the top, and typically 'driven' by one or more senior executives, using a traditional change management model. The big initiative is launched and is communicated to the layers of management. A big roll out is then planned, staged, and implemented. This often includes posters, shirts or jackets, gift cards, or online 'award points'. A tremendous amount of energy is pumped into the effort, especially at the outset. Some behavior changes can be witnessed, especially in the very beginning, because (1) people come to work wanting to do a 'good job' and (2) what's being focused upon is what's being perceived as a 'good job'. In the longer term, such initiatives often fall onto the heap of 'programs of the day'. This is because as time moves onward, the 'bloom falls from the rose'. Perhaps the sponsoring senior leader gets transferred or distracted by another initiative, a new CEO comes in with his new agenda, or the day-to-day busyness simply sucks energy, and focus gets shifted elsewhere. At some point, it is common to discover behaviors reverting to whatever they were before. This is an indicator that the culture has *not* actually changed. Workers were merely responding to what they were [temporarily] being told was a 'good job'.

Here's something to anchor in: When you initiate any efforts to change behaviors, if you do not succeed in transforming the culture, it's just like pumping water uphill. As soon as you turn off the pump, all of that water comes rushing back downward.

The other predominant school of thought regarding culture change is that you must 'grow' it from the 'Bottom Up'. In this scenario, working level teams are developed. The teams are given (or develop) charters, do brainstorming, and set priorities. You may have even taken the time to identify 'natural influencers' on the front lines and spend the money to bring in consultants and give them special training. Enthusiastically, they return to work role modeling new [desired] behaviors in anticipation that others will follow. And again, some of this may work...for a while. Unfortunately, in such scenarios, senior leadership often sets such a plan in motion and then moves onto other things. "But, it's supposed to grow from the 'bottom up', right?" you query. "Isn't this what 'organic growth' is all about?" Yes, it's part of it, but *only* part. In such efforts, workers (especially those who received 'special training') tend to launch with enthusiasm. However, because senior leadership has often merely 'checked the box' and moved onto other things, workers see no changes in behaviors of supervisors, managers, or senior leaders. Without consistent role modeling and reinforcement from the top, such efforts are typically doomed.

If you've ever been involved in a debate of whether 'Top Down' or 'Bottom Up' is the required method to successfully change culture, you can easily take the lead in the conversation by simply stating, "You must have both." Both elements- consistent role-modeling, sponsorship, and reinforcement from the top, AND worker involvement in growing it upward, are absolutely required for successful culture transformation. Even still, these are merely elements. Here's the *real* answer to how culture transformation is successfully implemented: **from the inside out.** Such is the reason why we spent so much time in Chapters Four and Five, developing and understanding what's going on 'inside' of the members of your team (yourself included).

A Huge Culprit

Culture change remains as an enigma (something hard to understand or explain) to many. A primary reason for this is the old-school approach of attempting to manage people like 'things'. This becomes blatantly obvious when you see organizations using the traditional change management model in an attempt to change culture.

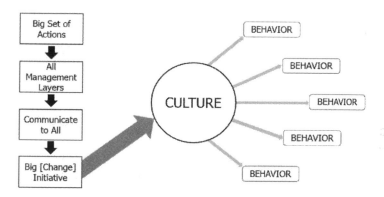

Traditional Change Management Model

You've likely seen a flowchart or model similar to the one shown above. This is classic, "Change Management 101." And it [supposedly] works like this:

A. Take vision from senior leadership (probably inspired by a book she just read or a great speaker heard at a recently attended conference), [maybe] interview 'stakeholders', and determine your set of actions. And since this is an organization-wide initiative, this is a BIG set of actions.

B. Conduct a management team meeting (typically down through department head / mid-level) to inform them of what's coming. Communications to lower levels (to supervisors, etc.) is typically left to the discretion of the mid-level managers.

C. Develop and launch a 'marketing campaign' (a communications campaign designed to inform all organization members of 'what's coming')

D. Conduct a series of 'All hands Meetings' and/or presentations via workgroup meetings, using the company intranet, etc. (whatever seems most expeditious) to inform 'all hands' of their newly expected behaviors, why this is good for the company, 'we're all in this together', etc.

E. *Anticipate* that the massive launching of the initiative will change organizational culture.

F. *Hope* that the change in organizational culture will translate into new/desired behaviors by [at least some of] the workers.

Not to entirely denigrate the change management industry, this model can work very well for change associated with…things. Say you are installing a new piece of company-wide software, or constructing a new facility. However, people are NOT things. Introducing an initiative designed to transform organizational culture using this model (or anything like it) is completely upside down. All you need do is simply recall what creates the culture in the first place, and this becomes blatantly obvious. So- if you are starting, or in the middle of, any efforts to change your culture, and this is your planned approach, stop right now. Do not go any further until you finish (at a minimum) reading, understanding, and digesting the rest of this chapter.

The Goal

A 'culture' essentially becomes its own 'thing'. It does not necessarily directly mirror nor represent the thoughts, feelings, or behaviors of any one member of the group. While it can be influenced by one or a few members, especially within a brand new team, a small team, or a team with one or more 'alpha' personalities, often the accepted behaviors and social 'norms' are what they have become over time. People come into the group. People leave the group. The culture tends to remain relatively static. This is one of the reasons why changing it is still considered 'hard to do' by so many. Culture will tend to remain as it is unless directly acted upon. And as we've been discussing, such 'acting upon' must dive *inside*. External pushing, expecting, and demanding will only, at best, result in temporary behavior change (which is not actually culture change at all).

If you were to stand back and ponder, "What would an ideal 'culture' look like? How would it work? How would people interact?" you'd likely come up with an answer something like, "An environment of ever-improving outcomes generated through a synergy of worker momentum, where positive behaviors are spontaneously prompted and reinforced through a sense of ownership and the proactive actions and interactions of team members." Okay, your words may be different, but the components of what you'd come up with would likely be very similar. This should be your goal. This is Viral Accountability®.

I've already introduced Viral Accountability® to you, first in Chapter Two (Third-Dimension Thinking), and then again in Chapter Five, where we developed the concept of Proactive Accountability® (the first element in the equation for its achievement). Just to refresh your memory (and because this is *really* important to your efforts to transform your organization's culture), here is a quick recap of the formula:

$$PA * PL * VC = VA$$

Where:

PA=   Proactive Accountability®

PL=   Peer Leadership

VC=   Viral Change

VA=   Viral Accountability®

We're now going to discuss the remaining two elements of Viral Accountability®- , Viral Change (VC) and Peer Leadership (PL). You will then be able to see how all of this fits together.

Viral Change (VC)

Individually, you and I are very unique. Put us together 'en masse' however, and there are characteristics that reveal striking similarities between us. While we may have directly opposing political or religious beliefs, or while I might be a vegetarian while you're always wondering, "Where's the beef?" when you put us together, especially with a bunch of others, commonalities emerge. For example, most people want to have some sense of belonging. This is why we identify with sports teams, join clubs, have company parties and family reunions. We like to feel respected. This is why every major religion on the planet promotes some form of the 'Golden Rule'. If someone does something for us (or gives something to us), we typically feel an obligation to 'return the favor'. This is known as reciprocity. For many, it seems almost a need to share information, especially that which has touched our emotions in some way. When was the last time you saw a movie you loved, or went to a restaurant that was horrible? What did you do? You likely shared this information with anyone who would stand still long enough to listen. And at work? What is the fastest communication system within your organization (one that often requires 'damage control' due to the rapid dissemination of *incorrect* info)? The rumor mill. Gossip.

And when it comes to these common characteristics of human beings, just like in everything else- what you focus upon expands. If you choose to look at them as problems, obstacles, and challenges, this is exactly how they will present themselves in your day-to-day operations. On the other hand look for the positives present in Human Nature and you will find them. Learn how to leverage them, and you are on your way to rapid changes in corporate work behaviors, and ultimately- culture transformation.

As an example of what I am talking about, here is a diagram of how information (and behavior change) [truly] occurs within an organization:

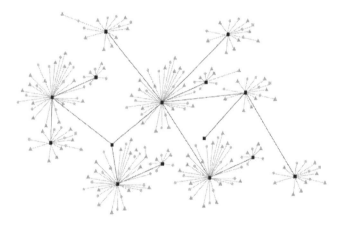

Viral Growth

The Viral Growth diagram is representative of that provided by the US Center for Disease Control to depict how an infectious disease spreads through a population. One of the features of viral diffusion is that nearly all (+90%) of those infected are *not* infected by the first to get the disease. So much for the charismatic leader who thinks she can do it all on her own.

In a study conducted in 2012 by Dan Goldstein (Microsoft Research) and Max Planck in Berlin regarding the 'viral' dissemination of information on the internet, what they discovered were relatively stable patterns in which a relatively small number of individuals were responsible for the bulk of information diffusion[1]. Both of these insights provide us with great opportunity. First, this is a natural phenomenon. It exists. The 'rumor mill' is a great example of how it can be very frustrating within an organization, and can even undermine things we are working to achieve. But...what if we can tap into the natural positive tendencies of Human Nature and leverage them to our advantage?

Secondly, the Goldstein/Planck discovery offers additional [substantial] leverage about the 'power of the few'. As an example, my wife, Suzette, has been developing a website for the past three years designed to help women improve their appearance (and self-esteem) by dressing properly for their body type and size. By the end of 2013, with the site still in the development phase, and having not yet been 'launched', the number of women who had somehow found the site online and created their virtual 'dressing rooms' had risen to about 4,500. In February of 2014, a "Power Pinner" (key influencer) on Pinterest 'pinned' Suzette's site (http://www.mystylerules.com). Within a few weeks, this number rose above 100,000. Bloggers and Facebook sharing entered the picture. Today, the site, mystylerules.com, has nearly a million women who are accessing the site, have created their private virtual dressing rooms, and are learning how to look younger, taller, and thinner by changing how they dress. Even more importantly, these women are learning how to feel better about themselves. So- what the heck does this have to do with improving your safety culture, quality, or reliability? Everything. This is a great representation of a natural aspect of Human Nature- how the 'few' help to influence the many.

A practical example of how we capitalize upon this within PPI when helping organizations implement Practicing Perfection®, is we encourage them to invite their Union Stewards (and/or key frontline leaders when no union is present) to Leadership Training. This is the first level of training you should provide in any effort to change human performance (as you will see in Chapter Ten). Think about it- these are your key frontline influencers. Getting them onboard before any formal training is provided to 'the troops' has an almost 'magical' impact upon your overall effort. If you'd like to hear a perspective on this directly from one of these influencers, watch the PPI Documentary and look for the guy in the black cowboy hat. His name is Victor. You can access the video here: http://ppiweb.com/home-2-3/ppi-documentary/

And now is where it really begins to get fun. In a few moments, I'm going to show you the model for *how* to do this, including *the* process for tying it all together. But first, we're going to talk about something that should be obvious- you cannot focus on 'everything' at one time. The great news is, you don't need to. In fact, you absolutely do not want to. All you need do, irrespective of where your performance improvement focus lies (safety, quality, etc.), is focus on a few key behaviors. We call these *vital behaviors.*

Vital Behaviors

According to the US Center for Disease Control and Prevention, 69% of adults in the country are overweight, and of this number, 35% are considered obese.[2] It should therefore come as no shock to hear that the diet and weight loss industry in the US was worth $69 Billion in 2014[3]. What does this have to do with improving performance within your organization?

When it comes to diets, you can find everything from low carb to no carb to the "Super-Carb Diet."[4] (I had to reference that last one because, on the surface, I couldn't believe it either.) You can 'travel' from South Beach to the Mediterranean to Asia via your diet choices, each 'guaranteed' to offer rapid and sustainable fat loss. You can 'Eat Right for Your Body Type', work to have a 'Clean Gut', go on a 'juice fast', or even go on the 'water diet'. And then, of course, there's the spectrum of exercise regimens far too numerous to mention. With all of these choices, and all of the money that's being spent on both diet and exercise, how can the statistics possibly be so horrendous?

I know the absolute 'secret' to weight loss, and I'm going to share it with you now. If you feel so inclined to send some of that $69 Billion my way as a 'thank you' for sharing this with you, there are plenty of places in this book where contact information can be obtained. Are you ready for some 'rocket science'? Here it is:

$$CW = CC - CB$$

Where:

CW = Change in weight

CC = Calories consumed

CB = Calories burned

Of course, you can get mired in the details of the types of calories being consumed, metabolic rates, genetic dysfunction, and the impacts of stress. And this only touches the surface. However, this very simple formula is the basis for whether your weight is going to go up...or down. It's true for you, it's true for me, it's true for virtually every human on the planet.

So now that we know the *science* behind weight loss, what behaviors might we possibly embrace in our efforts to keep from being (or becoming) part of the dreaded 69%? This is even more fascinating than the simple formula. The National Weight Control Registry has been conducting an ongoing study of over 10,000 individuals who have lost more than 30 pounds (the numbers actually range from 30 to 300 pounds), and have successfully kept the weight off for more than five years. In other words, successful, substantial, sustainable weight loss. And out of these 10,000+ success stories, they have identified (4) common behaviors. Hold onto your hat because these are really 'tough':

- 78% eat breakfast every day.
- 75% weigh themselves at least once a week.

- 62% watch less than 10 hours of TV per week.
- 90% exercise, on average, about 1 hour per day[5].

So, eat breakfast, weigh yourself regularly (this is your 'metric' to know how you're doing), don't watch too much TV (probably more of a lifestyle indicator than a 'prescription'), and...exercise regularly. It simply requires commitment and some very simple behaviors. It's not complicated.

And once again, you're probably wondering what in the world 'weight loss' has to do with improving performance. When you consider that success simply requires commitment and some very simple behaviors- everything. These behaviors, these fundamental things that *really* make a difference, are *vital behaviors*- high-leverage actions that are essential to achieving whatever it is you're seeking to do.

So what are the *vital behaviors* associated with next-level human performance? Well, before we get to the behaviors, we need to start with the science. And at this point, the science is merely a review from Chapter One:

$$HP = W(R + B)$$

Where:

HP = Human Performance

W = WHY

R = Results

B = Behaviors

As you should already be aware, putting this formula into words offers a simple, yet profoundly powerful awareness: *Human Performance is WHY we do WHAT we do the WAY we do it*. As a performance improvement professional, this level of understanding of what 'human performance' *is* and *how it works* puts you in the top 1% of the profession. I would imagine, however, that you're now wondering, "Is there a simple set of behaviors that I can promote that will generate successful, substantial, and sustainable performance improvement in my organization?" And the answer is- you bet! Here they are:

- Be proactively accountable
- Use the Error Elimination Tools™ uncompromisingly
- Engage one another based upon Principles
- Act upon lessons learned

I know there are some terms and concepts within these four behaviors that we have not yet covered. I will be covering the Error Elimination Tools™ in Chapter Eight, engagement based upon Principles in Chapter Nine, and taking action upon lessons learned in Chapter Ten. For now, simply recognize that these are the *vital behaviors* necessary for achieving and sustaining next-level performance. How do you get workers to actually do this stuff? Obviously, by getting them to *want* to. Hopefully you already *get* that part. As far as the mechanics for actually *doing* it are concerned, these will start to become clear as we work through the *Viral Change Model* and the mechanism for growing *Peer Leadership*. This truly is *not* complicated.

Viral Change Model

When I conducted the 'experiment' at the Vermont Yankee nuclear plant in 2003, I had the opportunity to test my 'theories' about how to sustainably enhance human performance within the nuclear environment. Following that success, as I established and began to grow PPI, I was able to further develop and refine what I considered to be the ideal 'recipe' for growing and sustaining the behaviors and types of outcomes we've been discussing thus far. With each success, we would learn, adapt, and improve; however, the basic recipe has never changed. This is because- it works. It wasn't until 2009, however, that I fully came to understand *why* the 'recipe' works so well. It was then that I happened across a book entitled, *Viral Change*, written by Leandro Herrero[6]. Digesting the information in this book was one of those 'happy dance' professional moments, because I now understood much of the underlying science behind *why* what we had been doing (and continue to do) has achieved such substantial and sustainable results. One of the things the author did was to explain how the traditional approach to change management, especially when the goal was a change in behaviors, was essentially upside down. He included a flowchart to help understanding of what he was discussing. Using this flowchart as a starting point, I developed the Viral Change Model, which you see below.

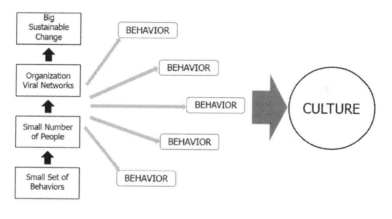

Viral Change Model

As you can see, the pathway to organizational culture transformation is essentially upside down from the traditional change management model. It begins with a small set of behaviors. These are your *vital behaviors*. Where do they come from? You let the members of the team decide. I'll explain how this works in the next section. You initiate/implement this small set of behaviors at the natural work team level- there's your *small number of people*.

Once you've initiated the small set of behaviors amongst the members of a natural work team, you allow one of the natural forces of Human Nature, the *viral networks* (already alive and well within your organization), to work on your behalf. Done the right way, you *will* see the proliferation of positive changes in behavior.

As changes in behavior grow amongst the population, the culture transforms. The result? A big *sustainable* change.

I speak with certainty about this model and its effectiveness because this is how the Practicing Perfection® approach to next-level human performance has been structured since its inception. This is the approach that has been used to generate the results I shared with you at the beginning of this book. It taps into, and leverages natural elements of Human Nature to everyone's benefit.

Peer Leadership (PL)

"A leader is best when people barely know he exists, when his work is done, his aim fulfilled, they will say: we did it ourselves." -Lao Tzu

As we've already discussed, achieving and sustaining next-level performance requires a different way of *thinking* and a different way of *doing*. And one of the key areas differentiating the 'old school' from the 'new' is in a re-defined understanding of what it means to be a *leader* within your organization. First of all, it has nothing to do with which box your name happens to occupy on the organizational chart. There are many whose names are in the upper tiers who are not *leaders* at all, but are merely [highly] overpaid managers. On the other hand, there are many on the bottom rungs (and everywhere in between) who demonstrate true *leadership* on a daily basis. Here is the next-level definition. A *leader* is:

Any individual who takes full ownership of his or her actions and behaviors, and who positively influences the actions and behaviors of others.

As I indicated [several times] before, this is not complicated. If you stop right now and consider this definition, and then do a quick mental scan of the members of your organization, I have no doubt that names and faces of team members who so conduct themselves will pop into your head. Here is an exercise for you: grab a highlighter and a copy of your org chart (one that includes names). Start at the very top, and highlight the name of each individual who currently fits this next-level definition of *leader*. If you are honest and truthful, you will likely find the results very interesting. Hopefully your name is highlighted. If not, this can be a great beginning to your *reflective self-assessment* (look in the mirror).

When doing this exercise, if you're a senior executive, and there are members of your leadership team whose names are not highlighted, this should be one of those 'things that make you go hmmm.' If you're a mid-level manager or coordinator, and there are names in boxes higher up on the chart that are not highlighted, this is likely a huge source of your current frustration with 'the way things are going'. If there are team members in position of frontline supervisor whose names are not highlighted, this should be a focus for immediate attention (we'll talk more about why this is so important in Chapter Nine). And, you are hopefully pleased with a number of highlighted names at the lower / frontline levels. Now- just imagine how your organization will function when the majority of names on your org chart are worthy of highlighting. Herein lies your opportunity to grow a magnificent pathway to Viral Accountability® and toward achieving and sustaining next-level performance.

Now to be clear, while the process I am about to reveal to you tends to bring out leadership qualities previously lying dormant, you will not likely turn the majority of your team members into 'natural born leaders'. The thing is, you don't need to. Science still seems pretty well agreed that the majority of us only use about five percent of our brain capacity over the course of our lives. Just imagine how much more powerful you or I could become if we just tweak our percentage of brain usage up a little bit. The same thing is true when it comes to leadership. There are intrinsic human desires and abilities within most people that make being a *leader* (as now defined) both appealing and rewarding. This does not necessarily mean that the majority want to 'take the helm', but it does mean that, especially amongst our peers, it is a natural part of healthy interaction and proactive relationship. This is called *Peer Leadership* (PL). Now…just as with the potential each of us has should we choose to notch up the use of our brains a percent or two, just imagine the impact upon your organization if we do the same with *Peer Leadership*. No longer is it about charismatic leaders, or the need to continually pump tons of positive energy in 'from on high'. When you get this right, Lao Tzu's philosophy will ring true within your organization. When your work is done, the people will say, *"we did it ourselves."* And I can tell you from personal experience- being a defined *leader* under these conditions is an absolute blast.

How do you get there? Keep reading and you'll see…

The Code of Honor

The *Code of Honor* brings together, internalizes, and 'puts feet to' everything we have discussed so far. In all of my professional life, I've never seen anything as powerful for transforming the culture of an organization. This process is the basis for my statement that culture change is *not* hard and it does *not* take a long time. Having personally facilitated the development of a few hundred Codes of Honor, and with PPI having helped facilitate a few thousand, I still remain amazed at the inward reaching, behavior transforming power of this process. To quote Frank Zappa, this truly is, "…the crux of the biscuit."

To begin, let's get back for a moment to why so many remain baffled and overwhelmed when contemplating 'culture change'. I have no idea how big your organization is, but for the sake of example, let's say you're running a facility with a population of approximately 500 employees. When you consider launching an effort to change the mindsets and behaviors of half-a-thousand people, this can be extremely overwhelming (especially when you have engineers, operators, and technicians to deal with, let alone people of differing ethnicities, and the attitudes of Generations X, Y, 'Why Not?" and "What the Heck?"). Attempting to transform a culture of 500 people is like turning an oil tanker in the middle of the ocean. For example, if such a large ship is traveling at normal cruising speed and it is decided that a 90-degree turn to port (left) or starboard (right) is in order, the ship must travel more than two nautical miles to negotiate the turn. Yes, it can be done, but it takes a tremendous amount of time, energy, and distance traveled.

Now, consider how long it takes to negotiate a 90-degree turn, at normal cruising speed, in a…speed boat. This can be achieved almost instantaneously. The Code of Honor process is facilitated at the natural work team level, essentially transforming your 500-person oil tanker into a fleet of speed boats. An organization of this size will likely have 60 to 65 natural work teams. When facilitated and implemented properly, each of these natural work teams will alter their course (transform their culture) in a very positive direction. The shift in course happens rapidly, is often quite dramatic, and is *owned* by those who created it (thus it is very sustainable). As each of the 'speedboats' alters its course, so is the direction of the 'fleet' (your 500-person organization) ultimately altered. Your organizational culture is thus transformed. It's *not* hard. It does *not* take a long time. It's *not* complicated.

Let's recall how true culture transformation is achieved- from the inside out. The Code of Honor process allows workers, the members of a given team, to set their own expectations, based upon what's important to *them*. The team members themselves essentially determine their 'ideal' work environment- desired behaviors, how they want to interact with one another, and what they are willing to commit to and be accountable for within their team. Once the facilitated process is complete, the team will have created a simple set of six to twelve (or so) bullets, each describing a behavior that every member of the team has (1) agreed that they will 100% commit to, and (2) agree to be accountable for. As an example of what a Code of Honor looks like, here is the Code that our PPI team created, and to which each of our members is accountable:

- Use timely effective communication
- Be the example

- Commit to and be responsible for the success of Practicing Perfection®
- Embrace CANI
- Learn, share, mentor
- Support mind, body, spirit
- Be willing to call and be called
- Express gratitude in everything you do
- Communicate crucial issues directly and promptly
- Live with passion!
- Celebrate all wins
- Create fun!

When we facilitate Code of Honor development, it occurs after training has been completed on essentially everything we've covered thus far in this book. This is critically important, because team members must be opened up to the possibilities of a different way of thinking and doing, and must understand the concept of Proactive Accountability® in order for the Code to be effectively developed and 'take root'. Beyond having received these insights, and showing team members our 'sample' code, we do not tell them what to put on their team Code of Honor. They get to decide this for themselves. We do, however, require one specific Code item. This is represented in the PPI Code by bullet number seven, "Be willing to call or be called." While teams are allowed to craft the wording of this item any way they so choose, it must be included, because this is the 'accountability' piece. This puts 'teeth' to the Code, moving from being a simple classroom exercise, to something team members are agreeing to live to (and be accountable for) when they go back to work.

Once a Code is created, the next part of the process involves person-to-person commitment. During this step, each team member commits to the Code, one-on-one with every other member of the team. They commit to live up to the Code, offer help if needed, and give the other team member permission to 'call them on it' should they exhibit any behaviors that do not live up to the Code. There are handshakes, sometimes hugs (depending upon the culture / makeup of the team), and often, even a tear or two.

When done properly, workers take this process very seriously, which is what you want them to do. This is literally 'inside out' culture transformation in progress.

While I can't take the time to go into much detail here, I will tell you that a huge part of the power of the Code of Honor comes through the process of its facilitation. With exposure to new insights and an expanded context through the training completed up to this point, it is amazing to see the 'stuff' that comes out when a skilled facilitator creates a safe place for people to be honest and forthright. I was facilitating a session one time with a crew of electricians at a power plant. We were working on their Code item dealing with 'respect'. During the conversation, one of the team members, who had long before been given the nickname of "Skinny Legs" decided to [finally] speak up. "You know," he addressed his teammates, "every time one of you calls me 'Skinny Legs', I hate it. I feel very disrespected." Now this was certainly not a team of what you would call 'touchy feely' types. And apparently, this individual had not previously felt 'safe enough' to express his true feelings. Use of the nickname had all been in fun, and apparently no one realized that it 'hurt' this guy every time it was used. I was amazed at the conversation that his comment initiated. I just stood back and listened. Needless to say, the use of "Skinny Legs" was, as of that moment, no longer part of the culture of that team.

We have countless stories of amazing things that have happened during these Code of Honor facilitations and the person-to-person commitments that occur afterward. I want to share a final quick story: I was facilitating a Code of Honor for an operating crew at a nuclear power plant on the east coast. Department leadership, knowing how the process worked, warned me that there were two members on this crew that had had a 'falling out' approximately two and a half years earlier. Because of this, they hadn't spoken a word to one another since. Knowing that we would be moving into the person-to-person commitment once the crew's Code was complete, leadership had no idea what might happen. Once the commitment process was explained and initiated, I stood back and watched the Department Head's jaw drop as these two guys shook hands and expressed their commitments to one another. As I mentioned earlier, this is the single most powerful process I have ever seen for transforming organizational culture.

If you're really thinking this through, one of the things you *must* be wondering at this point is, if each work team is allowed to set its own expectations, in other words if each 'speedboat' is given the power to direct its own course, how do you know they will all turn in the same direction? After all (visualize this), if the 'speedboats', traveling together, begin turning in different directions, you could have one heck of a mess. This is true, but this is also part of the 'magic' of this process. If you look back at the PPI Code of Honor for example, because we are a training organization on a mission to make the world a better place, there are a few Code items here that you might not see on the Code of...a crew of mechanics in a power plant. However, you will not see a single item that could conflict with another team's Code. In fact, irrespective of work discipline, ethnicity, generational differences, or seniority of any given team, you will see, that even though the words are different, the intent of all team Codes of Honor is essentially the same. Why? Because each and every team is made up of- people. And as we already discussed, 'en masse' people are very much the same. What essentially ends up on any given team's Code is their representation, in their own words, of natural principles that are important and appealing to our very Human Nature.

Consider the power of this within your organization. Because Leadership Training must occur first (as we have already discussed), the Executive Team develops its Code. Depending upon the structure of the organization, there will then be one or more Leadership Team Code(s). Beyond this, every natural work team has its own Code. This is *Viral Change* (VC). This is *Peer Leadership* (PL). When we look at the Viral Change Model, this is a *small set of behaviors* initiated amongst a *small number of people*. Relative to the 'science' of culture change, we have incorporated 'top down', bottom up' and most importantly 'inside out' transformation. Furthermore, this is *not* theory. This is a process that has been proven with tens of thousands of workers over the past ten years.

One final note: it takes (on average) about six hours to facilitate a Code of Honor. Think this might have anything to do with the title of this book?

Key Insights from Chapter Six

1. This is not complicated

2. Culture change is not hard and it does not take a long time (when done using the next-level approach)

3. If you attempt to use the traditional change management model (designed for managing the change of 'things') to change culture, you will, at best, see only temporary changes in behavior

4. You need not focus on 'everything' when changing culture. Focus on a handful of *vital behaviors*.

5. Rapid and real culture change is achieved using the Viral Change Model

6. The Code of Honor process ties all of this together while leveraging positive aspects of Human Nature to everyone's benefit

7. Do not attempt to initiate the Code of Honor process without first providing training on the other information provided in this book

8. This is not complicated

What can you do with what you just learned?

A. Recognize that culture change need not be complicated

B. Do the Org Chart exercise outlined in the section on Peer Leadership

C. Continue reading. We have just begun to tie the pieces together.

---

[1] *When information "goes viral", does it really spread virally?*; Choices & Inference; July 10, 2012

[2] *Health, United States 2013*; US Department of Health and Human Services; Table 64

[3] The U.S. Weight Loss Market: 2014 Status Report & Forecast; Marketdata Enterprises Inc. February 1, 2014

[4] http://www.goodhousekeeping.com/health/diet-nutrition/a25392/supercarb-diet/

[5] National Weight Control Registry; http://www.nwcr.ws/research/; March, 2014

[6] *Viral Change*; Leandro Herrero; 2006; meetingminds, UK

PART III: DO DIFFERENT

Chapter Seven: Production vs Prevention

"Culture eats strategy for breakfast, 'operational excellence' for lunch, and everything else for dinner"
-Peter Drucker

As I hope you've been gathering, the intent of the next-level approach to human performance is to leverage aspects Human Nature in a manner that offers tremendous positive potential for the performance of your organization. While process and structure are certainly necessary and important, these are not end goals. They are tools to be used (by humans) in the conduct of whatever it is your organization does. I think that leaders and practitioners sometimes lose sight of this. Handy as they might be, Human Performance is not a checklist or a toolbox or a set of procedures. Neither is your *safety culture*.

In this chapter, I will be directly addressing the operational aspects of organizational *culture*, specifically- *safety culture*, and *just culture*. Indeed, entire books can be written on each of these (and they have). At the time I was writing this, a quick look on Amazon.com revealed 23 books having *safety culture* in their title, some focused on specific industries (nuclear, food, and medical). While I will concede that there are many of them I have not yet read, a scan of their contents reveal a primary focus on structure and process.

Let's remember what *culture* is. It is essentially the accepted beliefs and behavioral 'norms' of a group; a product of the collective mindsets, thoughts, feelings, and behaviors of its members. As INPO cites in its document, *Traits of a Healthy Nuclear Safety Culture*, "Culture is for the group what character and personality are for the individual." [1] What you will find in this chapter is likely a different way of looking at both *safety culture* and *just culture.* As my good friend, Howard Sheard, put it during an 'aha moment' he shared while attending his initial Certification course, "What this is, is rather than 'telling people what to do', it's more like opening a door and inviting people to step through it." Brilliant.

Safety Culture

While this is certainly not a discussion designed to be specifically for (or about) the nuclear generation industry, I've referenced it frequently because (1) this is the industry in which I 'grew up', and (2) this industry has put more collective effort into *human performance* than any other. We therefore want to be aware of and benefit from the lessons learned. Likewise, the nuclear industry has taken the lead on *safety culture.* In fact, the first use of the term can be traced to a report issued by the International Atomic Energy Agency in 1988, following the Chernobyl nuclear accident.[2]

A few years ago, the US nuclear industry brought together representatives from the NRC (the regulator), INPO, and the industry in an effort to define *nuclear safety culture.* In addition, efforts were begun to develop traits and attributes for gaging its relative health within a given organization. In 2012, INPO published the following definition:

Nuclear safety culture is defined as the core values and behaviors resulting from a collective commitment by leaders and individuals to emphasize safety over competing goals to ensure protection of people and the environment.[3]

Again, my intent here is not to be too focused upon nuclear power, nor (in any way) to imply that you should run your operation like a nuclear power plant. This definition, however, does provide an excellent launching pad for our discussion on *safety culture.* To begin, here is our modified version of the definition:

The measure of core values, commitment, and collective behaviors of organization members to emphasize prevention over production to ensure protection of people and the environment

Let's dissect the components of this definition:

- *The measure of-* as a set of traits and attributes, your safety culture is something that can be measured and assessed. It is *not* static, and can be transformed from where you are to where you want to be
- *core values, commitment-* we'll talk shortly about *values* vs *principles*; however, the key here is that *safety* must lie at the *core* of how your organization and your team members conduct themselves
- *collective behaviors of organization members-* this is what creates your *culture*
- *to emphasize prevention over production-* these can be (and often are) directly opposing priorities. The bias must be toward prevention (we'll be discussing this in detail below).
- *to ensure protection of people and the environment-* the overall goal. If people or the environment are threatened or injured, the overall mission, irrespective of schedules or profits, has failed

Safety is NOT Your Top Priority

I attended a human performance conference a few years ago where the evening keynote speaker was a VP from the Southern Company. As we were being served our desserts, he was introduced, and then delivered his opening line: "At Southern Company, safety is *not* our top priority." There was a collective gasp across the room as he paused before he made his next statement, "Safety is a core value." It was brilliantly delivered. Needless to say, he got people's attention.

The dichotomy

Safety is not the "top priority" at the Southern Company, and I can guarantee you that it doesn't have the number one position in your organization either. There is simply no way that it can (irrespective of whatever industry you happen to be part of). Let me illustrate my point by asking you a simple question- what is the *safest* thing you can possibly do? The answer is-*nothing*. Any time you or I, or the workers in your organization do *anything*, there is some risk involved. Of course, if your organization did *nothing*, you wouldn't remain viable for very long (in other words…you'd go broke). So clearly, since you are still in business, your company has priorities above, beyond, and that take precedence over…safety. Oh, blasphemy! How can I possibly write such words?!

"Safety is our top priority," sure does sound nice though, doesn't it? Communications in place? Posters on the walls? Checkmarks on the *Safety Culture Check Sheet*. We've become so conditioned, that it even makes us (as leaders) feel good to say and hear it. But here's the *real* problem with "Safety is our top priority": In spite of the rhetoric, your workers know that it is simply not true. They hear the words (over and over and over), yet they know, for example, about that workaround in the plant, which is necessary because- actually *fixing* the issue would 'simply cost too much money'. You're sending a mixed message- it's confusing. And when confusion is registered by the *lizard brain*, it does what it does best- helps you survive. The choices are, fight it, run from it, or conserve energy (condense and discard most of it). Ever encountered any resistance to your latest safety initiatives? A confused mind says- no.

The Dynamic Balance of *Safety Culture*

As previously mentioned, the absolute *safest* thing you can possibly do is- *nothing*. However, doing *nothing* is simply not possible. You have electricity to generate or transmit, stuff to make or design or repair, planes to fly, patients to treat (or whatever it is your company does). *Production* is obviously necessary. The thing is, *production* itself directly opposes *prevention*. This is also true for each of the underlying elements:

- Production is *schedule driven*, while Prevention is *quality* driven
- Production is *task* oriented, while Prevention is *people* oriented
- Production is generally *short term* in focus, while Prevention has a *long term* focus

There is a dichotomy (directly opposing forces) between each of these elements. And since you need all of these to successfully run your organization, this brings us to what I believe represents your true *safety culture:* it is the dynamic balance between these priorities at any moment in time. And the balance *will* shift. As mentioned earlier, it is not static. As an example, consider a plant outage, where the loss of production is in the neighborhood of $1 million per day. The outage is scheduled for 18 days. You're twelve days into the outage, and due to a litany of conditions, you're two days behind schedule. How is this likely to impact the balance between *production* and *prevention*? Time pressure will be highly elevated. The *schedule* will tend to get more attention than *quality*. Across the organization, forces will naturally shift to the left (toward *production*) in any possible effort to make up time. When forces shift toward the left (*production*), they shift directly away from the right (*prevention*). The overall *safety culture* has been diminished. Like it or not, such tendencies are very real.

Values vs Principles

Since this 'dynamic balance' is the way things [really] work in the 'real world', what is the right approach to truly growing your *safety culture*? I'll get to that in a few moments. First, I would like to address the concept of *values*. Just as safety is *not* your top priority, it also should *not* be couched as a *value* (not even a *core value*). Why? Because as humans, we are constantly adjusting our values. For example, I've lived in New England for the past several years. In January in New Hampshire, I place high *value* on a nice warm coat *when* I'm headed outside. Not so much when I'm sitting in front of the fireplace. Come May, the heavy coats go into the closet, essentially having *no* value until sometime after Thanksgiving.

But, you say, "What about a *core* value?" Okay, consider this-preservation is the primary drive of any organism. We've discussed the function of your *lizard brain* many times, and how its primary purpose is your survival. In order to survive, you must eat. We could therefore say that *eating* is a *core value*. So, here's the question- how much *value* would you place on stopping by the In-N-Out Burger...right *after* you've finished eating a dinner at a fine restaurant? Okay, now compare this to 2:15 in the afternoon, you haven't had anything to eat since breakfast, and you're starting to feel light-headed. There just happens to be an In-N-Out Burger (with an empty drive through lane) directly in front of you as you pull through a parking lot. There's no other food in sight. You have a two-hour drive ahead of you. Get the point?

So if *safety* is not your top priority (which it's not), and it shouldn't be considered a *value*, how should it be addressed?

Safety must become a *Core Principle* of your organizational culture.

Values are fickle. Values are transitory. Principles are not. Principles form the core of who we are. My life- my priorities, my decisions, my choices, my actions are all guided by my principles. Your life is guided by yours. Principles predominate through each element of the Individual Performance Model (mindset/perception → thoughts → feelings → behaviors). They impact every decision you make, all the way from abrupt reactions (such as swerving in traffic to avoid an accident), to long drawn out decisions involving a great deal of internal reasoning and contemplation (and everything in between). Your *principles* are the bedrock that make you who you are- at your core. And the same is ultimately true for your organization. The way your company treats its customers, its workers, the environment; the way it chooses (or not) to attempt to influence lawmakers (and to what ends); its strategies, priorities, and ultimate objectives, all directly reflect its *Core Principles*.

Now- consider how your organization goes about conducting its day-to-day business. Can you honestly say that *safety* is a *Core Principle*? If so, outstanding. You are undoubtedly reaping the benefits in many ways. When Paul O'Neill took the helm of Alcoa in October of 1987, its profits had fallen, and many investors were worried whether he would be able to guide the company to overcome losses recently accumulated from launching unprofitable new lines of business. He began his first address to a group of prominent investors and stock analysts:

"I want to talk to you about worker safety", he said. "Every year, numerous Alcoa workers are injured so badly that they miss a day of work. Our safety record is better than the general American workforce, especially considering that our employees work with metals that are 1500 degrees and machines that can rip a man's arm off. But it's not good enough. I intend to make Alcoa the safest company in America. I intend to go for zero injuries."

You can imagine the confusion. Silence filled the room. Where were all of the buzzwords such as 'synergy', 'restructuring', 'excellence', and 'alignment'? Where was the promise to raise profits and lower costs? While he was pointing out where the safety exits were located, and what to do in the event that they had to evacuate the room, the silence was deafening. People looked around in bewilderment. A few hands began to go up. Questions about capital ratios, and inventories, and...

"I'm not certain you heard me," O'Neill responded. "If you want to understand how Alcoa is doing, you need to look at our workplace safety figures. If we bring our injury rates down, it won't be because of cheerleading or the nonsense you sometimes hear from other CEOs. It will be because the individuals at this company have agreed to become part of something important... Safety will be an indicator that we're making progress in changing our habits across the entire institution. That's how we should be judged."

After the presentation, several analysts advised their clients to sell all their stock in Alcoa (immediately). One of them told a client, "The board put a crazy hippie in charge and he's going to kill the company." This turned out to be horrible investment advice. A year later, Alcoa's profits would hit a record high. When O'Neill retired, thirteen years later, the firm's annual net income would be five times greater than it had been when he took the helm. His company would also be one of the safest in the world.[4]

Deming taught us many years ago that quality and profitability go hand in hand. People whose lives are lived upon solid principles tend to have great success. Organizations that conduct their affairs upon solid *Core Principles* lead their respective fields. *Safety* as a *Core Principle* is not only essential for a legitimately healthy *safety culture*, it positively influences virtually every aspect of how an organization conducts itself. When it comes to *principles* there must be no sidetracks, no detours, and no compromise.

So what does having safety as a Core Principle [honestly] do for your organization? Consider the following figure. Everything is biased toward *prevention.*

Safety as a **Core Principle**

As Paul O'Neill said, "If we bring our injury rates down, it won't be because of cheerleading or the nonsense you sometimes hear from other CEOs. It will be because the individuals at this company have agreed to become part of something important."

Become 'part of something important'. Firmly establish safety as a *Core Principle.* This will bias virtually everything your organization does, from strategic moves to day-to-day decisions, toward the right; toward *prevention, quality, people,* and *long term focus.* Understanding the 'dynamic' forces influencing your *safety culture,* where day-to-day challenges can tend to push you toward a *production* mentality (such as falling behind on a critical-path schedule), will then never overcome your *core.* When *safety* is a *Core Principle,* whether you're an Executive making a strategic decision to build a new facility, a Plant Manager weighing a decision to conduct an early plant shut down due to slowly rising vibrations on the turbine, or an operator in the field choosing to *not* proceed in the face of uncertainty, decisions and behaviors will remain- safe.

Principles, Traits, and Characteristics

Let us briefly revisit our definition of *safety culture*:

The measure of core values, commitment, and collective behaviors of organization members to emphasize prevention over production to ensure protection of people and the environment

First of all, the use of *core values* in the definition (rather than *Core Principles*) has been intentional. Since *values* tend to shift, they can be measured. So can commitment and collective behaviors. How? By considering and evaluating associated traits and attributes.

The International Nuclear Safety Advisory Group (INSAG) publication, *Safety Culture*, and the INPO document12-012, *Traits of a Healthy Nuclear Safety Culture*, identify exemplary safety culture traits along with associated desirable attributes. These documents identify three categories and associated traits as:

- Individual Commitment to Safety
  - Personal Accountability
  - Questioning Attitude
  - Effective communications related to safety
- Management Commitment to Safety
  - Leadership Safety Values and Actions
  - Decision-Making
  - Respectful Work Environment
- Management Systems
  - Continuous Learning
  - Problem Identification and Resolution
  - Environment for Raising Concerns
  - Work processes[5]

I have included this bulleted list to give you an idea of what can be measured relative to your current *safety culture*. As this book is being written, PPI is developing an online self-assessment matrix which can be used to gage the relative health of your current *safety culture*. If you have registered for your Book Bonuses, you will be notified as soon as it is available.

Just Culture

> *"It is exactly the friction between wanting everything in the open so you can learn, but not tolerating everything so that you can be 'just', that makes building a just culture such an interesting venture."*
> -Sidney Dekker

Concepts and dialogue regarding *just culture* span quite a spectrum. These range from organizations establishing 'blame free' environments in an attempt to promote open internal reporting and learning, to society's demands for 'justice' (civil and/or criminal), when an individual (or organization) is deemed 'guilty' or 'culpable'. In this section, I want to discuss *just culture* as it applies to achieving and sustaining next-level performance within *your* organization.

Here is the definition of *just culture*:

A culture where failure/error is addressed in a manner that promotes learning and improvement while satisfying the need for accountability

Is it 'safe'?

Dissecting this definition, let's first consider, *"where failure/error is addressed in a manner that promotes learning and improvement."* In order to *learn*, we must have information- open, honest, forthright information. In order to have such information, an environment must exist where (1) it is *safe* to offer/report it, *and*

(2) where people are freely willing to do so. Creating such an environment is a huge challenge for two reasons.

The first challenge to creating an environment of self-reporting is that past actions have often been riddled with subjective and inconsistent response. In addition, outdated systems designed to *control* (such as some of the mandatory rules of 'progressive discipline') have been ill-applied. Together, these have evolved many environments where there is little trust in outcomes or how people will be treated when something goes wrong. If you have no trust, no feeling of being *safe*, there will be no open flow of information.

The second challenge is that such information must be *voluntary*, in other words, if I am involved in an error or a 'near miss' (where something related to my actions could have gone wrong but didn't), I must be *willing* to report it. In order for me to do so, the perceived benefit (for my co-workers, my team, the organization, etc.) must be strong enough to overcome my sense of *self-preservation*. This is a tough one.

Many organizations remain mired in old-school systems of 'control'. In such systems, Human Resources (HR) manuals often *require* certain levels of discipline/consequences when an individual is involved in an error/event, irrespective of their actual *culpability*. Such levels often begin with a 'verbal reprimand', then move on to something such as a 'letter in the file', and progress upward in significance, to (and including) termination. Such systems can have a place, for example such as when a worker makes a deliberate choice to violate certain policies, or deliberately threatens/disrupts the conduct of business. However, the requirements of these systems are often inappropriately applied in conditions where a worker was involved in an error while doing their best to perform their work and 'get the job done'. It is at these times that 'punishment' is often seen as 'unfair' (and even 'unjust'), by not only the worker involved, but by [many] others as well.

I was involved in an investigation several years ago where an operator hung a "Danger- Do Not Operate" tag on a switch on the wrong unit. It was discovered during a second-check of the tags, prior to the start of any actual work. There were no consequences. A human error had occurred. From the organizational perspective, this was a 'near-miss', caught by the tag second-check process. In spite of this, it was a 'big deal' because (1) a Danger Tag on the wrong component can set up conditions for someone to be seriously hurt or killed, and (2) this was a two-unit nuclear plant with a known history of "wrong train / wrong unit" errors (so it was very 'political', both with INPO and the NRC). The non-licensed operator involved was a highly accountable upstanding worker. He had no prior issues of either negligence or lack of diligence. Because of the nature of the issue however, there was a lot of pressure to 'do something'. Such pressure typically resulted in, at a minimum, 'whacking' the individual involved.

Here were the conditions:

- The tag was placed on a switch on a motor control center (MCC) in a small outbuilding.
- This was one of two small identical side-by-side outbuildings. One housed a MCC for Unit 1, the other housed an MCC for Unit 2.
- There were entrances on each end of each of the outbuildings. Only one entrance on each outbuilding was labeled- the entrance on the far side of the building, away from the rest of the plant.
- Once inside either outbuilding, everything was identical. The only difference was the number "1" or "2" buried within the eight to twelve digit alpha-numeric labels for each of the components.
- It was pouring rain.
- The operator had a team of mechanics waiting on him in Diesel Generator Building.
- Just prior to leaving the Control Room to head to the Diesel Generator Building, the operator was asked to hang this particular tag, "while on his way."

Hopefully you are seeing a number of 'set ups' involved in the scenario. Yes, the operator did indeed hang the tag on the switch on the wrong unit. But did he deserve to be 'whacked'? Get a group of HR professionals, lawyers, human performance experts, and 'cause analysts' together in the same room, and we could debate the 'proper' outcome of this event *ad nauseum*. Under such conditions however, the thing to remember (and the thing that often gets lost amongst the agendas of the individuals involved), is the desired outcome: what response / corrective actions will minimize the potential for this (or anything like this) to ever happen again? I can tell you for certain that in this instance, 'whacking' the poor operator would not have in any way promoted that desired outcome. As a matter of fact, doing so would not have added any positive value to the organization whatsoever. He was now the most highly trained, least likely person to ever misread a label again.

Fortunately, that plant did not have 'hard and fast' requirements for 'punishment'. A sound operator's career remained untarnished (although I can tell you, he internally punished himself big time). On the other hand, MCC labeling was enhanced, color-coding was put in place (Unit 1- white, Unit 2- Blue), and the outbuilding doors on the plant side were [finally] labeled. In addition, similar conditions with other outbuildings were identified and corrected. Smart. Efficient. Effective.

Argue the outcome should you choose, however, had the operator in this 'near-miss' event been punished, how do you think this would have impacted the level of 'trust' in the system? Do you think his fellow operators, and anyone else involved would have been more (or less) likely to volunteer information in the future? I hope you get my point. All this considered, I am *not* proposing, as some organizations have implemented, a 'blame free' system. This brings us to the second part of the definition of *just culture:* "*...while satisfying the need for accountability.*"

The promotion of 'Blame Free' implies no accountability. Recall that in order for any culture (whether it's your family's, your company's, or your country's) to have a prayer of being *healthy* and highly *functional*, there *must* be a high level of accountability. Also recall what *accountability* is and where it resides. It is internal to the individual. It is not punishment, discipline, or retribution. If we understand this, then *accountability* is not the challenge when finding the balance between creating an open and trusting learning environment and dealing with specific levels/types of 'guilt' and/or 'culpability'.

When an error occurs during the course of *accountable* workers doing their best to 'get the job done', rarely, if ever, should there be applied consequences (aka *punishment*). It is simply not necessary and serves no positive/viable purpose for the future of the individual or the organization. There are times however, albeit rare in even moderately healthy organizations, when consequences become appropriate due to the negligence or ill-intent of choices made and actions taken.

Culpability is the degree to which an individual, group of individuals, or organization is blameworthy for their role in initiating or worsening undesirable conditions or consequences. We will be discussing how to objectively determine relative levels of *culpability* in the next chapter. When we do, you will see that next-level culpability determination involves 'broadening the scope'. For example, in the 'wrong unit' example above, there were obviously many organizational issues involved. Aside from the obvious labeling / human factors issues, was the operator properly assigned under the conditions indicated? Was there an inordinate amount of time pressure applied? Might someone else have been available to assist the mechanics waiting in the Diesel Generator Building? Asking such questions, answering them objectively, and using such a process consistently when things 'go wrong', goes a long way toward determining *appropriate* corrective actions and consequences (when appropriate), without destroying *trust*.

Is it 'worth it'?

Building an environment and culture where workers feel 'safe' to self-report takes time. Trust, once broken or tarnished, often takes a long time to heal. On top of this, there is another piece of the self-reporting dilemma that warrants brief discussion.

Let's say that you and I are out in one of the buildings in our facility, and we're in the process of starting up a line or a system. I am reading the procedure, while you are implementing the actions. At one point, you reach up and have your hand on the wrong switch. Just as you are about to turn the switch, I notice that your hand is on the wrong one, and I stop you. This is certainly a 'near miss' or 'close call'. Nothing actually happened. You didn't actually do anything. Do we report it? Putting myself into this scenario, I'll be perfectly honest with you- I don't know whether we would or not.

Some of you are undoubtedly now wondering, "How can he possibly be writing such a thing in a book? A book about…human performance?!" Because I am being totally honest. And all progress begins by telling the truth. Under such conditions, there are going to be many things to consider, the first of which is (see if you're having a moment of recall now): What's in it for me? The second thought (if I happen to like you) will be: What's in it for you? After all, in this situation, I was the 'hero'. I stopped you before the action actually occurred. If I don't like you, or if I am on the lookout for ways to make myself 'look good', I'll be more inclined to report. On the other hand, if we're 'buds', and my self-esteem and self-respect are such that I don't actively seek 'kudos' from the boss, I'll be [much] less likely to report.

We've talked about the function of the *lizard brain* quite a bit up to this point, enough that I hope you already see how it will come into play in our little 'report / no report' scenario. Much will have to do with (1) our perception of our culture (is it safe, what will the likely outcome be?), (2) our perceived relationship with one another and with the organization, (are we 'buds', do we feel respected by our peers and leaders?) and (3) our perception of 'self' in relation to our world- do we wallow in *scarcity* (seeing ourselves as *victims*), or do we live in *possibility,* where we are *accountable* and feel 'in control'? Based upon our internal processing of these questions, our *lizard brain* will calculate, at breakneck speed, a perceived level of threat. If the perception of threat is strong enough, it is highly likely that nothing will [ever] be reported. Nothing happened. No one else knows about this. The risk/reward ratio clearly signals- do NOT report.

Let's now say that circumstances pass the *lizard brain* threat assessment. There is still an additional hurdle that must be crossed in our decision of whether (or not) to self-report: *Is it worth it?* (Yes, once again we're into a variation of- WIIFM?) Even though this may not appear as a significant threat, I will still make my decision based upon my assessment of risk/reward. After all, at a minimum, self-reporting will cause some level of embarrassment. Even if the environment and the working culture is totally *safe,* I will be essentially 'ratting' on my fellow worker. I may be indicating that we weren't as focused as we might have been (after all, we were talking about how awesome Tom Brady was in Sunday's game). I may be implicating myself in not reading the instructions as clearly or loudly as I might have. It may simply be implying *your* carelessness. And then, of course, there's *your* perspective on whether or not we should report. What to do, what to do…

In order for me (or essentially anyone else) to take the time, put forth the energy, and endure [at least a bit of] the embarrassment involved, I must feel that the 'reward' is worth it. And in this case, I am *not* talking about receiving a gift card or tchotchke for self-reporting! (I sincerely hope, that after all we've discussed up to this point, such a thought did not cross your mind!) The 'reward' is my perceived benefit to the organization, to my co-workers: is there a lesson learned in this that can help us be better, safer, and more reliable? And if so, when I do report (pay attention to this one), will anything positive actually be done with the information that is reported? I have to believe that there will be some 'greater good' involved or I simply will not bother.

As the nuclear industry began its efforts to promote self-reporting, INPO began to imply that a minimum number of reports was required to consider a plant's 'learning environment' to be 'healthy'. We were told at one point that for a plant our size, we should be seeing 'at least 4,000' Condition Reports (the name of an entry into the reporting system) per year. While the intent of this was honorable (promotion of self-reporting), assigning such a number, and evaluating whether or not it was being met, was (in my humble opinion) ludicrous. Trends are indeed important. Are you seeing more self-reporting or less? Is the significance level of what is being reported going up or down? These are great indicators of whether you're making progress toward the *learning* aspect of *just culture* (or not). Assigning rote numbers as an indicator of whether (or not) 'enough' self-reporting is going on can have unintended consequences. (Remember our discussions regarding *cumulative impact*?)

I could write an entire book on how to set up, promote, and run an effective system for self-reporting, documentation of Conditions, and tracking of analysis and resolution. Such is beyond what I want to cover within this scope of promoting organizational learning. For now, since many organizations are currently looking at implementing such systems, I do want to offer a few simple things for you to remember as you consider your options. If you truly want to have a system that is going to add value (genuine return on investment) and promote *learning*, it must be:

- Readily accessible to everyone
- Fast, simple and easy to initiate a Condition / enter information
- Provided with an interface that makes it possible for anyone to quickly and easily run reports and determine trends

I'll be expanding upon this a bit in Chapter Ten.

Key Insights from Chapter Seven

1. Your *Safety Culture* is not a checklist, 'toolbox', or set of procedures

2. Your *Safety Culture* is: The measure of core values, commitment, and collective behaviors of organization members to emphasize prevention over production to ensure protection of people and the environment.

3. Safety is *not* your 'top priority'. Safety in your organization must be a *Core Principle*.

4. Your true *safety culture* is <u>not static</u>. It is the dynamic balance between *production* and *prevention*. Having safety as a *Core Principle* biases all decisions and actions toward the *prevention* side, ensuring that you remain safe.

5. *Just Culture* does not mean *Blame-Free Culture*. It is a culture where failure/error is addressed in a manner that promotes learning and improvement *while satisfying the need for accountability*.

6. Accountability is internal. It is not punishment, discipline, or retribution.

7. Overt consequences (*punishment* of any sort) is very rarely appropriate within an even moderately healthy culture.

8. The potential for any individual to self-report will be determined by (1) whether there is a *safe* environment in which to do so, and (2) whether the perceived outcome (reward) is worth the time, effort, and any embarrassment that might be involved.

9. Any system used for self-reporting must be:

   a. Readily accessible to everyone

b. Fast, simple, and easy to initiate/enter information
c. Provided with an interface that makes it possible for anyone to quickly and easily run reports and identify trends

What can you do with what you just learned?

A. Recognize that *safety culture* is *not* a set of processes, procedures, tools, or checklists.

B. Recognize that *Just Culture* does not mean *Blame-Free Culture*.

---

[1] *Traits of a Healthy Nuclear Safety Culture*; Institute of Nuclear Power Operations (INPO); 2013

[2] IAEA, (1991) Safety Culture (Safety Series No. 75-INSAG-4) International Atomic Energy Agency, Vienna

[3] *Traits of a Healthy Nuclear Safety Culture*; Institute of Nuclear Power Operations (INPO); 2013

[4] *The Power of Habit: Why We Do What We Do in Life and in Business*, Charles Duhigg (2012), Random House, New York.

[5] Traits of a Healthy Nuclear Safety Culture; INPO 12-012 (Revision 1); 2013

Chapter Eight: The Psychology of Human Error

> *"The biggest enemy of safety change is dogma."*
> -Todd Conklin

The intent of this chapter is to de-mystify some of the fundamental elements of the science of *human error*, and to bring them into the common sense context of next-level human performance. Again, numerous books have been written on this topic, some of them incredibly in-depth, such as James Reason's *Human Error*, and others incredibly insightful, such as Sidney Dekker's *The Field Guide to Understanding Human Error*. In this section, I am going to touch on the few areas that we have found directly instrumental to the successes we've helped PPI clients achieve over the past ten years.

I mentioned previously that the average member of your team (senior leader, manager, or otherwise) couldn't care less about the *science* of human performance. Well, they care even less about the *science* of human error. I know, as a performance improvement professional, you undoubtedly find this almost impossible to even conceive (again said in jest). It is likely, that unless you are a scientist, professor in a related field, or one of those extremely anal types that the world needs, knows, and loves, you probably have similar feelings. The hard core science of human error, while important for really 'digging in', is indeed but for the select few. So, I am going to keep this simple, and hopefully clear up some misconceptions along the way.

Errors and Events

It's appropriate to begin our discussion on the "Psychology of Human Error" by drawing a clear distinction between *error* and *event*. It's important to understand the difference, because your organization will never be 'error-free', that is…not as long as it has humans in it. Remember, human beings are *fallible*. On any given day, anyone of us can make a mistake. Even the best people make mistakes. As my friend Shane Bush likes to say, if you're working hard to be *error*-free, "You'll go broke, and you'll go insane." Your goal should be: to reduce human *error* to the lowest possible levels of frequency and severity, and to prevent *events* from ever happening.

An *error* occurs when a planned sequence of physical and/or mental activities fails to achieve its intended outcome.[1] It is an act, not a result or consequence. For example, I may be running late for a meeting, hurriedly heading up a flight of stairs. In my haste, I don't get my right foot quite high enough on the step just before the landing. This is an *error*. I stumble. Fortunately, I catch myself using the railing. I don't even spill my coffee. End of story.

An *event*, on the other hand, involves consequences. As we define it, an *event* is an undesirable outcome of significant negative consequence. For example, an *event* can be someone getting seriously hurt or killed, major equipment damage, inadvertent plant trip, wrong site / wrong patient surgery, environmental catastrophe, etc. E*vents,* which are often initiated by one or more errors, are preventable. When Cause Analyses are performed after an *event* has occurred, invariably there is a discovery of failed barriers/defenses, *landmines*, and/or conditions, which contributed to (or failed to prevent) the resulting consequences.

As an example, let's return to the stairs. Once again, running late for a meeting, I fail to get my right foot quite high enough, and I stumble. I grab onto the railing, however, it pulls from the wall due to loose/failed anchoring screws. I drop my coffee, which spills downward onto the steps. My right foot, slamming back onto the lower step, slips because the treading has long since worn away. My right knee slams into the next lower step as I fall. I end up six steps down before my head and shoulders smack into the wall on the opposite side of the stairwell, bringing me to rest. I need surgery on my right knee, and am required to wear a neck brace for six weeks (significant consequences). This is an *event*.

The important thing to notice is that the initiating act (the *error*), failure to get my right foot quite high enough, was precisely the same in each instance. The outcome or consequences, however, were quite different. An *error* is the act (or omission). An *event* involves consequences, often initiated by one or more *errors*.

Types of Errors

It can be useful to use common terminology when seeking to understand how/why a particular *error* occurred. This allows minds to collaborate and to collectively come to what are [hopefully] right and best conclusions. These conclusions can then be used to identify proper corrective actions to prevent recurrence (which should always be your primary goal of error analysis in the workplace).

To begin, *errors* can be designated as one of three 'types'. Doing so offers insight into where within a string of activities an *error* occurred, as well as into the types of mental and/or physical activities involved.

Mistakes

Mistakes generally occur on the front end, during the planning phase. Examples can include system design, when putting together a schedule, developing a procedure, writing a work instruction, or devising a checklist. They may involve deficiencies in judgement regarding a desired outcome, or in the specific instructions in how to achieve it.

When I was working at the River Bend nuclear plant, my outage job was to coordinate/schedule the Instrumentation & Control (I&C) test procedures (known as 'surveillances'). This was a mass of test procedures that could only be performed while the plant was shut down (and there were a *ton* of them). I was assigned this responsibility for the very first refueling outage at the station, which meant that no one at the plant had direct experience in doing this before. In other words, I didn't have anyone to tell me, "Look when I did this last outage, I learned..." I was handed this great big "P1" Schedule, which when tacked up on the wall, reached from floor to ceiling. I was given only one 'marching order'- "Don't become *critical path!*"

If you 'became *critical path*', this meant that the progression of the outage was directly dependent upon you. At a million dollars a day of lost generation revenue, trust me, you did *not* want to be the cause a delay. The testing I was coordinating was on plant safety systems, which have legal requirements for redundancy and operability, even when shutdown. It was therefore very important that logic diagrams and plant "Technical Specifications" (part of the operating license issued by the government) were considered when deciding which tests could be performed in parallel. Time pressure meant that you wanted to simultaneously be working as many surveillances as possible. By studying the logic diagrams and Tech Spec requirements, I could determine which surveillances could be done at the same time, and was essentially creating the entire department's daily surveillance work schedule. I was diligent with my logic analysis and Tech Spec compliance, and aggressive in my scheduling. My *mistake* came in my lack of awareness of component physical location. My specific instructions on how to achieve the desired outcome simply could not be completed. I had scheduled technicians to literally work atop one another. Technicians were returning to the shop, saying, "Hey, we can't do this." With time at a premium, I ended up with technicians standing by while I 'regrouped'.

Lapse

If we consider that a process/job begins with the planning/documentation phase, and ends with its execution (taking the action(s)), what we have in the middle is some period of time and level of mental processing. This is where *lapses* occur. The way I like to remember the meaning of *lapse* is through the common phrase, 'lapse of memory'. And oftentimes, memory is the direct culprit.

Think about this- you are in the middle of making a cake (from scratch). You have your brand new cookbook on your kitchen bar because you don't want to splash ingredients on it. You read the instructions, which say, "Two tbsp. Baking Powder". You turn, grab the baking powder off the shelf, open it, and then reach for the *teaspoon* measure (instead of *tablespoon*) because you [incorrectly] remembered "tsp." rather than the correct "tbsp." If you don't catch your error, which you're not likely to at this point, you'll find as you pull your cake from the oven, that it "cooked in the squat" (as Zig Ziglar used to say). In other words, with insufficient baking powder, you'll have a [very] thin cake. It simply won't rise, no matter what the temperature of your oven might have been. In this (highly technical) example, your mind processed / remembered something entirely different than what was intended by the 'procedure'. This is a *lapse*.

Slip

A *slip* occurs on the tail-end of the process when the action is actually taken. Technically, a *slip* is where the action is different that the intention. In the baking powder example used above, you *intended* to grab the teaspoon measure because that is what you remembered. On the other hand, if you had *intended* to grab the tablespoon measure, and inadvertently grabbed the teaspoon measure instead, this would be a *slip*.

The way I like to remember the meaning of *slip* relative to human error brings me back to wintertime in New Hampshire. When temperatures drop below 32 deg F (0 degrees for you Celsius types), water turns to...ice. Ice is very *slip*pery. So, as you walk across the parking lot in February, carelessly not paying attention to the patch of ice before you, you *intend* to place your right foot on the pavement. Instead, it lands on the ice and *slips*. Hopefully you're only embarrassed and not injured.

Just to help you anchor this in, here's how all three error types can occur in a sequence of events. This is another 'real-life' (cooking) scenario (hey- I like to eat!). My wife has a magnificent recipe for Southwestern Pumpkin Soup. It tastes great, and is super easy to make. In fact, there are only four ingredients: Canned pumpkin, chicken broth, light cream, and cumin. I love this soup, and on a particular Saturday, thought it sounded like a great idea for a quick, easy, and delicious dinner.

Suzette was scanning through the latest issue of Bon Appetite at the kitchen table. She was studying a recipe for "Decadent Chocolate Mousse" (which just happens to call for *heavy* cream) when I entered with my request for the soup. "Sure, sounds great," she said. "Let me jot down a list and Evie can run to the store." She took a nearby notepad and jotted down the following:

- Heavy cream
- Canned Pumpkin
- Chicken broth
- Cumin

Okay, we're off to a 'great' start. If you've been paying attention, you know that the recipe calls for *light* cream, and yet Suzette wrote down *heavy* cream. This was a *mistake*, which occurred in the *planning phase*.

Evie comes into the kitchen. Suzette hands her the note and asks her to go to the store. She was thrilled because she had just recently gotten her driver's license. She put the list on the table by the door and ran upstairs to put on her shoes and grab her keys. When she came back down, she glanced at the list. Only four things. She could remember what they were. She tossed the list onto the table and left.

When she got to the store, Evie grabbed a basket, headed back to the dairy aisle, and grabbed the *heavy* cream (check). She then found the soup aisle and grabbed a quart of chicken broth (check). Next- to the aisle with all of the baking supplies. The spices were half-way down on the left. She had not recollected that there were so many that started with the letter "c"- cinnamon, cilantro, coriander, cayenne... Yes, cayenne, that was it (and into the basket it went). So what have we here? The 'procedure' said *cumin* and what Evie is now remembering, after a bit of mental processing, is *cayenne*. This is a classic *lapse* [of memory]. One more item left, she spies the canned pumpkin down the aisle to the right. Anyone who has ever done much cooking knows that the *canned pumpkin* tends to be placed directly next to the cans of *pumpkin pie filling*. They're the same size, the same shape, and often even have very similar labels. Thrilled with her efficiency, Evie reached for the *canned pumpkin*, and inadvertently grabbed a can of *pumpkin pie filling*. Her *action* was different that her *intention*. This is a classic *slip*.

So, we ended up with the wrong cream (*mistake*), wrong spice (*lapse*), and no canned pumpkin (*slip*). What were the consequences of this grievous daisy chain of human error? We went to Panda North for Chinese food. No big deal for us; however, when one or more such errors occurs in a high risk environment, it can indeed initiate serious consequences.

As a final note on this, I get sloppy in my use of *mistake* as a synonym for *error*. If you're an analytical type, you may have already picked up on this. In fact, the only time I differentiate between the two is when I am either teaching this particular topic or involved in an analysis where the distinction matters. Here is a diagram to help you remember the science relating types of errors to where in the chain of activity they occur.

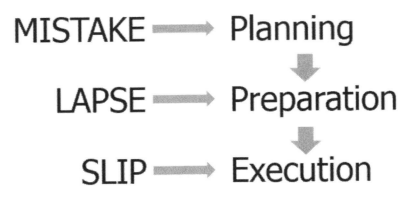

Types of Errors (and when they typically occur)

The 'Cognitive Control Hierarchy'

For those of you who prefer a non-technical approach to things, you're probably now thinking, "What the heck? The title of this section sounds like a play right of Reason's *Human Error.*" Fear not. Before we 'get to it' however, I do want to offer an example of the complexity with which some have attempted to teach this concept (as well as a lot of the science of human error) to 'regular' people within organizations. To quote James Reason:

"Although error correction mechanisms are little understood, there are grounds for arguing that their effectiveness is inversely related to their position within the cognitive control hierarchy. Low level (and largely hard-wired) postural correcting mechanisms work extremely well.[2]"

Yes, this *is* 'rocket science' and James Reason *is* brilliant. But for us mere mortals, we have found a way to keep peoples' attention while presenting this in a manner where *everyone* 'gets it'. I will demonstrate this shortly. This is important, because whereas the *error types* discussed in the previous section should probably be taught only to your leadership team, or maybe even just to your Performance Improvement staff, I believe this concept should be taught to- *everyone.* When you do it properly, it can actually be *fun.* It underscores the importance of one of your primary 'weapons' against human error: uncompromising use of the Error Elimination Tools™. These 'tools' represent Reason's *Low level (and largely hard-wired) postural correcting mechanisms.* When workers understand the *why*, they are much more inclined to *want* to do the right thing.

The *cognitive control hierarchy* sounds really complex, and as already demonstrated, can indeed be. However, when you recognize that it is really nothing more than the *modes* in which people perform tasks, it begins to become something you sink your teeth into. Check out the following diagram.

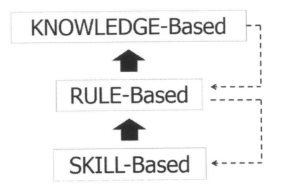

The Cognitive Control Hierarchy

As shown in the diagram, there are three basic [cognitive] levels within which people perform tasks. These levels are also known as *performance modes*, which is the term you may want to use should you decide to teach or explain this material going forward. The three levels, from lowest to highest level of conscious brain use (cognition) are: *Skill-based*, *Rule-based*, and *Knowledge-based*.

Skill-Based Performance

Driving your car. I'll bet you have the capability of driving your car along an Interstate highway at 70+ miles per hour (remember the *compliance* scenario?) while singing along with the radio and nursing an iced-Venti-three-pump-mocha from Starbucks®. All at the same time. How is this possible? We talked about how your brain works in Chapter Four, including all of the loops that accumulate as you learn things and develop *skills* throughout your life.

This is classic *skill-based* performance. Think about this. You're piloting one-and-a-half to two tons of steel, glass, and rubber down an asphalt lane at the rate of more than 100 feet per second. The majority of your conscious mind is consumed with the latest verse of Tom Petty's *Runnin' Down a Dream*, and ensuring that you don't spill any mocha on your new pants. Amazing. But here's the question- is this safe? Well, I can't answer specifically relative to your sipping or singing, but I can answer this with another question: When was the last time you had an accident under such conditions? Likely never. Therefore, based upon the data, we can speculate that yes, you are, in fact, a safe driver.

From a human error perspective, *skill-based* performance is actually the most reliable. Errors in this mode most often result from *inattention*. According to the US Department of Energy, the anticipated/average error rate when engaged in *skill-based* performance is approximately 1 in 10,000. [3] In the work environment, a common term used is 'skill of the craft' when referring to tasks that workers are allowed/expected to do without having explicit procedural guidance. Such are tasks falling within the range of what is 'expected' from a qualified operator, electrician, nurse, technician, etc.

Rule-Based Performance

Putting together your daughter's doll house on Christmas Eve. If you are a father (or mother), and you celebrate Christmas, or birthdays, or any holiday where gifts are given, you've likely had the extreme *pleasure* of doing your best to follow the instructions (the 'procedure') while putting together your kids' toys. From what I've seen, packaging and instructions have gotten much better in recent years. I remember a poor child riding around with the carrier on her Big Wheel tied up with twine because her [very tired] Dad misinterpreted the instructions and put it on backwards. And once it was on, it was *not* designed to be removed.

Rule-based performance simply means that work is being performed while following a procedure, a work instruction, a check sheet, etc. Such tasks are either deemed too complex or too significant to leave performance up to 'skill of the craft'. From a 'how the brain works' perspective, following a procedure while performing a task is much more complex than simply performing via *skill* alone. In this mode, some type of document must be read and interpreted, and then that interpretation turned into action.

Getting back to our 'driving a car' example, first consider driving down the Interstate under 'steady state' conditions. In other words, little traffic, consistent speed, no exits coming up, and no police or stalled cars on the horizon. This is classic *skill-based* performance. Your mind is free to do...other things. Now, compare this to navigating through New York City to catch a flight out of LaGuardia, during rush hour, using a...map. You turn the radio OFF. Coffee is certainly not an option. You need all of your faculties to interpret the map relative to your current position. You compare what [you think] the 'procedure' is telling you to do with current indications (road signs, upcoming exits, your odometer, etc.), and environmental conditions (traffic all around you). Based upon this assessment, you make moment by moment choices and take associated actions. Which of these driving conditions do you think is more 'error-likely'? This is a rather extreme example, but hopefully you get the point. On a 'per action taken' basis, *rule-based* performance is much more prone to error than *skill-based* performance. The accepted 'frequency rate' of errors in *skill-based* performance is 1 in 10,000. When functioning in *rule-based* performance, this rate increases by two decimal places to 1 in 100.[4]

With this in mind, it seems that it would be nice to have workers functioning in the *skill-based* performance mode whenever possible. Why do we even want procedures, checklists, and work instructions? Because of the limitations of the human brain. Documentation (procedures, work instructions, check sheets, etc.) is necessary for complex tasks. While the human mind may be very good at some things, such as adaptation and detecting movement, it typically can't remember more than seven discreet items, especially for any length of time[5]. When a procedure is in hand or nearby, memory issues are minimized. The issue that now pops up is interpretation and mental processing of the work document. The most common error in *rule-based* performance is misinterpretation of the instructions.

Before we move on, I have observed an overall trend of late, and I'd like to offer a quick note of caution. Organizations seem to be moving toward more prescriptiveness in their work practices. Perhaps you're in the process of doing this yourself. If you're doing this purely to reduce human error, you may want to go back and re-read the average frequency rates of error in *skill-based* (1 in 10,000), as compared to *rule-based performance* (1 in 100). If you're doing this because 'the regulator said so', it may be worth a bit of 'push back' on your part. While procedures, work instructions, and checklists are clearly necessary (and add value) in many applications, caution against 'going overboard' is highly recommended. First, you have an increase in the average frequency of error (by a factor of 100). Second, while reams of procedures lining a shelf or electronic library might *look* good, once you have created them, you've have given birth to a 'beast' that needs feeding and upkeep- forever. Let intelligence and common sense prevail. Only develop procedures and work instructions where truly needed, and where they truly add value.

Knowledge-Based Performance

"Do you have power?" This was the first step in the *Six-Step Troubleshooting Procedure* taught to us in Basic Electricity and Electronics School. It was, in my opinion, a fairly brilliant effort on the part of the US Navy to provide a logical methodical approach to electronic troubleshooting. It offered a flow path of simple yes/no, on/off, go/no-go steps to help the technician more efficiently solve what could be a very complex problem. The step-by-step approach helped minimize the potential of 'jumping to conclusions', which could lead you down the wrong path. It was a guide for effectively dealing with, and ultimately solving, the riddle of an 'unknown'.

Knowledge-based performance is basically- troubleshooting (solving the riddle of an 'unknown'). When the human brain is faced with something unfamiliar or unexpected, or forced to choose between several variables, it begins a search for familiarity. Because it wants to conserve energy, and because there is motivation to 'get the job done', the mind rapidly seeks to draw conclusions and 'get on with it'. Sometimes what is 'familiar' is very helpful, other times it can develop a completely inaccurate mental picture. The danger of having an inaccurate mental 'map' of course, is that it greatly increases the potential for error. Referring back to our efforts of driving to catch our flight out of LaGuardia, consider how accurate your actions and choices of turns/exits would be if the map you were using happened to be of...Chicago. You'd almost assuredly make a wrong turn or two. Yes, this example can seem a bit absurd (after all, who would possibly be stupid enough to attempt navigation through New York City using a map of Chicago?). However, inaccurate mental pictures (using the 'wrong map') frequently lead individuals down the path to error.

In *knowledge-based* performance, the average frequency rate of error is 1 out of 2. This is because you're 'testing' options. You either make the right choice, or the wrong choice. Make the *right* choice, and you're either lucky, or consider yourself brilliant (likely both). Make the *wrong* choice, and you can be- dead (or seriously hurt, hurt a patient or a co-worker, trip the plant, damage equipment, cause a spill or release, etc.). The potential consequences of *knowledge-based* errors in high risk environments can indeed be catastrophic.

In the work environment, workers most commonly enter *knowledge-based* performance when things 'don't go as planned'. Unfortunately, this happens fairly regularly (and it can be deadly). If you were to conduct a review of significant injuries and events that have occurred over the past few decades, you would find many that were initiated because a worker/workers 'proceeded in the face of uncertainty'. In other words, something wasn't going right, didn't look right, or didn't respond as it should have. Because of a strong motivation to 'get the job done', workers proceeded anyway. Wrong choices were made based upon on-the-fly assumptions and inaccurate mental pictures. Bad things happened.

How can you protect yourself and your organization from (1) the brain's desire to reach a quick conclusion, combined with (2) strong motivation to produce, to finish the work? By putting a 'pattern interrupt' into your work culture. By making it clear that when 'conditions of uncertainty' arise, *doing a good job* means to STOP; to place whatever it is that's being worked on in a safe condition. Then- taking the time to get an answer, to get resolution, BEFORE proceeding. Because of a predominant underlying *production* mentality (on behalf of workers as well as the organization), it will likely take some effort to get this embedded into your work culture. When we get to the Error Elimination Tools™ section of this chapter, you will see that there is a tool specifically designed to provide this 'pattern interrupt'- *STOP When Unsure*. It is one of the most powerful and important tools in the set.

Having Some 'Fun'

As I indicated at the beginning of this section, it is important for all team members to understand these performance modes, the error-likeliness of each, and how they tend to fit together during the course of doing work. This understanding helps workers be more diligent, more engaged, and will help them make better decisions when tempted to 'proceed in the face of uncertainty'.

The human brain is engaged when it is interacting and when it is entertained. I want to share with you how I present the *Cognitive Control Hierarchy* in a live setting. We have fun and it's engaging. It even draws the attention and understanding of the hardest-core crusty 'old timers'. Do this (or something like this) in your presentation of these *performance modes*, and not only will workers 'get it', they will be motivated to STOP the next time they find themselves facing an unknown. In the PPI curriculum, this is typically covered as an intro to teaching the *STOP When Unsure* tool. You'll want to develop the *Cognitive Control Hierarchy* diagram as you proceed.

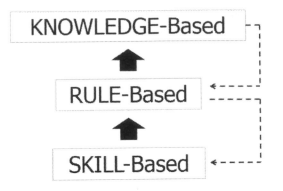

The Cognitive Control Hierarchy

"We're going to do a little mental scenario here. Play along with me, and we'll have some fun with this. I'd like you to mentally put yourself in a car, driving down a stretch of beautiful country road. The sun is warm, the grass is green. The weather is perfect and there's very little traffic. You're on a trip, and will be driving for some time. Under such conditions, what are you thinking about?

[You'll receive many different answers here as you engage the participants. Once you've queried a good cross section, then proceed.]

So, you're moving down the road at 50 or 60 miles per hour, singing along to the radio, thinking about [whatever]. Your brain is doing any of a number of things, *except* directly thinking about driving the car. Under such conditions, do you consider yourself to be a *safe* driver? [You'll get a mixture of yes and no answers.] Well let me ask you a question- when was the last time you had an accident under such conditions? I would assert that under such conditions you are a very safe driver. And if I were to place cameras in your vehicle and record you for a while, we would see that periodically you are checking your rearview mirror, and checking your side-view mirrors. Your hands will be rocking the steering wheel slightly side to side, keeping your car in the center of the lane. Your foot is maintaining just the right amount of pressure on the gas pedal to keep your speed within a narrow band- you are a very safe driver. And yet, you're thinking about essentially anything *other* than driving the car.

Let me ask you another question- the first time you ever drove a car were you able to drive like this? [no] Of course not. It was more like white-knuckling the steering wheel, over-starting, over-stopping, and if you had a manual transmission, the classic lurch...lurch...kill the engine, restart, lurch...lurch...kill the engine (until you got the hang of coordinating correct pressure on the gas pedal as you let out the clutch). The point is, you can now drive a car, very safely, with little conscious effort. This is because you have developed the *skill* of driving your car. This is called *skill-based* performance.

So, a little further down the road, you see an intersection with a traffic light. And as you approach, the traffic light turns from green, to yellow, to red. Red means what? [Stop]. Did you know that "red" meant "stop" the day you were born? [no] Of course not. This is a *rule* you learned somewhere along the way. And this change in conditions, initiated by your knowledge of the first *rule*, kicks off a set of actions (as prescribed in your car owner's manual)- your foot eases up on the gas pedal, moves over to the left, applies a bit of pressure to the brake pedal, and your car comes to a stop at precisely the right place. A set of *rules*, properly implemented, results in the desired outcome. This is called *rule-based* performance.

Now if this happens to be a really l-o-n-g red light, and you're sitting there for a while, where are your thoughts inclined to go? The car is stopped. It doesn't require much conscious effort to keep it stopped, so your brain moves back down to *skill-based* performance. This is because our brains like to conserve energy- they are basically 'lazy'. After a period of time however, the light *will* turn green. Green means what? [Go] Another *rule*. Your foot will lift off of the brake pedal, move over to the right, and begin applying pressure to the gas pedal as it becomes your turn to move forward.

So now you're traveling down the road again. *Tom Sawyer* (by Rush) just came on the radio, and you're singing along. You're just getting into the chorus of, "…though his mind is not for rent," when you recognize another intersection approaching. And as you get closer, once again, the light turns from green, to yellow, to red. Red means what? [Stop]. Right. So your foot eases up on the gas pedal, moves over to the left, and applies a bit of pressure to the brake pedal. A little more pressure…a lot more pressure, and your car does not slow down. What are you going to do?

[This is the fun part of the scenario. As you rapidly call on people, they feel pressured to come up with a response (not unlike 'when things don't go as planned' on the job). You will find that of eight (or so) people called upon, you'll likely get five or six different answers. And then you proceed.]

In our previous interaction with the stoplight, we all did the same thing. Now, when things have not gone as planned, I just asked [8] people what they would do, and I got [6] different answers. This is called *knowledge-based* performance. When we enter this mode, we don't have a clue what any given person might do on any given day. Thankfully, in the work environment we're usually not attempting to stop a speeding car from crashing through an intersection. However, because there are so many unknowns, what do you think would be the best thing to do the next time you're performing a task and things don't go as anticipated?"

[You will invariably get the answer of "STOP" to this question, which can then lead you directly into a discussion of the *STOP When Unsure* tool.]

[I like to cap this off by congratulating the participants. As I am drawing attention to the diagram…] "If you paid attention, and played along with me through this scenario, you now know more about how to prevent catastrophic human error than 99.9% of the people on the planet." And they do.

Drift and Accumulation

History has shown that, no matter how brilliant your initial implementation, human performance is subject to (just like virtually everything else) the natural law of- gravity. What this means is that you must periodically pump a bit of positive energy into the system, otherwise human performance, and performance in general, will tend to drop off. This phenomenon is referred to as *drift*. If allowed, it will occur at the individual level, and consequently, at the organizational level. It typically involves a drop in level of engagement, in diligence, in verbatim compliance, and in the perception of risk.

Perception of Risk

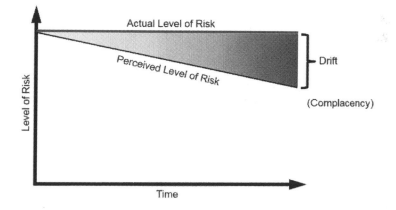

DRIFT in Perception of Risk

When it comes to *drift,* your continued success doesn't do you any favors. Let's consider a job or evolution that is performed regularly and involves a relatively high level of risk (as indicated by the horizontal *Actual Level of Risk* line at the top of the chart). Each time this task is repeated successfully, the *lizard brain* will tend to perceive a lower level of threat. This is a natural psychological phenomenon of Human Nature, and occurs for a couple of reasons. Perception of a threat heightens awareness. Heightened awareness consumes energy (and remember, part of the *lizard brain's* mission is to conserve energy). Secondly, perception of a legitimate threat causes stress. Stress pumps cortisol into your system. Chronic infusions of cortisol are very unhealthy, so your *lizard brain*, again tasked with your survival, will seek opportunities to place 'normal' / 'routine' things into a 'lower threat' category. Successful completion of a job/task, especially repetitive successful completion, provides such opportunity. Unchecked, the effect, over time, tends to reduce your level of engagement and diligence in whatever the task happens to be.

This lowering level of engagement/diligence is a product of the line in the diagram labeled *Perceived Level of Risk*. As you can see, repeated successful performance of the task, the job, or overall operations, tends to create a downward slope. Unfortunately, the *actual* risk has not changed. An emerging difference (or 'delta') now exists between the *actual* risk and the *perceived* risk. This 'delta' is known as *drift*. The resulting behavior, which is a natural tendency of Human Nature, is *complacency*. This *will* occur unless efforts are directly taken to counteract these natural tendencies. The greater this delta for any given job or task, the greater the potential for an *event* (an error of significant consequence) to occur.

The 'Way we do it Around Here'

In most organizations, there is a difference (delta) between the '4.0' *expectations* of how workers are to complete their assigned tasks and 'the way it's [actually] done around here'. This is another form of *drift*.

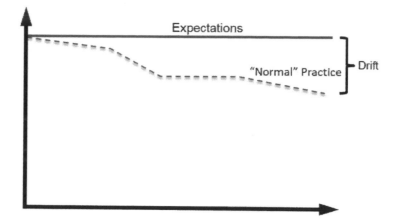

DRIFT in How Work is Done

Within your organization, I have no doubt that there are *expectations* to do certain things. Show up on time, fulfill the responsibilities of your job function, be respectful, etc. I would imagine that one of these *expectations* is to follow procedures (the Safety Manual, work instructions, checklists, etc.). In the scheme of things, these *expectations* should represent the optimum ('4.0') means of doing [whatever it is].

As I am certain you are aware, no procedure or 'way of doing things' is necessarily 'perfect'. In addition, there is oftentimes more than one way of performing a particular task. You may prefer one way, I might prefer another, while yet another approach is preferred by other team members. Emergent issues often require 'workarounds' in the way things are done. And let's not forget- if a human being can find a way to achieve a result with less effort, it is Human Nature to take the 'path of least resistance'. What this all adds up to, as shown in the figure, is a general departure, over time, from the 'expected' way of completing tasks and jobs. From a human error perspective, this is important. The greater the departure from the 'ideal', which should be where your *expectations* are set, the greater the likelihood for an error to occur. And again, for all of the reasons cited above, *drift* will tend to occur unless overt ongoing efforts are taken to stem its insidiousness nature.

When we combine the *drift in perception of risk*, which increases the potential seriousness of an error, with the *drift in how work is done*, which increases the potential for more errors to occur, we have a compounding negative (more error-likely) effect.

Accumulation

If you've ever lived in one place for very long, and then moved, you recognize how 'stuff' tends to *accumulate*. We recently cleaned out the house in which I grew up, and in which my parents lived for 56 years. Talk about stuff!

The same thing occurs within organizations. The longer a plant, facility, or organization has been around, combined with the number of mergers, acquisitions, and various forms of [right-sizing, down-sizing, and/or re-engineering] it has endured, the more 'stuff' it will have accumulated. Relative to human error, we're talking specifically about the *accumulation* of *landmines* and *roadblocks*.

Practicing Perfection Precept #2 is: *84 to 94 percent of all human error can be directly attributed to process, programmatic, or organizational issues.* What this means (as we discussed in Chapter 3) is that the lions' share of the time human error occurs in the workplace, some thing or things have set the individual up for failure. As you should recall, the technical term for these 'things' is *Latent Organizational Weaknesses*; however, we call them-*landmines*.

Roadblocks, on the other hand, are requirements, processes, and/or physical constraints that inhibit getting things done. Examples in the workplace might include:

- A safety requirement to wear gloves when working in a certain area, and yet gloves can only be acquired on the other side of the plant (*after* getting a requisition signed by a supervisor).

- Conduct of a procedure requiring periodic communications with the control room, yet the only phone is on the opposite side of the building
- A requirement to wash your hands before touching a patient, yet there is no sink in the room

Roadblocks are directly related to the potential for human error because they cause frustration and stress. When frustration results from a job being delayed, many will look for ways to 'cut corners'. Face it- people come to work wanting to do a 'good job', and one of the primary aspects of doing a 'good job' is getting it completed. Onerous administrative requirements and cumbersome logistics tend to prompt people to take 'make up time' short cuts wherever they can find them. This increases the potential for human error.

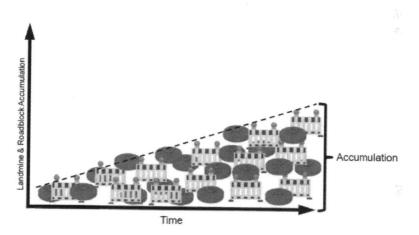

Accumulation

Just as *drift* is a natural phenomenon of Human Nature, *landmines* and *roadblocks* tend to *accumulate* over time as a result of many issues and conditions: They accumulate as a result of ongoing organization operation, maintenance, and modification. Equipment is updated, added, and removed. Procedures are added or altered. New regulations require new policies and 'ways of doing things'. New senior leaders interject their preferences and seek to 'make their mark' on the organization.

In reality, no system is perfect. And every time a system is altered, opportunities exist for the insertion of unintended consequences, oversights, and flat-out latent errors. In the dynamic environment in which every business exists and operates, the myriad efforts to change and 'improve' almost always results in the creation of additional *landmines* and *roadblocks*. I may not know you. And I may have never heard of your organization. But I can just about guarantee you that your organization, at this very moment, is littered with *roadblocks*. They're causing worker delays, and frustration, and prompting the 'cutting of corners'. I would also bet big money that your organizational landscape is strewn with *landmines*, lying in wait for the unwary, and the non-engaged. And as time goes on, unless actions are taken to dig these things up and remove them, they continue to accumulate.

Now consider the combined effects of *drift* and *accumulation*. While *drift* lowers diligence, engagement, and work standards, *accumulation* increases vulnerability to *landmines* and the taking of 'shortcuts'. As shown in the diagram, this combination sets the stage for an *event*.

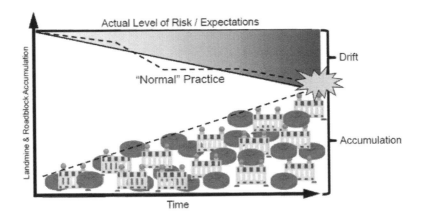

Combined Potential of Drift and Accumulation

In Chapter Nine, I will give you the precise recipe for promoting engagement and alignment in a manner that directly combats both *drift* and *accumulation.*

Human Error Traps

Landmines are physical, administrative, or organizational setups for human error. *Roadblocks*, due to the frustration they cause, tend to promote behaviors that have a greater potential for error. *Traps* are conditions of the work environment, which because of how they impact cognitive and decision-making abilities, make human error more likely.

In this section, I am going to briefly cover the eleven (11) most common traps in present-day work environments. Many of the perspectives offered are based upon the tens of thousands of workers we have surveyed and interviewed as part of PPI's Culture Profile process. If you'd like more information about this process, you may go here:

http://ppiweb.com/home-2-3/culture-profile/

Time Pressure

Whether actual or perceived, *Time Pressure* is a prevalent trap. In healthier organizations, for example where *safety* may honestly be promoted as a core value, we have found it intriguing that the message coming from 'the top' may sincerely be, "Take whatever time is necessary to do the work safely. If you think something might be unsafe, or you're unsure, stop and get your issue resolved before moving forward." And yet, on the front line, there can still be an overt sense of urgency to 'get the job done'. I have often heard comments from senior leaders who are baffled as to why such a sense of *time pressure* still exists on the front line. There can obviously be a spectrum of reasons for this. For example, there are generally layers of leadership between 'the top' and the front line, each of which is likely adding its 'spin' or bias to the *production* vs *prevention* message. However, at the most basic level, the thing to remember is that workers come to work wanting to do a 'good job'. And just as the organization exists to *produce*, a typical worker's perception of how 'good' a job she is doing is tied to her productivity, to getting [whatever it is] done. This naturally generates a sense of *time pressure* for many workers.

Whether real or perceived (remember from Chapter Four- *my perception of reality is my reality*), *time pressure* increases the potential for human error. Here's a simple example: You're running late for work. For whatever the reason, you got out of the house late. You're twenty minutes out (in normal traffic), and you're supposed to be there in ten. Traffic's a little heavier than normal. There's a school bus right in front of you. Chances are, your sense of *time pressure* will cause you to drive [a bit] more aggressively than normal. You'll take more risk (especially to get around the school bus). Taking more risk can [greatly] increase your potential for an *event* to occur. Similar types of scenarios play out frequently in the work environment. This is another reason why having *safety* firmly established as a *Core Principle* is so important. It provides an internal governor to the 'risks' people are willing to take, even under an acute sense of *time pressure*.

Distraction/Interruption

Without exception, the PPI Culture Profile process has revealed *Distractions/Interruptions* and *Multi-tasking* (the next *trap* to be discussed) as the top contributors to error-likely environments amongst the organizations analyzed[6]. The following figure offers insight into the mental functioning that takes place whenever a primary task is interrupted.

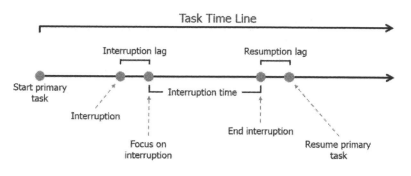

Task Interruption Processing[7]

To illustrate how this works, let's say a technician is verifying voltage readings on a terminal strip. He is following a procedure (*rule-based* performance), verifying that each of the readings falls within an allowable range. His cell phone rings. Mental focus has now been interrupted. The technician must now shift from focus on the placement of his voltage probes, to the ringing cell phone. This is the *Interruption lag*. He now looks at the phone, recognizes that it is his supervisor calling, and answers it. The supervisor is calling to see how much longer before this job is complete (by the way, such questions almost always elevate a sense of *time pressure*). The technician answers the question, ends the call, and returns his cell phone to his left front pocket. The *Interruption time* has ended. Now the technician must regain focus on his primary task, as he does his best to remember which terminal he was targeting prior to the interruption. This is the *Resumption lag*. The reliance upon memory as the technician returns to the primary task is a classic point for human error (missed or repeated step).

So what's the big deal? Science has shown that the recovery process (the resumption lag) following an interruption during the type of task used in the example is typically a minimum of 15 seconds[8]. On the other hand, say for an engineer in the middle of a calculation, there is (on average) a 25-minute lag before returning to the level of mental focus that was present prior to the interruption. And in an office environment, the typical worker is interrupted about every eleven minutes[9]. If you do the simple math on this one, it is easy to see the increased potential for human error (let alone the loss of productivity).

Do we know how much *Distractions* and *Interruptions* directly impact error rates? Recent studies within the medical industry provide disturbing insight. In the emergency department, doctors failed to return to 19% of interrupted tasks.[10] Interruptions and distractions have been reported as a factor contributing up to 11% of medication-dispensing errors.[11] On hospital wards, interruption to nurses administering medications was associated with a 12% increase in procedural failure, and a 13% increase in clinical error.[12] Interruptions also have a time cost. In one study, clinical staff in an emergency department spent 24% of their time dealing with interruptions.[13]

Irrespective of your industry, or the type of work your organization does, *distractions* and *interruptions* greatly increase the potential for human error, while also diminishing productivity. The rapid advancement of technology, the proliferation of smart phones as one example, has only served to increase the frequency of these substantial *traps* for human error. Based upon our experience, most organizations simply seem resolved to, "Well, that's just the way it is. In *our* business, there's no way around it." I don't believe this has to be the case. The 'world' and the demands of the work environment will inevitably cause *some* level of *distraction* and *interruption*. However, it will serve you well to look for and initiate measures to diminish their frequency while your team members are doing their work.

Multi-tasking

The Commodore Amiga A-1000. Launched in 1985, this was the first 'home computer' with the capability to do something extraordinary- to perform more than one function at a time, in other words- to 'multi-task'. This seems like ancient history, doesn't it? As I write this, I am using three different screens connected to my HP Z-Book. I have eight files open, seven tabs open in my Chrome browser, and nine programs running simultaneously. Computers have become marvelously capable of doing many (multiple) things (tasks) at the same time.

For anyone beyond the age of 20, we have seen our world transformed by technology. Do you realize that 'smartphones' are less than eight years old (the first iPhone was introduced in 2007)? How was life even possible without the ability to text, access the internet, and conduct video chat over our phones?! And if you keep up with Wired® Magazine, or have read the book *Bold*, by Peter Diamandis and Steven Kotler[14], you are well aware that 'we ain't seen nothin' yet'! Technology is supposed to make life easier, and when it comes to communicating, researching and number-crunching, it certainly has. When it comes to our overall lives, however, I think it has done a better job of simply making them 'faster'. And to 'keep up', we do our best to attempt to 'multi-task'.

The thing is, only a very small percentage of the population has the brain wiring to allow them to truly multi-task. I sure as heck know that I don't have it. Attempting to do so is a classic human error *trap*. According to our data, more than 80% of workers indicate the need to 'perform more than one task at a time' within their roles at work.[15] This is a significant likely contributor to human error, because for most people, the brain does not actually 'multi-task'. It segments, jumping back and forth from one task to another. It therefore rarely has the time to fully focus on any one task. When people attempt to complete many tasks at one time (actually alternating rapidly between them), errors are substantially increased. It also takes far longer, often double the time or more, to get the jobs done than if they were done sequentially. This is largely because "the brain is compelled to restart and refocus", much as we discussed when talking about *distractions* and *interruptions*[16].

A 'final word' on *multi-tasking*? Philip Stanhope, also known as the Lord of Chesterfield, wrote a series of letters to his son between 1746 and 1754. The collection became known as, *Letters to His Son on the Art of Becoming a Man of the World and a*

Gentleman. One of his letters, which I think involves sage advice for everyone, included the following:

> *"There is time enough for everything in the course of the day, if you do but one thing at once, but there is not time enough in the year, if you will do two things at a time. This steady and undissipated attention to one object, is a sure mark of a superior genius; as hurry, bustle, and agitation, are the never-failing symptoms of a weak and frivolous mind."*

Overconfidence

As we discussed during our conversation on drift, success at doing a thing can work against us. This is because the more times we successfully repeat a task, irrespective of the actual risk involved, it becomes less of a perceived 'threat'. As such, we tend to 'lower our guard'. Our minds are less engaged. They process fewer questions about the surrounding environment and associated conditions relative to [whatever it is] we happen to be doing. This is called overconfidence.

While an appropriate level of 'confidence' is healthy, overconfidence creates a trap because environmental and associated conditions are rarely static. They are dynamic. And even though we might have completed a given task successfully 98 times previously, time number 99 is performed under a different set of conditions. Overconfidence makes us less likely to notice the different conditions, increasing the potential for human error.

Vague or Interpretive Guidance

Inaccurate / out-of-date procedures, drawings that do not accurately represent as-built conditions, policies and procedures that contradict one another, and procedures with multiple actions embedded within a single step- of themselves these represent *landmines*. Such setups for human error need to be 'dug up' and gotten rid of; however, most organizations do not seem to have the resources (or easy-enough-to-use systems) to allow for keeping things updated and getting errors fixed. This is one of the reasons why I urge so much caution on the trend to become more prescriptive in your work processes.

These *landmines* become *traps* when people are forced to use these documents in the course of doing their work. Having guidance that is vague, out of date, or contradictory forces the user to interpret and to draw conclusions. As I hope you recall, the need to interpret or draw conclusions while performing a task moves the worker into *knowledge-based* performance. And the potential for error when in this mode is…1 out of 2.

What to do? Fix your frickin' procedures! If your system makes this very difficult to do, fix your system! Engage workers in making these things better. Remember (Precept #4)- the people who do the work are the ones who have the answers. In the interim, deploy (and highly encourage the use of) the *STOP When Unsure* tool (see the next section of this chapter).

First Shift / Last Shift

This *trap* is a natural by-product of Human Nature and its relation to the work cycle. Think about it. If you work Monday-Friday, and it's after lunch on Friday (*last* shift), what are you thinking about? Chances are pretty darn good, you're thinking about heading out for the weekend. The same thing is true on Monday morning (*first* shift): your focus will tend to be on either how great the past weekend was, or upon how frickin' long it is until next Saturday! In 24/7 operations, 12-hour shift rotations often involve a seven-day stretch of time off as part of the rotation. Just before (and after) these seven-day stretches offers an even more acute *trap*.

The way to deal with this particular *trap* is to (1) be aware of it, (2) steer away from high-risk work and scheduling of critical tasks during these periods, and (3) be extra-thorough and overtly engaged when briefing and conducting work.

Peer Pressure

Peer Pressure can be a means of helping spread positive behaviors, as well as a human error *trap*. On the positive side, team members 'taking the lead' and exhibiting new/desired behaviors (*Peer Leadership*) will be noticed by others. Some of these others, in turn, will modify their behaviors. This happens based upon the [positive] influence of their peers (*Viral Change*). On the other hand, Peer Pressure can be a strong negative force. It can inhibit the adoption of new/desired behaviors, as well as promote behaviors that increase the potential for human error. Let's use the Error Elimination Tools™ to provide an example of each behavior:

Positive

In a power plant, all communications typically go through the Control Room. Operators in the Control Room therefore have a grand opportunity to role model and reinforce the use of the *Effective Communication* tool, which includes three-part communication and use of the phonetic alphabet. As workers in the plant engage in conversation with the Control Room, the new behaviors tend to rub off. This happens because (1) the techniques are simple and easy to use, (2) they really do minimize the potential for verbal communications errors, and (3) people come to work wanting to do a good job (they do not want to make mistakes). In a short period of time, the use of three-part communication and phonetics (positive/desired behaviors) will become more and more prevalent throughout the organization. This isn't theory. We've seen this happen time and time again.

Negative

Another of the Error Elimination Tools™, perhaps the single most powerful one, is *Questioning Attitude*. This is a tool that can save more lives, prevent more injuries, and alleviate more grief (all by itself) than perhaps any other. However, it must be well received and respected. For example, if I have the courage to ask a question, this reveals that there is something I don't know. It might be something I 'ought to know'. Perhaps I was trained on it 18 months ago, or an email was sent out last week. Maybe it's in the 'night order' book. If I anticipate that my question will be met by my peers with jokes, ridicule, and/or a 'suck it up princess' attitude, it is very likely that I won't ask it. This can create a dangerous *trap*, because I may now proceed in the face of uncertainty, potentially putting myself, others, or the facility at risk.

The best way to deal with *Peer Pressure* is to look for and positively recognize the behaviors that you want to promote/encourage. Remember- what gets recognized gets repeated. This will support and accelerate growth through *Viral Change*. On the flip side (countering *negative* peer pressure), overtly and genuinely recognizing positive/desired behaviors, wherever and whenever you observe them, will help shift 'old attitudes' of the majority of your team members. Again this is not theory. It works. I'll be providing you with a simple 'recipe' for how to maximize positive interactions in Chapter Nine.

Change / Off-Normal

A change in conditions or a change in routine generates this *trap*. For example, if your facility has been shut down for some period of time, right after you start back up, this *trap* can be quite prevalent. During shutdown, lines may be static, systems may be depressurized, and piping may be cool. After these conditions have existed for a while, they become 'normal'. Start back up, and the moving lines, rotating machinery, high pressures and hot temperatures present 'new' hazards. Our brains guide us through most of what we do using a series of 'loops', and these 'loops' create our mental 'maps'. If you still have a 'shutdown map' in your mind after the plant starts up, it can prompt you to take actions without much thought. Such actions can have serious consequences.

The way to combat this particular *trap* is to overemphasize the new conditions / change in routine, both *before* they occur, and for some period afterward. Depending upon your specific conditions / situation, there may be physical 'mental cues' you can put in place such as blatantly obvious signs or placards, computer desktop warnings, flashing lights, etc.

Physical Environment

Here we're talking about things that 'grate' upon or distract the human psyche and detract from the ability to focus upon the task at hand. For example, have you ever tried to read a book on an airplane while the two teenage girls in the seats next to you banter on incessantly (for the entire flight) and every other word is 'like'? This is one reason why I always travel with my iPod and my noise-cancelling ear buds.

In the work environment, this *trap* is often incurred through high noise, heat, cold, cramped spaces, not enough lighting, extremely bright light, or a combination of these. High risk and industrial environments are often filled with many such environmental *traps*. When working in such areas / under such conditions, the physical discomfort tends to cause mental distraction, as well as induced time pressure (to hurry up and get the work done so you can get the heck out of there). There are also aspects of physical limitation and impact to consider, such as heat stress, exposure, etc.

When such environmental factors are present, an awareness of the heightened potential for human error is critical. This should be incorporated into planning and *Pre-Job Briefing*, as well as through orchestrated efforts to minimize (wherever possible) the time workers are exposed to such conditions.

Mental Stress

All of the *traps* we have discussed thus far essentially add to mental stress on the job. In addition, most everyone has things outside of work that are adding stress to their lives. There is 'chronic' stress, that which occurs over a long period of time, and there is "acute" stress, such as occurs in an emergency. The thing to remember about *mental stress* is that it is cumulative. In other words, when we come to work, we bring the rest of our lives with us- every day. When stress accumulates, all stages of our mental processes- perception, attention, memory, decision making, problem-solving, and response execution are candidates for degradation[17].

Clearly, an entire book could be written on stress and its impact upon the mind and the body (and many have). Remembering that our focus is upon human performance in the workplace (safety, reduction of human error, reliability, etc.), I want to confine our discussion to the impact of stress on the potential for human error.

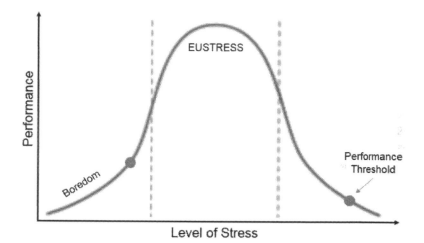

Stress and Performance

You may be familiar with the work of Hans Selye, regarding what he coined as "eustress". The prefix *'eu'* is derived from the Greek word meaning either "well" or "good." Selye's work identified that there is an 'optimum' level of stress at which performance capabilities are at their peak. This is a fascinating area of study; however, related to human error, simply realize that at extremely low levels of stimulation, the potential for human error does indeed rise. This is due to 'boredom', which tends to cause a lack of engagement and awareness. At the peak of the eustress curve, which is considered the 'ideal' level of stress, the brain is engaged on all cylinders, and the potential for human error is at its minimum. Beyond this peak, performance begins to degrade and the potential for error rises. When stress rises beyond an individual's *performance threshold*, human error becomes highly likely.

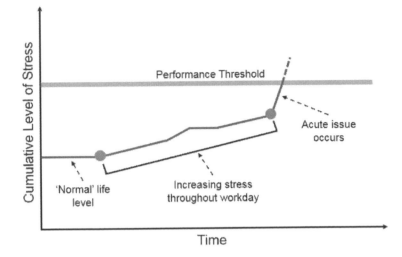

Stress Performance Threshold

The Stress Performance Threshold diagram is designed to illustrate how stress tends to accumulate. Each and every one of us has some level of stress simply due to 'life'. We have bills to pay, family issues, things that need to be repaired, feeling like 'life is passing us by', etc. According to the latest Gallup polls, 68.5% of American workers are either 'disengaged' or 'actively disengaged' from their jobs[18]. It is likely that for a good percentage of workers who fall into this category, stress levels rise when they walk through the door at work, and continue to rise throughout the day. For the sake of keeping things simple, let's say that an acute issue occurs for such an individual, causing their cumulative stress level to rise above their *Stress Performance Threshold*. This means that the person's level of stress has reached a point where normal cognitive functioning is nearly impossible. Under such a condition, this individual is highly likely to make mistakes.

The reason I wanted to include information on the *Stress Performance Threshold* is- we've all been there. Simply think of a time when you were so stressed that you couldn't even think straight. In high risk environments, it's important to recognize when someone has crossed their *threshold*. This is an acute condition, and (thank goodness) doesn't happen very often. But when it does, it's our responsibility to ensure that such an individual is not involved in nor assigned any tasks where he might place himself, or anyone else, in danger. It's also important to evolve a culture where it's *safe* for an individual who recognizes they're 'maxed out' to be able to say so; to be able to ask for help if they need it, without being chastised or ridiculed. This may sound like we're entering into 'group hug' territory, but nothing could be further from the truth. While awareness, recognition, and creating a *safe* environment for one another does involve a level of compassion and caring, it is also critically important to safety and reliability.

Fatigue

When I get tired, I make lots of mistakes. The same is true for...most everyone. As a matter of fact, the science shows that fatigue-related impairment is very similar to the effects of drinking alcohol. Research in this area has indicated that after 17 hours on the job, fatigue-related impairment on a hand-eye co-ordination is equivalent to a blood alcohol concentration

(BAC) of 0.05%. After 24 hours on the job, impairment was equivalent to a BAC of 0.10%.[19]

Fatigue delays response and reaction times, negatively impacts logical reasoning and decision making, and impairs hand-eye co-ordination. These are all critical safety issues in high risk environments. A significant body of research has concluded that fatigue is rapidly emerging as one of the greatest single safety issues now facing many sectors. For example, recent research in the USA, Europe and Australia suggests that somewhere between 20-30% of all heavy vehicle accidents can be directly or indirectly attributed to fatigue-related impairment of the driver[20].

Fatigue has the following effects upon an individual:

- Cognitive performance impairment, leading to a decreased ability to process information and make timely, appropriate decisions and actions

- Alertness impairment, leading to a decreased ability to remain engaged, and in extreme conditions, to remain conscious

- Mood changes such as increased irritability, decreased motivation, and lowered morale

Twenty years ago, *fatigue* was not identified as one of the more common human error *traps*. Changing work conditions and demands, combined with societal and family demands (for example the growth in the predominance of two-income families) have conspired to make this a substantial workplace consideration.

What can you do about it? First, be aware of it. Watch for the signs of fatigue, for yourself as well as your co-workers. Encourage (and expect) use of the Error Elimination Tools™, especially during extended work periods. Depending upon your industry, consider implementing work hour limits. For example, the US NRC has specifically defined work hour limits for nuclear workers. NRC work hour limits are:

- 16 work hours in any 24-hour period
- 26 work hours in any 48-hour period
- 72 work hours in any 7-day period[21]

Error Elimination Tools™

In the early 90s, the US nuclear generation industry began placing acute focus on 'human performance'. Through the information sharing, guidance, and material development provided by INPO, operating units across the country began developing and refining means and methods by which to reduce human error and increase reliability. The results were extremely successful. In 1990, the industry capacity factor (the ratio of actual power produced as compared to all industry units operating at 100% for the entire year) was approximately 70 percent. In 2013, it was 90.9 percent. In 1990, the average duration of a plant refueling outage was 104 days. In 2013, this number was down to 41 days. And *safety culture*? In 1997, the industry's average OSHA recordable rate was 0.38. By 2013, this number had dropped to 0.04[22]. A focus on human performance played a key role in achieving these substantial improvements in economy, safety, and reliability.

Part of the evolution of 'human performance' during this period was the creation, development, and refinement of simple 'tools' that could be used to influence worker behaviors and enhance reliability. Over about fifteen years, these 'tools' were created, tested, and refined across 100+ nuclear operating units. By sharing information through INPO, the industry was able to identify the 'tools' that worked, while discarding the ones that didn't. By 2005, the 'tools' had been refined to a 'set' of fifteen.

As I mentioned, these 'tools' are specifically designed to increase the reliability of human interactions, as well as behaviors at the point of task execution. Recall Practicing Perfection Precept #2: *84 to 94 percent of all human error can be directly attributed to process, programmatic, or organizational issues.* These 'tools' primarily address the [other] 6 to 16 percent- human fallibility.

Now recall James Reason's statement regarding the "Cognitive Control Hierarchy": *Although error correction mechanisms are little understood, there are grounds for arguing that their effectiveness is inversely related to their position within the cognitive control hierarchy. Low level (and largely hard-wired) postural correcting mechanisms work extremely well.* These 'tools' are *low level postural correcting mechanisms*. When they are well implemented (*largely hard-wired*), they work extremely well; however, their effectiveness is *inversely related to their position within the cognitive control hierarchy*. In other words, when properly used, these 'tools' are very effective in *skill-based* and *rule-based* performance; however, they tend to be far less effective once the *knowledge-based* mode has been entered.

It is important that you understand the information in the previous two paragraphs. If you didn't 'get it'- please read them again. These 'tools' while extremely effective when properly used under the right conditions, are *not* the 'fix all cure all' for human performance. They are simply 'tools'. Merely giving workers an hour or two of training, sending them back to work with their "HP Tool Kit" and expecting error-free performance, would be like giving a group of people an hour or two of 'basic woodworking', sending them out with a hammer and a saw, and expecting them to be master craftsmen. You will *not* get the results you are seeking.

The reason I am bringing this up is because we have seen many organizations who think that implementing these 'tools' is *the answer* to the challenge of human error. When I hear that an organization has addressed error reduction by providing their workers with some introductory training and an "HP Tool Kit" (which usually means a set of some or all of these 'tools'), I get the same queasy feeling as when I hear a senior leader say, "I support human performance." Bring the bowl, we can now wash our hands. Another box checked on the list of 'politically correct' things to do. This may sound a bit harsh, but worker frustration (at all levels), the waste of resources, and the continued injuries and heartache caused by not properly approaching and addressing *human performance* is, in my opinion, no longer forgivable now that all that is known is known.

Okay, I'll now step down off of my soapbox and get back to the 'tools' themselves. The 'refinement' that took place across 100+ operating nuclear units offers a great advantage to all industries. The 15 'tools' that rose to the surface and were subsequently published and promoted by INPO- actually work. This is not text book theory or the result of scientific tests conducted on college undergraduates. These tools represent the collective efforts of many very smart and very dedicated people, working diligently to reduce human error within the most highly regulated industry on the planet. The wheel does not need to be created. It already exists.

Of these 15 tools, seven should be considered *fundamental*, which means that they ought to be used *at all times* while workers (at all levels) are doing their work. The other eight are *situational*, which means they should be used whenever appropriate for the task/situation at hand. Within our world (PPI), we refer to the entire set as the *Error Elimination Tools™*. The tools are shown in the following graphic.

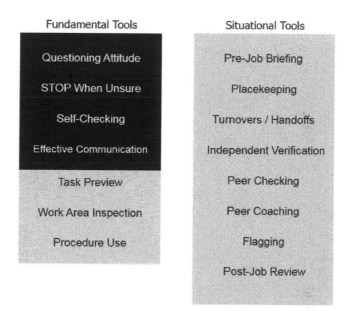

Fundamental Tools

Questioning Attitude

STOP When Unsure

Self-Checking

Effective Communication

Task Preview

Work Area Inspection

Procedure Use

Situational Tools

Pre-Job Briefing

Placekeeping

Turnovers / Handoffs

Independent Verification

Peer Checking

Peer Coaching

Flagging

Post-Job Review

Error Elimination Tools™

I am not going to go into detail on all of these tools; however, I do want to provide you with an overview of their basic 'hierarchy', and their usefulness/effectiveness. This information is based upon my experiences within the nuclear industry, as well as what we have learned working with PPI clients over the past ten years. Again, my intent is to provide you with insights you can put to direct use to make the most rapid progress and greatest return on investment for your efforts.

Let's face it- 15 tools are…a bunch. This is one of the reasons to designate some as *Fundamental*, and others as *Situational*. You should also notice that the first four *Fundamental Tools* are bolded and contained within their own box. These are the 'mother tools', having the broadest and most powerful impact of all. If you are to limit your efforts to a bare minimum, or simply want to start with 'some' of the tools, these are the ones you should begin with.

Fundamental Tools

The seven *Fundamental Tools* should be used at all times when work, or communications about work, is in progress. As shown in the figure, the Fundamental Tools are:

- **Questioning Attitude**
- **STOP When Unsure**
- **Self-Checking**
- **Effective Communication**
- Task Preview
- Work Area Inspection
- Procedure Use

When used *uncompromisingly*, the four 'mother tools' (those bolded in the list above) are incredibly powerful and effective at minimizing human error. Because of this, I wanted to offer a few insights regarding each of them. At the end of this section, I am providing you with access to detailed information on all of the tools.

Questioning Attitude

One of the biggest challenges in workforces today (as you've seen in some of the Gallup Survey results previously mentioned) is- *engagement*. To be *engaged* in a job or a task is to be mentally involved, committed, and greatly interested. When the brain is engaged, it is naturally attentive, searching for effectiveness, solution, and resolution. In other words, it is attentively questioning- conditions, circumstances, alternatives, how to be more effective or efficient, etc. The 'tool' that is used to promote such engagement is *Questioning Attitude.*

When safety professionals interview injured workers regarding *how* they managed to get hurt, the most common answer they hear is, "I just wasn't paying attention." By promoting and recognizing *Questioning Attitude*, you achieve two things: (1) a higher level of worker engagement during task performance, and (2) the uncovering and exposure of *landmines* and *roadblocks*. Error reduction is thereby achieved directly at the point of making choices and taking actions. It is also achieved in the broader context of making the overall workplace, processes, and protocols better and safer (through the elimination of *landmines* and *roadblocks*).

Questioning Attitude is what prompts the use of many of the other tools. For example, by continually questioning while conducting a task, the brain may very well come to the conclusion, "Something doesn't seem right here. Why is that light on when this whole cabinet is supposed to be de-energized?" This would then kick in the use of another tool, *STOP When Unsure*, prompting the individual to stop and get the issue resolved before continuing with her task.

Shortly after completing Practicing Perfection® Mastery Training, an operator at a coal-powered generating station was 'racking out' the 4,160-volt breaker that connected power to one of the coal conveyors. The 'racking out' process is where a tool is inserted into a socket in the front of the breaker cabinet. By rotating the tool, the breaker is lowered, and is ultimately disengaged from its ability to connect power from the source of electricity to the 'load' (in this case, the coal conveyer). As the Operator inserted and began rotating the racking tool to lower the breaker, she noticed that a light energized on the cabinet. This light indicated that the conveyer had started. She *questioned* the light, was now unsure, and stopped. She called the Control Room to see what was going on. When the Control Room Operator checked his indications, he realized that the conveyor had somehow started (all by itself). As it turned out, a worn bushing inside the breaker caused the conveyer to inadvertently start during the rack-out process. Had the operator continued (without a *Questioning Attitude*), she would have ended up racking out the breaker 'under load'. Had she done so, because of the electrical arc/flash that would have occurred, she would likely have been killed or seriously injured.

In the PPI Culture Profile, there are several survey items designed to measure whether *Questioning Attitude* is being encouraged within the current culture. There are also items that measure how questions are received / responded to when they are asked. The metrics and comments associated with these particular items provide tremendous insight about the relative health of the associated work team / organizational culture. In a healthy culture, workers at all levels are encouraged to question *everything*. Just as having a *questioning attitude* likely saved that Operator's life, so too is it a key element to achieving and sustaining greater overall safety, efficiency, and reliability. Remember- no one of us is as smart as all of us

STOP When Unsure

When 'things don't seem right', or when a worker is simply 'unsure' about the next step he is supposed to take, what would you want him to do? Clearly you would want him to stop and get the issue/uncertainty resolved before he proceeds. In many manufacturing facilities, any worker has the power to stop the line if they feel it is warranted. In the nuclear industry, by virtue of being issued their license by the NRC, a Reactor Operator is given both the authority and the responsibility to shutdown ("scram") the reactor at any point if he feels things have gotten unsafe. These are extreme (yet important) examples of *STOP When Unsure*.

The intent of this tool is to stop further progress, and get questions and issues resolved PRIOR to taking any further actions associated with the associated task or evolution. The basic concept is:

"Whenever you're unsure, or things just 'don't seem right'":

- **STOP**
- Place [whatever it is you're doing] in a safe condition
- Notify your supervisor / appropriate 'expert(s)'
- Resolve the issue PRIOR to proceeding

When a worker is 'unsure' or 'things just don't seem right', he transitions into *knowledge-based* performance. Recall that in this [troubleshooting] mode of mental processing, the average error rate is- 1 out of 2. The intent of this tool is to remove the danger (STOP and place things in a safe condition), and do the 'troubleshooting' (resolve the issue / get clarification) while things remain safe. Only after getting answers/resolution will the worker then proceed.

This just seems to be common sense, right? It is. However, consider several of the things we've discussed thus far:

- People come to work wanting to do a 'good job'. Doing a 'good job' means getting the work completed. STOPPING stands directly in the way of that.

- It takes courage to ask a question. It takes even more courage to take action on your question (stop the process).

- In many organizational cultures, if you stop work inappropriately, there will be negative repercussions. At a minimum this may include embarrassment, a conversation with your supervisor, and/or 'ribbing' / jokes from your co-workers

This tool is critical to saving lives and preventing catastrophe. It must be overtly promoted. When someone uses the tool and actually STOPs a task or evolution, such behavior must be strongly [positively] recognized in order to overcome the [cultural] forces working against it. I am aware of one time in my nuclear career where a Reactor Operator, unsure about what the reactor was 'doing', stood up, announced, "Scramming the reactor!" and then proceeded to hit the button to shut it down. The operator was immediately relieved from his station and interrogated. For several hours, the implications were that he was incompetent and had over-reacted. That is, until analysis of computer files indicated that the reactor had initiated an automatic shutdown 0.43 seconds before he 'hit the switch'.

Once the computer analysis news was revealed, the Operator was immediately transformed from potentially losing his license, to being the station hero. I found the whole thing quite disgusting. If you are a member of your leadership team, you *must* recognize that such reactions will never promote right behaviors. Remember, people come to work wanting to do a good job. If you've told them that doing a 'good job' means stopping when unsure (and I sure as heck hope you're telling them this), whenever they do so, even if after-the-fact it is deemed that stopping was not necessary, you want to [positively] recognize them for doing the 'right thing'.

Self-Checking

This was one of the first, and is likely the most well-known of the 'tools'. During my tenure at the Brunswick nuclear plant, we rolled this out site-wide as part of our *Human Performance Group* efforts. This tool forms the last barrier between a worker and an error. It is incredibly effective, providing the worker is intending to 'do the right thing to the right thing'. I'll give you an example of what I'm talking about in a minute.

Self-checking uses a well-known mnemonic (you ever wonder who came up with the spelling for that word?!), which is: S-T-A-R. This stands for Stop → Think → Act → Review. It is designed to help you 'do the right thing to the right thing'. It works like this:

- Before you take action (do the thing to the thing), you STOP and THINK about the thing you're going to do the thing to (this is *engagement*, and should involve *Questioning Attitude*)

- Once you're mentally clear that this is in fact the thing you want to do the thing do, you then ACT (do the thing to the thing)

- Once you've taken the action (done the thing to the thing), you do a quick mental REVIEW to ensure that what was supposed to happen when you did the thing to the thing is what actually happened (again, *engagement*, and *Questioning Attitude*). Once everything is in order, you then move onto the next step.

If you're not familiar with *self-checking*, this may sound cumbersome and complicated, but people who are conscientious about their work are likely already doing this (or something very similar). The mind can process all of this very quickly. You should be able to see how this forces a higher level of mental engagement, which is essentially the biggest benefit of 'tool' use in the first place.

Just like with anything else, *self-checking* is certainly not the 'be-all-end-all' defense against human error. If the worker is *intending* to do the 'wrong thing' to the 'right thing', OR the 'right thing' to the 'wrong thing', and if there are no other indications that might stop them, this 'tool' will help them do it more assuredly. Are you totally confused?

Remember when we sent Evie to the store to buy the ingredients for Southwestern Pumpkin Soup? There was a *mistake* in the planning process, and 'heavy cream' ended up on the checklist, rather than 'light cream'. Even if Evie had the checklist in front of her when she arrived at the dairy case. Even if she had STOPPED and mentally connected the item on the list with what she saw in the cooler (THINK), when she ACTed and reached into the cooler, she would have done so with the intention of doing the 'right thing' (grabbing the container) to the 'wrong thing' (the container labeled, "Heavy Cream"). *Self-checking* in this case would have helped her more assuredly end up with the wrong result. Even if she now, as part of her REVIEW, compared the container in her basket to the checklist, the desired end result, the ability to make the soup, was still doomed.

I present this in this way for two reasons. First, because when things go wrong, there is still a relatively strong tendency to blame the person 'on the sharp end of the stick' (the person that actually did the thing to the thing). Second, to point out that even though *self-checking* is a very powerful error reduction tool, and is indeed the 'last point of defense', it only works when the worker is intending to do the right thing to the right thing.

Effective Communication

The first three of the 'mother tools' involve the internal thought processes of an individual as he/she interfaces with a task or action amidst surrounding conditions and circumstances. This tool, *Effective Communication*, enters into a whole new world of complexity- the interaction between two people. Now we have two brains in action. The potential for error is therefore compounded. In fact, if you were to take all of the Root Cause Analyses that have been generated throughout modern work history, put them into a great big pile, and then took the time to sit down and *read* them (that would be *fun*, wouldn't it?), you would find *communications* as either a root cause or a significant contributing cause to a very large percentage of the events analyzed.

If you're married, think about how easy it is to miscommunicate with your spouse. And this is someone you likely know very well. In the work environment, you must communicate with many different people, some you may not directly know at all. Some may have accents that make them hard to understand. For others, English may not even be their primary language. The work environment is very dynamic, often fast-paced, and from time to time…rather stressful. None of these serve to promote accuracy in communications.

Use of the *Effective Communication* tool involves two very simple verbal communications behaviors- the first is 'three-part' communications, the second is use of the phonetic alphabet.

The first verbal behavior, 'three-part' communications, works like this: (1) the sender sends the message to the receiver, (2) the receiver repeats the message back to the receiver *in her own words, and then (3) the sender, after listening to the repeat-back and mentally confirming that what was understood by the receiver is what was intended, provides verbal confirmation to the receiver, such as, "That's correct." This simple set of behaviors is powerfully effective.

I want to quickly address the "*in her own words" statement in the previous paragraph. The reason this is important is because the human brain has the ability to hear and parrot-back sounds without truly understanding their meaning. By having the receiver repeat the message back in her own words, it reveals *what* she understood. Her brain has processed the information, rephrased it, and is presenting back her interpretation of the message. This should be the general rule for the second part of the three-part process. There are conditions, however, where verbatim repeat back of position designation and alpha-numeric nomenclature is more appropriate. An example would be communications between an operator in the field and a Control Authority when providing specific directions for in-field component manipulation.

The second technique associated with the *Effective Communication* tool is use of the phonetic alphabet. Adapted from the military, the standard phonetic alphabet is shown in following figure.

A	Alpha	N	November
B	Bravo	O	Oscar
C	Charlie	P	Papa
D	Delta	Q	Quebec
E	Echo	R	Romeo
F	Foxtrot	S	Sierra
G	Golf	T	Tango
H	Hotel	U	Uniform
I	India	V	Victor
J	Juliet	W	Whiskey
K	Kilo	X	X-Ray
L	Lima	Y	Yankee
M	Mike	Z	Zulu

Standard Phonetic Alphabet

Communicating using the phonetic alphabet tends to feel awkward at first; however, once it becomes a habit, it will bother you when others do not use it. For example, it used to drive me crazy when on a plane approaching a destination, and the flight attendant would come onto the PA system and announce the gates for connecting flights *without* using the phonetic alphabet. With the drone of the plane engines, and the (lack of) fidelity of the speakers, it was very difficult understand what was being said, let alone being able to distinguish between "B15" and "D15". This doesn't bother me so much anymore because (1) Flight attendants have gotten much better at using the phonetic alphabet, (2) I've gotten much better about not letting 'silly things' bother me, and (3) the proliferation of airport monitors and the Trip-It info on my smartphone gives me the needed info anyway. By using phonetic pronunciation, there can be no confusion or misinterpretation. In the pronunciation of airline gate announcements, for example, while "B15" can be easily confused with "D15". There can be no confusion between "Bravo-one-five" and "Delta-one-five".

When your team members use the *Effective Communication* tool uncompromisingly, the potential for verbal (spoken) communication errors (one of the most common causes of significantly bad consequences) will be virtually eliminated.

Situational Tools

The *Situational Tools* are so-named because they are to be used as appropriate for specific situations/opportunities that arise during the scope of doing work. The eight *Situational Tools* are:

- Pre-Job Brief
- Placekeeping
- Turnovers / Handoffs
- Independent Verification
- Peer Checking
- Peer Coaching
- Flagging
- Post-Job Review

As I previously mentioned, we have taken this entire set of 'tools', and formatted them into a fast, simple, and easy-to-use Error Elimination Tools™ handbook. During PPI training classes, every participant gets a personal copy. PPI will be happy to send you a free copy of this handbook (all you have to pay is shipping/handling). To grab your free copy, go here: http://www.6hoursafetyculture.com/resources/ee-tools/hb/

In addition to the handbook, PPI has also put together an Error Elimination Tools™ User Guide, which provides detailed information on every one of the tools, including 'things to watch out for' and insights on how to effectively observe and coach/mentor each of the behaviors. The User Guide also includes a turn-key implementation plan, sample forms that you can reproduce and use, and additional tools specifically for managers and supervisors. This User Guide is available for immediate download by going here: http://ppiweb.com/?p=334

Culpability

Earlier in this chapter, in the section on *Just Culture*, we talked about the difference between *accountability* and *culpability*. To refresh your memory, *accountability* is the *internalization* of personal responsibility for one's actions and behaviors, including ownership of associated outcomes. It comes from *within*. *Culpability*, on the other hand, is the degree to which an individual, group of individuals, or organization is *blameworthy* for their role in initiating or worsening undesirable conditions or consequences. This is typically an assessment made from *outside* the individual or organization.

There have been significant shortcomings and misunderstandings over the years regarding the differences between culpability, punishment, and "holding someone accountable." First, if you understand what *accountability* truly is, you now know that it is not possible to "hold someone accountable" for anything. With that cleared up, we're left with the differences between *culpability* and *punishment*. The degree to which an individual or organization is *culpable* is the degree to which they are *blameworthy* for their role in [whatever it is]. Based upon this determination, then whoever is making the determination will typically determine whether any consequences (aka *punishment*) are appropriate. The determination and application of such consequences is w-a-y outside the scope of this book. What's left for us to discuss then, is a means by which to fairly, objectively, and consistently assess *culpability*.

In 1997, James Reason published *Managing the Risks of Organizational Accidents*[23]. Unlike his seminal work, *Human Error*, which was written for academia, this work was written for the practitioner. One of the things that he did was to make (what I believe was) the first effort at providing a 'decision tree' for objectively determining culpability. Many are still using Reason's tree today.

In 2008, Andrew Hobbs wrote a white paper entitled, *Human Performance Culpability Evaluations: A comparison of various versions of the Culpability Decision Tree from various Department of Energy sites*[24]. His research gathered together variations and enhancements to Reason's original decision tree. Studying the different variations, he then created a new decision tree that incorporated the 'best' elements devised by users and practitioners over the previous eleven years. Hobbs did an excellent job. The decision tree he developed in this whitepaper formed the basis for the Culpability Decision Tree currently used and taught by PPI.

Culpability Decision Tree

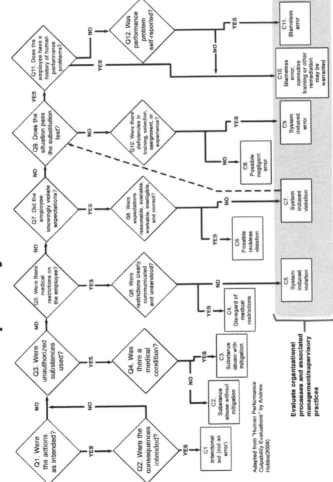

Adapted from "Human Performance Culpability Evaluations" by Andrew Hobbs(2008)

As you can see, the *Culpability Decision Tree* utilizes a series of YES/NO questions, beginning on the left and working toward the right. The questions are numbered Q1 through Q12. As you answer the questions, at some point you will arrive at a conclusion. The conclusions are numbered C1 through C11. When assessing *culpability*, the higher the conclusion number, the lower the level of *culpability*. For example, C1, the highest level of *culpability*, is an *Intentional act (not an error)*. This level of *culpability* is where the negative consequences were intended when the action was taken, and could also be termed *sabotage*. On the other end of the spectrum (to the far right), C11 concludes that this is a Blameless error. In other words, the level of *culpability* is zero.

I would like to draw your attention to Conclusions C5, C7, C9, C10, and C11, which are located in the shaded box toward the bottom right of the figure. When any of these conclusions is reached, it is appropriate to do further analysis to evaluate organizational processes and associated management/supervisory practices that may have contributed to the error. This level of analysis is what separates 'old-school' from next-level thinking and doing. Expanding your analysis beyond the person 'on the sharp end of the stick' is essential in a highly accountable culture, and is critical to having a true learning culture (and a *Just Culture*).

Because the *Culpability Decision Tree* graphic is difficult to read in the format that can be provided in this book, I am providing you with access (free of charge) to a full color (letter size or 11X17) copy available for immediate download. You may access your   copy   here: http://www.6hoursafetyculture.com/resources/culpability/

Rather than have you go back and forth between a detailed explanation of the Decision Tree in this text and your downloadable copy, you may also download the associated *Culpability Decision Tree Guidelines*, which contain details and amplifying information for each of the questions and conclusions. Again, this is free of charge. You may download the Culpability Decision   Tree   Guidelines   here: http://www.6hoursafetyculture.com/resources/culpability/

Recommended Reading

We have covered a LOT of territory in this chapter. I have highlighted what I consider to be the most important elements associated with the *psychology of human error*, and the determination of *culpability* as they relate to next-level human performance. Because 'inquiring minds need to know', and many of you will want to dig more deeply, I encourage you to check out the *Human Error Reduction* section on the Recommended Reading page of the PPI website. You may access the page here: http://ppiweb.com/?p=2738

Key Insights from Chapter Eight

1. The three 'types' of errors are: *mistake* (which occurs in the *planning* phase), *lapse* (which occurs in the *preparation* phase), and *slip* (which occurs in the *execution* phase).

2. The three modes in which people perform tasks are: *skill-based*, *rule-based*, and *knowledge-based*. Whenever a worker enters *knowledge-based* mode during task performance, they should STOP.

3. Successful conduct of operations tends to promote *drift* in both individual and organizational behaviors. At the same time, *landmines* and *roadblocks* tend to *accumulate*. Without overt effort to stop/correct this, the combined effects of *drift* and *accumulation* increase the potential for (and potential significance of) human error.

4. *Traps* are conditions of the work environment that increase the potential for human error. There are eleven *traps* commonly seen in today's work environments:

   - Time Pressure
   - Distraction/Interruption
   - Multiple Tasks
   - Overconfidence
   - Vague or Interpretive Guidance

- First Shift / Last Shift
- Peer Pressure
- Change / Off-Normal
- Physical Environment
- Mental Stress
- Fatigue

5. There are fifteen 'tools' that have been proven to effectively modify human behaviors while performing tasks. When used uncompromisingly, these tools virtually eliminate the potential for human error in *skill-based* and *rule-based* tasks. These 'tools' are:

Fundamental Tools

- **Questioning Attitude**
- **STOP When Unsure**
- **Self-Checking**
- **Effective Communication**
- Task Preview
- Work Area Inspection
- Procedure Use

Situational Tools

- Pre-Job Brief
- Placekeeping
- Turnovers / Handoffs
- Independent Verification
- Peer Checking
- Peer Coaching
- Flagging
- Post-Job Review

6. Out of the 15 'tools', there are (4) 'mother tools' that are, by far, the most powerful. If you are only going to implement a small number of 'tools', your set should absolutely include these:

- **Questioning Attitude**
- **STOP When Unsure**
- **Self-Checking**
- **Effective Communication**

7. *Culpability* is *not* 'accountability' or 'punishment'. It is the degree to which an individual, group of individuals, or organization is blameworthy for their role in initiating or worsening undesirable conditions or consequences. It must be determined objectively.

8. Next-level *culpability* determination includes 'extent of condition' assessment of culpability (beyond just the person on the 'sharp end of the stick'). Areas assessed include organizational processes and associated management/supervisory practices.

What can you do with what you just learned?

A. Recognize that a couple of hours of introductory training and a 'tool kit' will never give you the human error reduction results you desire.

B. Train all workers on *skill-based*, *rule-based*, and *knowledge-based* performance (in a manner that is *fun* and *engaging*)

C. Begin to actively look for examples of *drift* in work standards and *drift* in perception of risk within your work culture

D. Recognize that your organization is chock-full of *roadblocks* and *landmines*. Initiate efforts to dig these suckers up and get rid of them

E. Begin to actively look for and minimize human error *traps* within your work environment

F. Request your free copy of the Error Elimination Tools™ Handbook. Study its fast, simple, and easy format. Download the Error Elimination Tools™ User Guide. Study it thoroughly. THEN decide how you want to move forward with 'tools' implementation (or modification) within your organization. You can access a free sample of the Tools Handbook here: http://www.6hoursafetyculture.com/resources/ee-tools/hb/

G. A downloadable copy of the Tools User Guide can be acquired   here: http://www.6hoursafetyculture.com/resources/ee-tools/ug/

H. Immediately download the Culpability Decision Tree and associated Guidelines (they're both free of charge). Begin using them immediately in your assessments of *culpability*. You can access them here: http://www.6hoursafetyculture.com/resources/culpability/

---

[1] *Human Error*; James Reason; Cambridge University Press; 1990

[2] *Human Error*; James Reason; Cambridge University Press; 20th printing, 2009; page xi

[3] *Human Error Performance Modes*; US Department of Energy; 2007

[4] *Human Error Performance Modes*; US Department of Energy; 2007

[5] Short Term Memory; Saul McLeod; 2009

[6] Culture Profile Data Base; Practicing Perfection Institute, Inc.; 2015

[7] [Adapted from] Trafton JG, Altmann EM, Brock DP, et al. Preparing to resume an interrupted task: effects of prospective goal encoding and retrospective rehearsal. Int J Hum Comput Stud 2003;58:583–603

[8] *Timecourse of recovery from task interruption: Data and a model*; Altmann and Trafton; Psychonomic Bulletin & Review 2007, 14 (6), 1079-1084

[9] *Meet the Life Hackers*; Thompson, Clive (16 October 2005); New York Times

[10] *The impact of interruptions on clinical task completion*; Coiera E, Dunsmuir WT, et al. Westbrook JI; Qual Saf Health Care 2010;19:284–9

[11] *Prospective study of the incidence, nature and causes of dispensing errors in community pharmacies*; Ashcroft DM, Quinlan P, Blenkinsopp A.; Pharmacoepidemiol Drug Saf 2005;14:327–32

[12] *Association of interruptions with an increased risk and severity of medication administration errors*; Woods A, Rob MI, et al.; Westbrook JI; Arch Intern Med 2010;170:683–90

[13] *Variation in communication loads on clinical staff in the emergency department*; Spencer R, Coiera E, Logan P; Ann Emerg Med 2004;44:268–73

[14] *Bold: How to Go Big, Create Wealth, and Impact the World*; Peter Diamandis and Steven Kotler; Simon & Schuster; 2015

[15] Culture Profile Data Base; Practicing Perfection Institute, Inc.; 2015

[16] *The Myth of Multitasking*; Christine Rosen; The New Atlantis; Spring 2008

[17] *Stress And Cognition: A Cognitive Psychological Perspective*; National Aeronautics and Space Administration; Grant Number NAG2-1561; Lyle E. Bourne, Jr. and Rita A. Yaroush; February 1, 2003

[18] Majority of U.S. Employees Not Engaged, Despite Gains in 2014; Amy Adkins; Gallup

[19] *Shift Management: The Role of Fatigue in Human Error*; Dr. Drew Dawson, Director, Centre for Applied Behavioural Research, The University of South Australia; 14th Annual Human Factors in Aviation Maintenance Symposium

[20] ibid

[21] Title 10, US Code of Federal Regulations; 26.205- *Work hours*

[22] Source: Nuclear Energy Institute; http://www.nei.org

[23] *Managing the Risks of Organizational Accidents*; James Reason; Ashgate Publishing; 1997

[24] *Human Performance Culpability Evaluations: A comparison of various versions of the Culpability Decision Tree from various Department of Energy sites*; Andrew F. Hobbs; University of Tennessee–Knoxville, Masters in Safety Management Program; November 2008

Chapter Nine: Engagement and Alignment

> *"All organizations are perfectly aligned to get the results they get."*
> -Arthur W. Jones

We've talked about mindset and perceptions, and how these impact the thoughts, feelings, and behaviors of the members of your organization. We've talked about how these combine and interact to create your team, department, and organizational cultures. We've been through a bit of the science of human error, and the components of building and sustaining a learning culture, a *Just Culture*, and ultimately a *Safety Culture*.

We're now going to 'bring it home'. Between this chapter and Chapter Ten, I'm going to bring all of the pieces together, and talk directly about what you can (and must) *do* to grow and sustain next-level performance.

Alignment

Alignment is the proper positioning or state of adjustment of parts in relation to each other[1]. Think about a simple mechanical relationship- the wheels on your car, or the coupling between a motor and a pump. Alignment is critical to smooth operation. If you've ever had an 'out of alignment' front end, you know that your car either pulls to the left or right, or "wobbles" at certain speeds. An 'out of alignment' coupling can cause lots of noise, and rapid destruction of rotating machinery. On the other hand, when components are aligned, equipment runs quietly, smoothly, and efficiently.

Does your team, department, or organization have a bit of a 'wobble'? Does it make a lot of 'noise'? Does it tend to pull to one side or the other, especially when you take your hand off the steering wheel? *Alignment* of your team, your department, and your entire organization (the proper positioning and adjustment of 'parts') is just as critical to its ability to efficiently function as it is to any piece of equipment. Fixing organizational dysfunction (misalignment) is not quite as simple as spending $99 at the auto garage, or taking readings with a micrometer and making a few mechanical adjustments. However, it can (and must) be done if you are to ever achieve, let alone sustain, next-level performance.

A Key Insight within the PPI curriculum is an adaptation of the Arthur W. Jones' quote provided at the beginning of this chapter: *Every organization is perfectly aligned to get exactly the results it is getting.* This includes *your* organization- from your overall mission or sense of purpose (your organizational *why*), to the current results you are achieving (your *what*), to the relative synchronicity (or dysfunction) with which you achieve those results (your *how*). And just as it is the 'front end' that typically needs alignment on an automobile, so too have we found this to be the case in most organizations. Once you're steering in the right direction, and you have the front end properly aligned, the rest of the organization tends to follow along very nicely.

Who (or what) is Driving Your Ship?

There are two sets of forces that ultimately determine a ship's course: the natural forces of the environment (the waves, the wind, the tides, and the currents), and the ship's propulsion and course of direction. The interaction/counteraction of these two sets of forces determines the speed and efficiency with which the ship arrives at its destination (or not).

The same thing is true for your organization. There are external forces to contend with such as regulation, competition, and economic cycles. There are internal forces such as *drift* and *accumulation*. And there is the natural force of *organizational entropy*. This is a measure of the wasted energy (chaos) within your 'system'. And just like *drift* and *accumulation*, the disorder of *organizational entropy* naturally increases over time unless you take direct action to counter its insidious nature.

All three of these forces- external, internal, and natural, directly impact (and often oppose) your day-to-day navigation (operations). In fact, just like a ship in a storm at sea, you may find that much (if not all) of your day-to-day energy is consumed reacting to waves, currents, and shifts in wind direction. If so, you have a problem. It's a *culture* problem. If this is your current 'state of affairs', you are living proof of the following: If you don't manage your culture, your culture will manage you. As Peter Drucker said, *"Culture eats strategy for breakfast, operational excellence for lunch, and everything else for dinner."*

External forces are just that- you must respond to them. However, the internal forces (*drift, accumulation,* and *organizational entropy*), are being directly created or allowed to happen on a daily basis. Recall Practicing Perfection® Precept#1: *Things are the way they are because they got that way.* If 'things' are not the way you want them to be, you have the power to change them. In order to alter your course (to achieve next-level performance), you must directly confront and address these forces. Let's now talk about how to do precisely that.

Your Rudder

External challenges will forever ebb and flow, wax and wane. You have no choice but to deal with them if you want to remain in business. But wouldn't it be wonderful if these were essentially the only significant challenges you had to face? Wouldn't it be great if you had an organizational culture that remained on the lookout for and spontaneously combatted tendencies toward *drift, accumulation,* and *entropy*? Not only would this eliminate much of the daily 'firefighting' you may now be facing, it would likely be a culture that would also present a united front to whatever external challenges arise.

How can you get there? You need to begin at the beginning- at your core. You must define, and make a solid commitment to live by a set of *Core Principles*. Thomas Carlyle gave us, "A man without a purpose is like a ship without a rudder." I would assert that any organization that does not solidly know, commit to, and live by its *Core Principles* is as well adrift on the sea. Without such a rudder, the external challenges, internal challenges, and natural challenges are free to batter you about. All you can then do is to react to them.

Your organization likely has a *vision statement*, a *mission statement*, and perhaps even a mnemonic of some sort that defines your ideals. I've seen hundreds of these. Many lose me with lofty corporate speak about 'excellence'. Others are simply 'kitschy', obviously poised for political correctness (and that's about it). I've seen a handful that are very well done. Even in these cases though, I have yet to experience an organization (other than PPI) where the majority of employees have internalized the intent and are actively living to the precepts. The thing is, a poster on the wall is just...a poster on the wall.

Four-thousand-five-hundred-forty-three words. This is the number of words in the original Constitution of the United States (including signatures). Short. Not complicated. This document offered a set of *Core Principles*, upon which was built what was to become the greatest and strongest country in history. Yes, far from perfect, but filled with more freedom and opportunity for more people than had ever before existed on planet earth.

This set of Core Principles provided for (and promoted) the *spontaneous cooperation of a free people*. People from all over the globe coming together, working together, playing together. One of the things that has made the USA unique, and certainly a core reason for its success, has been that because of this set of *Core Principles*, the country became an ethic, not an ethnicity.

So, what does this have to do with your organization? If a simple set of *Core Principles* can have worked so well for so many years across an entire country, think of the possibilities for your team, department, or organization. My perception is that external challenges are only going to increase in the near term. In order to thrive, you are going to need an internal *culture* that is stronger than ever. In spite of generational differences. In spite of continued increases in diversification of ethnicities, of social preferences, of values. Here's what it comes down to: running your organization based upon *principles* provides the framework (the rudder) for people with different *values* to work together effectively.

What does a set of *Core Principles* look like? Short. Simple. To the point. I'm [just a bit] biased, but I'll show you the best set I've seen to date. These are the *Core Principles* of the Practicing Perfection Institute, Inc.:

Proactive Passion

Constant and never-ending motivation to improve performance, grow relationships, enhance conditions, and elevate circumstances

Independent Thinking

Be responsible to/for yourself by questioning everything; seek to understand and innovate

Honesty

Complete transparency; not even a 'white lie'

Integrity

Do the right thing, in the right way, for the right reasons- no matter what

Safety

External protection of and internal caring for self and others at all times

Sanity

The simplest workable resolution is likely the most appropriate

Simplicity

Make the complex simple and tangible

So there you have an example of a set of *Core Principles*. If you have never identified and defined your *Core Principles*, this should be the first step you take in your efforts to become a next-level organization. You have my explicit permission to use these as a starting point if you like. Based upon your industry, you'll likely have additions and deletions. But remember to keep to the *core*. For example, PPI is a learning / human performance company. Notice that neither of these words are included in the Core Principles; "core" means *core*.

As many team members as possible should be involved in, and have a voice in, the identification and definition of your *Core Principles*. Once your *Core Principles* are determined, they must be communicated, communicated, communicated. Even more importantly, they must be interjected into your corporate conversation, referenced during meetings, brought forward often (especially in the beginning), and overtly role-modeled by those in positions of authority. And finally, when questions and potential conflicts arise, your *Core Principles* should be used as the framework for discussion and resolution.

Do you recall our discussion in Chapter Six regarding the *Code of Honor*? You may remember me referring to this as the 'crux of the biscuit' regarding organizational culture change. Now I'm referring to *Core Principles* as your organizational 'rudder'. A logical question would be, "How do these fit together?" I'm glad you asked...

If we use the example of the US Constitution as the *Core Principles* of the United States, then each *Code of Honor* (depending upon the size of your company) would be like a state constitution, or perhaps even a town charter. The *Code of Honor* is created by and for the 'local' level, the natural work team. And when you look at the items that end up on the individual *Codes of Honor* within your organization, you will see that they align with, support, and reinforce your *Core Principles*. The simple brilliance in this arrangement is that it achieves global alignment with your *Core Principles* while generating ownership at the local level.

Your Linchpin

According to Webster, a 'linchpin' is, "one that serves to hold together parts or elements that exist or function as a unit.[2]" In 2010, Seth Godin wrote *Linchpin: Are You Indispensable?* In which he describes 'linchpins' as, "...indispensable, the driving force of our future.[3]"

When I designed my initial error reduction efforts thirteen years ago, I targeted a position within the organization that I believed would have the greatest impact upon how work was actually being done on a day-to-day basis- the Frontline Supervisor. This worked spectacularly well. I shared the success with you in the Prologue (87.5% sustainable reduction in human error rate). Based upon the success of this inaugural effort, we retained and further developed this focus as we built the Practicing Perfection® approach.

Let's not get confused with terminology. Frontline supervisors (FLS) are the leaders of your natural work teams. If you are my FLS, I generally get my work assignments from you. You provide me with guidance and oversight. If your company still uses performance appraisals, you are the one who determines if I am "average", "above average," or whether I "need improvement." I directly interface with you in the conduct of my work. At work, you will therefore generally have a far greater impact upon my mindset and perceptions about [whatever it is] than anyone else. Our relationship is direct. Rather than emails or intranet correspondence from 'corporate' or 'senior leadership', information and communication (and the bias and filtering of that information and communication) coming from you is 'close to home'. It specifically impacts...me.

In 2009, Dan Anderson, a visionary leader at Northeast Utilities, shared a study with me. This study quantified the relative impact of key organizational elements upon the potential for an accident (safety related incident) to occur. Since human error is involved in 95% of all work-related accidents and injuries[4], the data in this study[5] provided the information needed for me to develop what we refer to as *The Accident Propensity Model*.

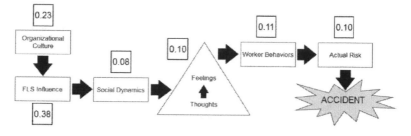

Accident Propensity Model

The Accident Propensity Model includes the organizational factors that tend to have direct impact upon the potential for an accident to occur. Using the data from the study, I created a proportion representing the relative contribution of each element. In this model, if you add up each of the numbers indicated, you will see that the sum equals 1.0 (or 100%). Under 'perfect' circumstances, with all elements the best they can be, we're at 100% (the 'safest' possible condition). As any of the elements departs from the ideal, the sum lowers, and the potential for an accident to occur rises.

Looking at the numbers in the model, you can see that one element has far greater impact than any other single element- the influence of the Frontline Supervisor (FLS) (38%). The empirical evidence gathered by PPI over the past ten years, combined with the data provided within the *Predictors of Work Safety* study clearly indicate- the FLS is your *linchpin* within your efforts to take the performance of your organization to the next level.

Unfortunately, many Frontline Supervisors have been given little (if any) training on *how* to lead. Most have risen from subject matter expert, and been promoted into the ranks of defined leadership. In other words, your best electrician becomes the Electrical Supervisor. The most talented nurse becomes the Nursing Supervisor. The best operator becomes a Shift/Crew Supervisor. The thing is, the skill set required to be a *supervisor* is completely different than that needed to be a top notch electrician, or nurse, or operator.

It has been my experience that (1) most organizations provide grossly inadequate leadership training (if any) to their Frontline Supervisors, (2) new supervisors are often tasked with supervising the folks who used to be their co-workers, and (3) FLS are given a tremendous amount of responsibility with very little authority. On top of this, a large percentage of supervisors are so burdened with paperwork that they have very little opportunity to actually...supervise.

I was conducting a Code of Honor facilitation for a natural work team of 49 people in 2007. Since most natural work teams are comprised of five to twelve members, I recognized up front that this might be a bit of a challenge. As I hope you recall, in order for an item to end up on a team's Code of Honor, every team member must commit to being 100% accountable to its context and intent. We were working on the sole 'required' Code item of, "Be willing to call and be called." The team had agreed upon the wording. After four iterations of discussion, when I asked for a show of hands regarding those who were willing to 100% commit, there were still only 48 arms raised. Pointing to the item on the wall, I then directly asked the technician whose arm was not raised, "What is your problem with this?" Here was his response: "There's a member of this team who I have so little respect for, I don't want him calling me on anything!"

I don't remember how we successfully completed the Code (with this item intact), but we did. What I do remember is being pulled aside by one of the Department Managers following its completion, and being told, "The person he has 'so little respect for' is the team supervisor." This was a classic example of the 'top technician' being promoted into a position of *supervisor* and not having the requisite 'people skills' to be effective. Fortunately, the company had the wisdom shortly thereafter to effect a lateral transfer. This 'super smart / top notch' technician was moved into a position where his talents and abilities could add much more value to the organization. He was happy. The technicians on this particular team were happy. The company was happy. The individual who replaced him had excellent 'people skills', and went on with great success, being promoted to Department Head prior to his retirement.

Within the Practicing Perfection® approach, we insist that Front Line Supervisors be treated as members of the Leadership Team. Considering that the FLS has more impact upon how work actually gets done than any other position within the organization, it makes no sense to treat them any other way. Frontline Supervisors get the same Leadership Training as the more senior leaders within the organization. Finally, we place a tremendous amount of Proactive Accountability® directly on the shoulders of the FLS through a process that we call the FLS Challenge. Details on this process are provided in Chapter Ten.

A Players, B Players, and C Players

"The ability to make good decisions regarding people represents one of the last reliable sources of competitive advantage, since very few organizations are very good at it." -Peter Drucker

We have now established:

- Your *culture* is driving your ship
- Your *rudder* for navigating to next-level performance is provided by your *Core Principles*. These must be identified, developed, role modeled, and communicated.
- The Code of Honor generates ownership at the local (natural work team) level that directly support/reinforce your Core Principles.

- The success (or lack thereof) of your efforts to achieve and sustain next-level performance rests heavily upon on the shoulders of your *linchpins*- your Front Line Supervisors (FLS)

We are now going to address another organizational reality. Unless you are extremely unique, your team roster consists of a combination of 'A Players', 'B Players', and 'C Players'. And I am not just talking about your 'frontline' workers. All three levels can likely be found amongst your leadership ranks, management ranks, and your supervisory ranks as well. I want to highlight this up front. I have found that without doing so, folks in positions of authority tend to think only about 'front line' workers as we dive into the 'meat' of this discussion. And the thing to remember here is that the higher on the 'org chart' an individual resides, the greater the leverage of their influence. Having anything other than 'A Players' on your leadership team (FLS and above) can have a tremendously negative impact upon your efforts. Unfortunately, up to this point only about 25% of people promoted in most companies turn out to be 'A Players'.[6]

What are 'A Players', 'B Players', and 'C Players'? These designations represent the combined level of talent and commitment of the members of your team. 'A Players' are the top producers, the biggest contributors to your overall effort. When a solid idea comes along, they are the 'early adopters'. They will take the lead in solving problems, finding solutions, and making things better. In a 'typical' organization, 'A Players' comprise about 10% of the population. 'B Players' are solid workers. They come to work wanting to do a good job. They will generally follow the lead of the 'A Players'. In a typical company, 'B Players" make up about 80% of the population. And then we have the 'C Players'. These are typically looked at as the 'low performers', the 'attitude problems', or both.

If you do the math, the 'bottom dwellers', the 'C Players', tend to make up the balance of the organization (the bottom 10%). Relative to *human performance* however, we have found this number to be a bit high. Our experience has shown that a decent percentage of those acting like 'C Players' are not really 'C Players' at all. They are highly intelligent, highly frustrated workers. As we discussed when talking about Precept #3 in Chapter Three (*People come to work wanting to do a good job*), many such workers have simply become disgruntled. Rather than quit and go work somewhere else, they have (for whatever reason) chosen to stick around and be...negative. Unfortunately, this doesn't serve them or the organization. We have countless stories of watching so-called 'C Players' transform from being thought of as a 'pain in the ass', to becoming solid valuable contributors. In many cases, we've seen them rise to 'A Player' status once things start to make sense- once the leadership, management, and 'people' practices I've been describing throughout this book are put into place.

The continued presence of 'C Players' in your organization (or those conducting themselves as 'C Players') is an indicator of the relative health of your overall *culture*. On a natural work team, the presence of 'C Players" can have a profound impact upon the *social dynamics* of the team. If we revisit the *Accident Propensity Model*, we can see that these two factors, *Organizational Culture* and *Social Dynamics*, together have a substantial impact upon the potential for an accident to occur (0.31). In addition, if you allow 'C Players' to remain, your improvement efforts can only go so far. Take a look at the following figure, which was adapted from a similar diagram provided by Quint Studer, in his book, *Results That Last: Hardwiring Behaviors That Will Take Your Company to the Top*[7]

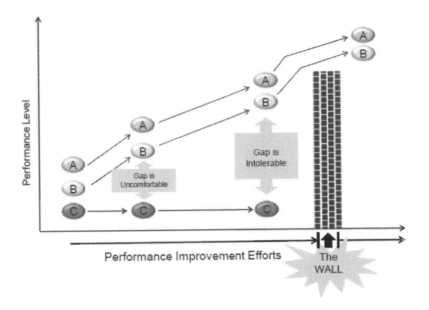

The Wall

You've likely experienced this before. You have something 'great' that you are promoting or implementing (or wanting to promote/implement). If [whatever it is] makes sense and obviously 'adds value', your top performers, your 'A Players', take the ball and run with it. The 'B Players' will generally follow the lead of the 'A Players'. As shown in the figure, they move upward and so does overall performance. Then there are the 'C Players'. As shown, these team members do nothing different. In fact, behind the scenes, they are likely doing what they can to stifle your efforts. Fortunately, they are such a minority that overall performance will continue to improve- to a certain point.

At some point, the 'cracks' in your *culture* (as evidenced by the fact that 'C Players still exist), combined with the social tension generated, will reach a level that becomes intolerable within the fabric of your day-to-day operations. At this point, your performance improvement efforts will hit *The Wall*. There will be no additional performance improvement. Unless- you get rid of your 'C Players'.

Now, while some are cheering, others are likely thinking, "What the heck?! Sounds like a lawsuit waiting to happen!" When you do this correctly, there are no lawsuits. In fact, everyone (with the possible exception of a 'hard core C Player' or two) appreciates this approach. This being said, this is *not* about a 'witch hunt' within your organization. I'd like to ask you a question: what do you think is the best way to 'get rid of a C Player'? I hope the answer is obvious- help them transform into becoming either a 'B Player' or an 'A Player'. These are human beings. They have families. They may still have children at home, or kids in college. What a gift you are giving these individuals, and whoever they return home to every day, by helping them get out of *Suckers' Swamp*, and to rise into a proactive world of *Possibility*.

Within the PPI approach, we present *The Wall*, and talk about 'A Players', 'B Players', and 'C Players' to all organization members (not just 'management'). We present during the first session of our primary training courses on the morning of Day One. We lay it right on the table. And all of our facilitators are trained to use the phrase, "You must get rid of your 'C Players'." Sound contentious? Sound like labor and unions might rise up in arms? Not when you present this properly. When done correctly, this is a 'breath of fresh air', appreciated by all. I have discovered that people, no matter what their station, are sick and tired of putting up with the 'loads' (the true 'C Players' who are flat out 'jerks' and/or add little actual value). This is especially true when such individuals are found at higher levels within the organization.

Several years ago, I was working with a coal powered generation facility in rural Pennsylvania. This was a bargaining unit organization. At the time, a moderately contentious relationship existed between management and the union. A few of their management team members had been through our Certification Course, and were well aware of *The Wall*. As we were putting the pieces together for rollout of Practicing Perfection® at their facility, these folks attempted to convince me that I probably shouldn't talk about *The Wall*, especially in the worker-level training. They were afraid it would upset the union members. Fortunately, I was able to convince them otherwise, and *The Wall* was left in the learning experience.

Our learning regimen begins with the Leadership Learning Experience. We encourage facilities to invite their Union Stewards and any other key natural leaders/influencers to attend. Because these folks have tremendous influence on the larger worker population, this provides a great 'head start' to the overall effort (remember the phenomenon of *viral change*)? Prior to the very first Leadership Learning Experience, I was warned that one of the most 'contentious' Union Stewards would be participating. I told them this was fine, and asked them not to identify who this person was prior to class.

We took our first morning break at around 9:15AM, by which time I had already covered *The Wall*, where I did indeed say, "We must get rid of the 'C Players'." I was grabbing a cup of coffee when I was approached from behind. The man introduced himself. He was the Union Steward I had been warned about. As he extended his right hand, he said, "I want to thank you. It's about time someone said these things around here." He was one of the most engaged, most supportive members of that particular class. What do you think he had to say to his constituents when he returned to work?

Our experience has proven that workers and their labor representatives are every bit as fed up with the 'C Players' as anyone else in a facility, perhaps even more so than 'management'. After all, workers have to directly 'live' with their negative attitudes, and have to cover for their lack of productivity. At another of our client companies, we did a follow-up *Culture Profile* one year after full site implementation. This was also a bargaining unit facility. A prominent worker-level question that showed up, both in the online survey and in the interviews, was, "How come we haven't gotten rid of all of the 'C Players'?"

I believe we're seeing a major shift in perspective in the workplace. Organization members at all levels are sick and tired of feeling like their hands are tied when it comes to dealing with 'C Players'. Your hands are not tied! Proper implementation of a next-level approach to human performance will undo the negative conditioning of many of your 'highly intelligent / highly frustrated' workers who have been acting like 'C Players'. We've seen this happen over, and over, and over again. These workers, in turn often become some of the most proactive members of your team.

But what about the 'legitimate C Players'? The chronically lazy? Those who lack integrity? Our experience has shown that many of them will turn in their resignations once they 'get the message' that this is now going to be a highly reliable and highly accountable work environment. We've seen people resign the very next morning following their completion of the Mastery Learning Experience. We've seen people 'buy out' early retirement because they simply did not want to live and work to such standards.

What about those 'legitimate C Players' who don't leave of their own accord? This is where management and HR need to be accountable. You must have the courage to do 'the right thing' for the sake of the other 98-99.5% of the organization. You must get rid of your 'C Players'.

Command & Control → Observation & Coaching

"Not everything that matters can be measured, and
not everything that can be measured matters."
-Albert Einstein

The 'old school' approach, the 'old paradigm' of dealing with people in organizations has centered around 'command and control'; of managing people like 'things'. Hopefully you're enlightened enough to recognize there is a much more effective (and enjoyable) way of being a leader. You should be managing 'things' and leading people.

Observation and Coaching programs have been prominent in nuclear power plants for the last twenty years. Over the past few years, such programs have become popular, or at least have 'come onto the radar of things to do' in many other industries. The 'upside' to this is that direct correlations have been seen between leadership presence in the field and work performance. As leadership 'time in the field' rises, so do performance levels. The 'downside' has been that the 'old paradigms' have remained alive and well in many organizations' efforts to *Observe and Coach*. Many have approached their effort as a 'program'. Designated individuals are required to complete a certain number of observations per a given time period (month, quarter, etc.). Those doing the *observing* are either turned loose to do so with little or no training, or are armed with checklists ('coaching cards') identifying precisely what to look for. The bias is toward looking for the 'negatives'. For organizations who have an *Observation & Coaching Database,* these 'negatives' are entered electronically. The hope is that there will eventually be enough data, or some emerging 'trend'. The computer can then tell *management* where they need to focus in order to *fix* the workers.

The "Shiny Box" Revisited

I have 'railed against' the *shiny box* for the past fifteen years. In my last nuclear power position, as *Corrective Action Manager*, I was responsible for two of the large *shiny boxes* onsite- the *Corrective Action Program* database, and the *Observation & Coaching* database. I saw tremendous input of time, energy, and resource in both of these areas without a commensurate return on investment. Every nuclear power plant in the United States is required by law to have and maintain a *Corrective Action Database*, and it serves a good purpose. I simply saw many ways in which the entire process could provide much more value with much less effort. The *Observation & Coaching* database, however, was another story. I said it then, and ten years into our experiences at PPI (with clients all over the world), I can still say the same thing: I have yet to see an *Observation & Coaching* database that has provided *any* real positive value to an organization.

The basic problem is that when you take leaders in high risk industries, industries that use lots of technology, there is a tendency toward and a natural attraction to, a 'technology fix' for virtually everything. Unfortunately, we've seen this same tendency toward *Observation & Coaching*. In many (if not most) organizations that have incorporated such a 'system', it has become about the 'system', about the collection of data, and the production of graphs and multi-colored bar charts. In such cases, measures of success tend to be focused upon [monthly] quotas, and total numbers of observations completed. This is totally missing the point. The focus within any *Observation & Coaching* effort should be upon behaviors and relationships. This is how you achieve *engagement* and *alignment*. No database required.

Interestingly, as I previously indicated, in 2014, the number one concern of Chief Nuclear Officers (CNOs) across the entire US nuclear industry was *cumulative impact*. When a first look was made at where savings in time, energy, and resources could be made (without sacrificing safety), two of the first areas identified were the 'programs' associated with: 'Corrective Action' and *Observation & Coaching*. At the 2014 Utility Services Alliance (USA) Executive Summit, the INPO Senior VP of Operations admitted that the organization has had "a few missteps along the way." After years of 'requiring' nuclear plants to build databases and display numbers and metrics regarding their *Observation & Coaching* programs, they have come to the conclusion that perhaps this has not provided a solid return on investment. They are apparently re-thinking their position. Bravo. All progress begins by telling the truth.

Looking For Negatives

Before we get into how you can derive tremendous organizational value by doing observations and engaging with those observed, I want to touch on one other aspect that has seemed to dominate this arena since its inception: looking for negatives.

In our early years in PPI, we did a good job of driving home the point that leadership team members should spend more time in the field. We did not, however, do a good job of teaching those leadership team members how to effectively use their time in the field, what to look for, or how to proactively engage with workers in a manner that not only promoted desired behaviors, but built positive relationships in the process.

In the initial Culture Profile for one of our early clients, one of the 'messages' that came from the frontline was that workers wanted to see more management presence in the field. The organization took this to heart. Managers (assistant department heads and up) began spending time in the plant. Twelve months later, the follow-up Culture Profile provided us with new insight. Workers now told us that they felt like, "they had 'targets' on their backs."

So what happened? The organization decided to make it a requirement that each member of the leadership team conduct a minimum of 20 observations per month. This was the first mistake. Management time 'in the plant' (or 'on the floor') is a wonderful thing (when done properly); however, setting a required number of observations per [month] is a bad idea. Why? Irrespective of where your title and job responsibilities fall on the 'org chart', I imagine you are busy. You have a lot to do. If we now add a required number of observations to your 'pile' of things to do, here's how it tends to play out for most people. You wait until then end of the [month], and in the last few days available, you rush out into the plant (or onto the floor) and do a series of 'drive by' observations. Yes, you fulfill the requirement. Most likely, however, you've added zero value to overall operations, and you've likely done zero to promote a healthy positive relationship between yourself and those you 'observed'. What's the alternative? If you want to set minimum requirements, which is a good idea, establish a required amount of *time* in the plant / on the floor (versus a required number of observations). Remember- the objective is *not* the collection of data. It is the opportunity to positively influence behaviors, build relationships, and to grow an aligned sense of *one team*.

The second thing that went wrong within this organization is, because our training (at the time) was lacking in how to properly observe and engage, the leadership team members did what came 'naturally'. They went out looking for negatives (simple negatives). For example, a substantial focus during their implementation was upon the use of the Error Elimination Tools™. Use of the tools, the behaviors, was indeed something that could be observed. However, somehow a 'requirement' developed that workers had to have their tools handbooks in their possession while doing their work. So what do you think became a focus point of the observations? Workers were getting 'gigged' for not 'visibly' having their tools handbooks on their person while engaged in their tasks. Shame on us (PPI) for not providing better guidance. Without proper training and insight, the leadership team members were defaulting to looking for tangible things they could see and document, with a 'natural' bias of looking for things that were wrong (rather than acknowledging all the things going [very] well).

I hope you remember the lesson in the story I relayed to you earlier about the wise man outside the ancient city of Babylon: *you're going to find whatever it is you're looking for*. This is true in every aspect of life, including your workplace observations. Look for negatives- you're going to find them. "But," you counter, "Isn't that the point? Isn't the purpose of going into the plant, or onto the floor, to find and document what workers are doing wrong?" No. No. No. This is not the purpose. Approaching observation and subsequent engagement in this way only serves to harm relationships. Workers will tend to slow down, stop work, or even 'hide' when they know you're coming. And why wouldn't they?

The *Real* Value

The true value in any *Observation & Coaching* effort lies *not* in the observation of 'silly' things (like whether or not a worker has her tools handbook with her). I have yet to see a single error prevented because a worker had her tools handbook sticking out of her pocket. True value does *not* come through documentation. It does *not* come through the accumulation of data. It does *not* come by solely looking for negatives. The true value lies in the interactions between the observer and those being observed. Let me repeat this, because it is so important (and counter to what most organizations have been doing):

The true value of doing observations and engaging with those observed lies in the interaction between the individuals involved.

Into the Third Dimension: Principle-Based Mentoring™

The overall intent of the next-level approach to *human performance* is ultimately to achieve substantial long-term sustainable performance improvement. Doing so requires a departure from a focus on rote 'compliance' and 'managing people like things'. It requires developing a culture of *desire* that is *aligned* to a central set of [*core*] *principles*. The Principle-Based Mentoring™ (PBM) process provides a simple and consistent approach for role modeling, communicating, and reinforcing the behaviors necessary to achieve a healthy aligned working environment.

Whenever you interface with another person with the intent/desire to *influence*, you are entering into a *transaction* with them. Recall that in order for any transaction to be sustainable, both parties must profit. In order for your influencing efforts to 'stick', the person you are wanting to influence must feel that they are 'profiting'. As such, they will *want* to do [whatever it is] because there is 'something in it for them'. Every transaction has a beginning, a middle, and a conclusion. The PBM approach provides a simple three-step process that fulfills the requirements for a healthy win/win transaction.

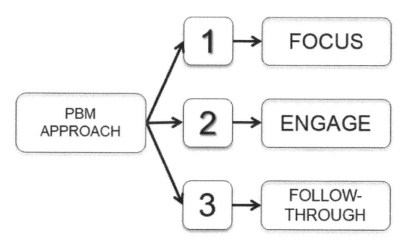

The Principle-Based Mentoring™ Approach

If you have experience with *observation & coaching*, your initial thought may be that this doesn't look any different than what you've already been doing. You will find, however, as you understand the intent and interaction associated with each of the three steps, that this is quite different from any approach you've likely used/experienced before.

FOCUS — Upon what should you be focusing when conducting any type of *observation* (whether formal or informal)? This is an area where many are completely missing the mark.

ENGAGE — Once you have insights that you want to share, you have a grand opportunity to interact with the individual(s) you observed. When done properly, your interactions build rapport, relationship, and mutual respect.

FOLLOW-THROUGH — Normally missed in the standard *observation & coaching* process, this is where you have an amazing opportunity to role model; to promote and demonstrate *ownership*, and to grow a *one team* mindset.

FOCUS (What to Look For)

Recall that 84 to 94 percent of human error can be directly attributed to process, programmatic, and organizational issues. What if, as an observer, rather than looking for workers 'doing things wrong', you were to take a holistic view of a given task, evolution, or process? What if you were to approach your observation, not as a 'supervisor' or 'manager', but rather as a fellow team member, with the same ultimate goals as the worker(s) you are observing?

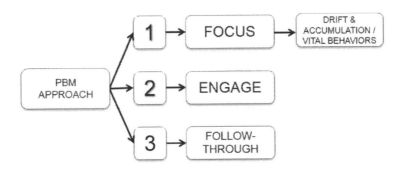

The PBM Process (Step One): FOCUS

Rather than using a prescribed checklist (because this is what the database requires). Rather than checking a series of (-) or (+) 'ticky boxes' while looking for 'evidence' that someone is (for example) actively 'self-checking'. Rather than simply 'going through the motions' and completing your 'required number' by the end of the month. What if you were to truly and honestly engage your brain? And in doing so, what if you 'judge' everything you see against a consistently simple context- your *Core Principles*? Do you think any of this might give you a slightly different perspective? If you've never done this before, trust me, it's like arising from Lasik surgery, able to see clearly without the aid of glasses or contacts, for the first time in your life. You'll recognize that you and the worker(s) have the same goal: the safest, most efficient, most reliable, and highest quality completion of [whatever it is].

People Doing Stuff Right

Yes, I know, 'people doing stuff right' is not 'grammatically correct'. And if this bothered you, let this serve as an example of how most of us are 'biased' to pick out the negatives. We can read a well-written 10,000 word manuscript, and what tends to stick out is the horribly bad grammar used at the beginning of section three, and the back-to-back typos on page 27. It doesn't seem to matter that the remainder of the text is brilliant. This is how we've been conditioned. And this conditioning (to look for the negatives) tends to be especially strong when we're in a 'boss' or 'oversight' position, and we're observing work in progress.

Every time I fly, I marvel at how this magnificent piece of machinery has just carried me hundreds (or thousands) of miles, perhaps across the country or to the other side of the world. All I had to do was sit there, read my Kindle, watch a movie, or...sleep. The tens of thousands of mechanical, structural, and electronic components, all of which were designed, manufactured, assembled, and maintained by [people], functioned perfectly. The pilots and navigation systems guide us safely to our destination. The flight attendants take care of our every need.

As we safely land at our destination and the pilot pulls the aircraft up to the gate, it is carefully guided into place by the 'baton dudes'. Simultaneously, in spite of the often crappy weather, a small army of dedicated workers hits the tarmac- offloading our piles of over-stuffed luggage, checking and servicing vital components, and refueling and refreshing the plane for its next trip. All of this magnificence has occurred and is occurring, and all the guy behind me can do, all the way down the Jetway, is continue to complain to his wife about how they ran out of the Asian Chicken Salad before the flight attendants got the cart to his row (two hours ago).

I suppose we can lay a little 'blame' on Human Nature for the overwhelming lens of negativity with which so much of humanity tends to perceive the world. It may be part of our lizard brain's mission to help ensure our survival. But I can only believe that a tiny slice of these tendencies can be classified as 'natural'. I believe the rest, by far the majority, is a result of *conditioning*. We've been conditioned by our parents, our teachers, our friends and colleagues, and certainly by the evening news (does anyone still watch that by the way?). And when it comes to being a 'boss', we have certainly been *conditioned* to look for what's *wrong*. I have even heard of some organizations that have configured their *observation & coaching* software to only allow for input of *negative* information. Amazing.

Your organization could not function without the vast majority of your team members working their tails off to do a 'good job'. How refreshing might it be, the next time you decide to do a bit of observing, to purposefully look for the things workers are doing *right*? What if you began to recognize how, in spite of the *roadblocks* and *minefield* of *workarounds* within your work environment, that the majority of tasks and jobs are completed safely and on schedule? The reality is, unless you're in an extreme state of dysfunction, the folks in your organization are already doing a darn good job. Your plant, facility, organization simply could not function otherwise. Why not start recognizing the positives? Remember- what gets recognized gets repeated.

The proper mindset with which to approach any observation is to actively look for the positives, while remaining neutral (unbiased) in your expectations. In other words, make an overt effort (especially as you transition from the 'old' way of doing things) to recognize all of the good things people are doing.

When we put Leadership Team members through our Group Mentor-the-Mentor process (following their completion of training on Principle-Based Mentoring™), their assignment for the first week is to conduct observations and look for nothing but positives. It's amazing how this begins to turn things around. This being said, in the grand scheme of things, being neutral in your 'expectations' leaves your eyes wide open and unbiased. 'Expecting' to find the 'good' can bias you toward the proverbial 'rose colored glasses', blinding you to symptoms of *drift* or sub-standard behaviors. 'Expecting' to find the 'bad' leads you directly down the negative pathway we were discussing earlier, a direction that can ultimately do more harm than good.

As much as possible, you want to come from a 'neutral' place (no expectations), making note of everything you observe. When you do, you will generally find *far more* 'good' than 'bad'. However- whenever symptoms of *drift* or sub-standard behaviors are noted, you must ensure they are addressed. You must remember that what you allow, you teach. Should you notice any substandard performance, and allow it to pass by unaddressed, you are essentially teaching the individual(s) involved that such behaviors are okay. This is what allows personal *drift* to grow into organizational *drift*.

Drift & Accumulation

We have already spent quite a bit of time discussing *drift* and *accumulation*- *drift* in work standards and perception of risk, and the *accumulation* of *landmines* and *roadblocks*. Observing work in progress is your best opportunity to identify, and ultimately address these negative internal forces.

As you observe, specifically watch for departure from "4.0" work practices and the currently prescribed way of doing things. Remember, when you notice deviations, these must be addressed during your subsequent engagement with the worker(s). I can imagine that you might be thinking, "Okay, he said to look for positives, but he keeps talking about 'not letting anything slip by'. How is this *really* any different than what we've been doing?" Stand by. When we get to the section on *how* to engage workers following your observations, you will be given a 'recipe' (the Core Four™ process) for ensuring that everything you observed is addressed (in a manner that is almost 'magical').

Properly addressing the *accumulation* of *landmines* and *roadblocks* provides you with a grand opportunity to build relationships and promote the *one team* approach. Think about it. As a 'boss', which you likely are if you're doing *observations*, your goal should always be the safest, most efficient, highest quality, and most timely completion of [whatever it is]. What are the goals of the folks actually doing the work? First, they do not want themselves or their co-workers to get hurt. Second, they want to do a 'good job'. This means that they are *motivated* to complete their work in a quality manner, by the most efficient means possible. <u>Your goals are the same</u>!

When do *landmines* and *roadblocks* tend to rise to the surface? During the course of performing tasks / doing the work. If you have the same goal as those doing the work, and a *landmine* or *roadblock* happens to rear its ugly head during the course of one of your *observations*, what do you think you should do? First, you make sure it's identified. Second, you do whatever you can to help the workers involved dig that sucker up and get rid of it! I'll cover more about *how* to do this when we talk through the next two steps of the PBM process (ENGAGE and FOLLOW-THROUGH). At this point, simply consider what such an approach on your part will do to (1) demonstrate desired behaviors, (2) enhance your relationship with the folks you're observing (you're helping *them* remove one of *our* challenges or workarounds), and (3) promote a sense of *ownership* and the *one team* approach.

"Common Ground"

In high risk environments there are areas that you should always consider whenever conducting *observations*. We refer to these collectively as *common ground*. Examples include:

- Use of Personal Protective Equipment (PPE)
- Use of Error Elimination Tools™
- Industrial and process safety procedures and protocols
- Security protocols
- Fire protection
- Housekeeping
- Adherence to written instructions
- Rigging and Lifting

In your particular industry, you may have a few you want to add to this list. Several of the elements listed directly relate to the *drift in work standards* we discussed previously. Before we leave this topic, there are two aspects of *common ground* I want to touch upon.

When doing *observations,* you want to let workers know that they're being observed. You certainly don't want to 'hide' or be perceived as a 'spy'. This being said, you want to be as unobtrusive as possible. Stay out of the way. Do not create distractions or interruptions- with one exception. If you happen to observe unsafe conditions or behaviors, you must intervene- immediately. Err on the side of caution if necessary. When workers understand that you are truly concerned about their safety, they'll actually come to appreciate your efforts.

Another area I want to specifically touch on is- *housekeeping.* Housekeeping says a *lot* about the *culture* of an organization. When general areas and work areas are kept clean and neat, this indicates a sense of caring and ownership on behalf of those involved. If your organization has already crossed this hurdle (as many have), and your housekeeping is in great shape, wonderful. If not, begin to bring the issues up during your engagement and follow-through steps.

Paying attention to (and actively promoting) good *housekeeping* offers a grand opportunity to role model the behaviors you want to see in others. When you see good *housekeeping* practices, note them, recognize them. In addition, think about the influence of (for example) picking up a piece of trash you see on the floor, and disposing of it. Others are watching your behaviors. They want to do a 'good job'. When they see you, a 'boss', doing such things, they will follow in kind. After all- you're *one team.* You have the same goal. Our PPI Master Mentors have many stories about how proactively doing such 'little things' during their in-field observations has had substantial positive influence on the attitudes and behaviors of workers.

Vital Behaviors

As we wrap up the first part of the three-part PBM approach, we want to get to the specific behaviors that you should be looking for (and role modeling) during your *observations*. Please pay attention here, because what we're about to discuss is your simple yet direct path to ongoing alignment and ever-improving (CANI) performance.

We discussed the concept of *vital behaviors* in Chapter Six. Now we're going to identify the specific *vital behaviors* associated with each of the elements of the HU Factor®.

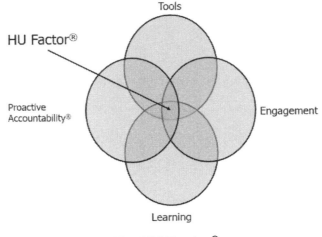

The HU Factor®

As you should recall, the four elements of the HU Factor® create your 'system' for achieving and sustaining next-level performance. When these elements are combined in the right proportions under the right conditions, 'magic' happens. If you are unclear about what the specific elements are or how they fit together, please go back and review the section entitled, *The System*, in Chapter Three.

After years of helping people understand each of the four elements of the HU Factor®, we decided to take this concept to the 'next-level ourselves. "Wouldn't it be great," we thought, "If we could isolate key (observable) *behaviors* for each of the elements?" So with the input of our team members, especially Roger Knisely and Lee Lane, we constructed a simple set of truly proactive next-level behaviors, three for each element of the HU Factor®.

The HU Factor® defines your 'system' for achieving and sustaining next-level performance. Since these represent the 'ideal' behaviors associated with each of its elements, they become your set of next-level *Vital Behaviors*. These are the behaviors you should be role modeling, recognizing, and promoting during the three steps of the PBM process. As you should recognize when you see the following list, these *Vital Behaviors* not only offer your best opportunity for natural and organic performance improvement, they also provide your very best defense against *drift*, *accumulation*, and *organizational entropy*.

Proactive Accountability® Vital Behaviors

- Work safely with ownership and purpose (recognize and correct personal *drift*)
- Focus on doing the 'right things' in the 'right way'
- Identify and remove *landmines* and *roadblocks* (CANI)

Tools Vital Behaviors

- Fully engage with task and procedure
- Proactively consider and use appropriate Error Elimination Tools™
- Challenge assumptions, inconsistencies, or lack of clarity

Engagement Vital Behaviors

- Be AWARE- Focus on actions and surroundings
- Support and encourage others
- Ask questions / get answers

- Be curious and ask questions
- Document *learning* using appropriate methods
- Share lessons learned; look for mentoring opportunities

ENGAGE

When you engage another human being with an intent to *influence*, this constitutes a *transaction*. Remember that in order for any *transaction* to be sustainable, both parties involved must profit. Everything you do must be approached from a WIN/WIN perspective. Also remember that you cannot 'motivate' another person to do anything. You can force them, manipulate them, or inspire them. The only sustainable pathways of true *influence* are through the upper levels of Maslow's Hierarchy (appealing to their self-esteem and self-actualization).

What you are directly seeking through Principle-Based Mentoring™ is behavioral transformation that is aligned with your *Core Principles* of the organization. That is the desired outcome. We also know that in order for such behaviors to be pervasive and sustainable, in other words, behaviors that will exist even '*at 3:00AM when no one else is watching*', they must come from a place of personal *desire*, not through force or manipulation.

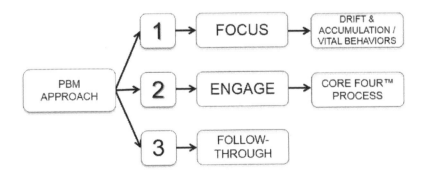

The PBM Process (Step Two): ENGAGE

We have defined 'what to look for' in the previous section. Let's now move on to *how* to engage others in a manner that promotes 'right' behaviors (those aligned with your *Core Principles*), exhibited for the 'right reason' (because the individuals involved *want* to do so).

Behavior Change Defined

As I've already mentioned, everything about this overall approach to next-level human performance flies in the face of, "It's *hard* and it takes a *long* time." Consider the classic approach of the *observation & coaching* database, even the peer observations typically associated with 'Behavior-Based Safety': information accumulates, trends are evaluated, and then some type of 'global' action is taken to 'stem the negative tide'. This can take months, and often ends up with a stigma of 'programmitis', becoming 'just another thing that 'management is making us do'. Why not effect positive change and reinforcement of *Core Principles* at the point of engagement? Why not do this immediately following any type of observation? The impacts of doing so are profound. And as I've mentioned previously (at least a couple of times)- no database is required. We have found the PBM approach to be so rapid and so impactful, that we've crafted the following definition of Behavior Change: *What can be done today that we can see working today?*

Before we get into the actual *engagement* process, I want to touch on the three basic types (or methods) of *influence* typically employed in the workplace. Since the metaphor of 'wearing different hats' is common relative to different roles and responsibilities, this is the terminology I'll be using.

The Three Hats

The use of each of these 'hats' is situational. There are times when each is appropriate and necessary. Generically speaking, however, I like to think of the *boss* hat as the 'old school' method of 'command and control'. The *coach* hat is the typical present-day method used by most in *observation & coaching* (where the primary focus is upon looking for and correcting negatives). The *mentor* hat, on the other hand, is the future. This is the WIN/WIN transaction approach to *inspire* (rather than coerce or manipulate). This is your ticket for engaging and aligning sustainable next-level performance.

Boss

The *boss* hat is worn by the "person in charge". Its impact is represented by a high level of *command and control*, where the predominant form of communication is *telling*- directive communication from 'superior' to 'subordinate'.

On the surface, you would think that this hat would have the greatest level of influence. However, while *telling* can result in immediate response / behavior change, when the 'subordinate' feels coerced or does not [truly] agree with the 'boss', such changes in behavior are likely to last only while the boss 'is around'. In organizations with a high focus on *compliance*, this tends to be a hat frequently worn. It's necessary to ensure workers 'follow the rules'.

Far from promoting *one team*, the approach of, "Do this because I said so, because I'm the boss!" tends to promote 'us-vs-them' division and separation. It is the classic 'old paradigm' of *managing people like things*. This approach places primary focus upon the rules, not upon the people. Next-level performance is neither achievable nor sustainable when this is the predominant method of attempting to influence.

Coach

Many organizations have come to recognize that strictly wearing the *boss* hat does not generate or sustain desired levels of performance (especially when the 'boss' is not present to monitor worker behaviors). Therefore, the *coach* hat has become a popular method for attempting to proactively promote desired behaviors.

The *coach* hat is often worn by a manager or supervisor in the process of complying with the requirements of an *Observation & Coaching* Program. The definition of *coach* is: one who instructs or trains[8]. The primary forms of communication associated with this method of influence tend to be *telling* and *correcting*.

Because of its contemporary popularity, the *coach* hat represents the most common current method for directly engaging individuals in behavioral performance improvement. When used properly, this method of influence can be far superior to wearing the *boss* hat. However, as we've already discussed, the majority of *coaching* currently in play within most organizations typically emphasizes:

- looking for "less than 'excellent' behaviors"
- documenting those behaviors
- providing corrective feedback to the individual(s) being *coached*

Ultimately, because of the predominance of *telling* and *correcting*, this approach also tends to have the limited impact upon sustainable behavior change.

Mentor

I've previously mentioned (several times) that the only way to achieve long-term sustainable performance improvement is by shifting from a focus on *compliance* to a culture of *desire*. At the engagement level, this requires a transformation from 'telling' and 'correcting' to that of, "...*opening a door and inviting people to step through it.*" I hope you get this. This is how you create win/win transactions. This is how you effect sustainable change.

Let us now consider the 'next-level' method of influence- the *mentor* hat. A *mentor* is: a trusted counselor or guide[9]. She uses the predominant communications of *asking* and *sharing*. A dialogue involving *asking* and *sharing* is perceived entirely differently by the lizard brain. There is no perceived 'threat' or 'loss of sense of control'. Consequently, defenses are lowered. The doorway to *influence* is opened. You have moved completely away from 'enforcing compliance', and toward recognizing and promoting *desire* to do the 'right' things.

The predominant focus within the Principle-Based Mentoring™ approach is to catch people doing things 'right', primarily recognizing them for doing so. This applies at every level of an individual's ability. Think about when one of your children was just learning to walk. They take their first step or two, and...fall on their fanny. Did you say, "Oh, only two steps. You can do w-a-y better than that! Get up and do it again!" Not likely. (If you did, I sure as heck wouldn't have wanted to be your kid!) I'm certain it was more like, "That was great! You are such big boy!" Encouragement. Recognition. Remember- what gets recognized gets repeated. Very likely, your child got up [immediately] and tried it again. Within a few days, they've gone from walking to running (and you're having to chase them around the house). Do you get the point?

As far as positive recognition is concerned, it is every bit as much appreciated by adults in the workplace; however, it must be delivered appropriately, especially during a 'one on one' interaction following *observation*. The difference lies in the *experiences* workers have had in the past, much of which has likely resulted in negative conditioning. If you simply charge in with nothing but "Rah Rah" praise and approbation (there's a 45-cent word for you), a typical worker is likely to figure you're just 'blowing smoke'. Even though it might be a refreshing change from the negative feedback they typically receive, they'll not likely take it very seriously. It will therefore have little (if any) lasting influence on future behaviors.

As previously mentioned, the communication approach used by the *mentor* is that of *asking* and *sharing*. Rather than simply 'telling' an individual what she did well, as a *mentor* you first share a few of your favorite things you observed. You then *ask* the worker to identify what else she did well. Rather than 'telling' her noted areas where she can improve, you first ask, "What could have gone better?" This gives the worker the opportunity to self-identify any behaviors during task/job performance where she feels she could have done better. It also allows her to point out *landmines* and *roadblocks* she encountered along the way. If she is apparently unaware of one or more areas needing improvement, you then ask probing questions to draw the individual toward awareness and proactive conclusions.

Approaching engagement as a *mentor* (1) generates an overall positive interaction, (2) fosters open and honest communication, and (3) creates a platform for sustainable influence. The influence is sustainable because first, relative to recognition of the positives, *what gets recognized gets repeated*, and second, because insights relative to doing things better evolved from within, rather than the person feeling directed, corrected, or controlled. This is true *influence*. This is true *leadership*.

A Final Note...

In the Principle-Based Mentoring™ approach, the *mentor* hat should be worn *almost* all of the time. Because of conditioning, and perhaps even some of your prior training ('old' and 'current' paradigms regarding *observation & coaching*), it will be easy (and feel natural) to drop the *mentor* hat and don either the *coach* hat or the *boss* hat during the *engagement* process. Until you get used to the 'next-level way' of doing things, this will be especially tempting when addressing areas for improvement. Be cautious of this. This being said, 'changing hats' may become necessary if:

- You observe that a worker is about to do something that is unsafe
- After exhausting your probing questions, the individual remains unaware of *key* (substantially important) risks, *drift*, or *landmines*
- The worker is totally unresponsive or becomes confrontational

Interaction- the Core Four™ Method

The Principle-Based Mentoring™ method of engagement following observation uses a set of four *Share/Ask* interactions. The sequence is specifically designed to provide positive recognition of desired behaviors, while directly promoting a 'one team' approach to constant and never-ending improvement (CANI). Within this method, you will find that by far the majority of 'areas for improvement' are brought forward by the individual(s) being observed. This is much more powerful, and has a much more 'stickable' impact than when people are simply being told 'what they did wrong'. At PPI, we use a simple 'recipe' called the *Core Four™*. Using this 'recipe' provides a consistent, simple, and extremely effective method for interaction. The sequence of interaction between the *mentor* and the *mentee* looks like this:

1	SHARE-	Top Three Positives
	ASK-	What else did YOU do well?

2	SHARE-	Any additional positives
	ASK-	WHAT could have gone better?

3	SHARE-	Any additional KEY drift, risks, or landmines
	ASK-	How can WE proactively resolve these?

4	SHARE-	Offer personal proactive leadership insights
	ASK-	How else can I HELP you?

The Core Four™ Share/Ask Sequence

FOLLOW-THROUGH

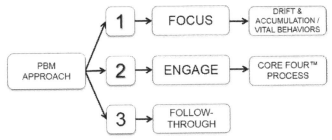

The PBM Process (Step Three): FOLLOW-THROUGH

Unfortunately, this is typically the most neglected aspect of many existing *observation & coaching* 'programs'. It is also a huge missed opportunity. Think about this. Let's say you're the Maintenance Manager. You're doing an observation of an Operator performing a task to shut down and drain a system. During your engagement/mentoring following your observation, the Operator makes you aware of a legitimate *landmine* is present within the evolution she just completed. It's a potential safety hazard caused by confusing wording in Step 16 of the procedure. Simple to fix, right?

Well…the procedure has 'been this way' for six years. It's a job that is done once per quarter, which means that, to this point, workers have had to 'work around' this step 24 times. The worker you observed is newly qualified. This is the second time she's completed this particular task. During your Core Four™ interaction sequence, she was very vocal about Step 16. She pointed out that if she had interpreted it 'this way', rather than 'that way', she could have potentially been seriously injured. She let you know that the last time she did this task, she discussed the Step 16 problem with her supervisor, and was told, "Yeah, we've been trying to get that fixed for years." What do you do?

In the standard world of 'busyness' and reliance upon software, you might include this in the comments section of your database entry. You may recommend that the Operator write a Condition Report on the issue (and let *that* system/database take care of the issue). But wait a minute. Step 16 is a true *landmine*, a legitimate potential safety hazard. How can, "Yeah, we've been trying to get that fixed for years," possibly be an acceptable answer? In an organization that is honestly seeking to achieve and sustain next-level performance- it *can't*. So upon conclusion of your Core Four™ interaction sequence, you tell the Operator to get a 'clean' copy of the procedure, and to mark it up with her recommended corrections to Step 16 (as well as for any other *landmines* she's aware of in that particular procedure). Because you know that it 'takes forever' to get anything through your [current] procedure revision process, you ask her to bring it by your office.

While you're waiting for the marked up procedure, you stop by and talk with her supervisor about the issue. "This is only one of *many* such issues we have to deal with," you're told, "we can't seem to get any procedures fixed." This is clearly a larger issue, but let's confine our conversation to the 'Step 16' issue.

The next morning, the marked up procedure is sitting on your desk when you get to your office. Thumbing through the markup, it's obvious that the Operator put a lot of thought and work into it. You call her and thank her for her diligence. Using the clout that you have as a Department Head, you then talk directly with the Document Control supervisor and the Operations Manager, and get this through the [nearly broken] procedure revision process in short order. Once the new procedure is approved and 'on the shelf', you call the Operator and let her know, again thanking her for her efforts to make things safer and better.

Who wins in this approach? The Operator, the Operations Department, the Organization, and...you. How do you think this has impacted your relationship with that Operator? How do you think this has influenced her perceptions of (1) the *Observation & Mentoring* process, (2) the Maintenance Department (since you're its manager), or (3) a *one team* approach to the operation of the facility? How do you think her mindset has been affected regarding bringing issues, *landmines*, and *roadblocks* to the surface in the future? How do you think this has made her feel about herself and her role in the organization? How about you? It feels pretty good to 'make things better', doesn't it? Finally, who wins in this scenario? EVERYONE.

I cannot stress strongly enough what a leveraged opportunity you have whenever you follow-through to help strengthen defenses, dig up *landmines*, and remove *roadblocks*. Of course, you might be thinking, "I sure as heck don't have time to do 'stuff' like that!" Really. How many of your current 'hours in the day' are spent dealing with the aftermath of *not* taking care of such issues? It's not a matter of time. It never is. It's a matter of priorities. Do you *truly* want to get better...or not?

Achieving Zero Events

We have already discussed all of the elements necessary to drive the incidence of human error to its lowest possible levels of frequency and severity, and to absolutely minimize the potential for an *event* to ever again occur at your facility / within your organization. The interactions afforded through Principle-Based Mentoring™ bring all of these elements together as one team, with common purpose, driven by a solid set of *Core Principles*.

If you're an engineer or a hard core Six Sigma analyst (or both), you'll love this next part, because I am going to introduce you to the *Zero Events Formula*. If you're not into math, you're in luck, because there's no actual math involved. In fact, as you will see, the formula is not even an equation, it is simply a 'potentiality statement'. This being said, I have seen looks of 'horror' blank the faces of class participants when we first reveal this formula. So consider this before I show it to you. I am not including this to give you something else to remember or regurgitate. The whole point is to show how the behaviors and ongoing activities that we've been discussing fit together, especially relative to the interactions and follow-through associated with Principle-Based Mentoring™.

Here's the formula:

$$(\Delta R + \Delta W) - (B_{Re} + B_{Md}) \sim E$$

Zero Events Formula

Where:

$\Delta R =$ the difference between perceived and actual risk

$\Delta W =$ the difference between '4.0' expectations and 'how it's actually done around here'

$B_{Re} =$ Behaviors directly related to reducing errors

$B_{Md} =$ Behaviors directly related to managing defenses

$E =$ Event

When engaging others using the PBM approach, every element of the Zero Events Formula is addressed in a manner that aligns behaviors with your *Core Principles*. As previously mentioned, this serves to naturally and organically improve safety, efficiency, and reliability. The elements directly address the forces of *drift*, *accumulation*, and *organizational entropy*, which would otherwise drag you down.

First, notice that this is a 'potentiality statement', *not* an equation. The entire point is to demonstrate how the associated elements and behaviors make the occurrence of an *event* more (or less likely). So here's where the [very minimal] math comes into play:

- If ΔR goes up (in other words, the perception of risk further departs from the actual risk), the potential for an *event* to occur- INCREASES

- If ΔW goes up (in other words, 'how work is actually done around here' gets further and further from '4.0' expectations), the potential for an *event* to occur- INCREASES

- When B_{Re} increases (in other words, workers begin using the Error Elimination Tools™, causing diligence, focus, and mental engagement to rise), the potential for an *event* to occur- DECREASES

- When B_{Md} (in other words, *roadblocks* are being removed, *landmines* are being dug up, and defenses are being bolstered), the potential for an *event* to occur- DECREASES

Here are some insights into how these elements are directly addressed within the Principle-Based Mentoring ™ approach:

ΔR	This is the difference between the actual risk and the perception of risk. As *drift* occurs in this space, it leads to *complacency*. A *mentor* will recognize diligent engagement and Questioning Attitude (what gets recognized gets repeated). He will ask questions to draw out insights that were either missed or not thought all the way through.
ΔW	Within our environment where the general overall perception is, "more is better," and "faster is better," workers tasked to perform naturally look for ways to get jobs completed more quickly. This can lead to shortcuts and marginalization of safety and procedural precautionary measures. A *mentor* will recognize behaviors that refuse to deviate from guidance and that meet/exceed expectations, while assisting as necessary to help eliminate *landmines* and *roadblocks*, and make procedures/processes safer and more efficient.
B_{Re}	Behaviors directly involved with Reducing Errors include such things as uncompromising use of the Error Elimination Tools™. *Mentors* will (1) Role model use of the Tools at all times, (2) recognize others' use of the Tools, and (3) ask questions to draw out where more diligent use of the Tools may be / might have been appropriate.
B_{Md}	Behaviors at Managing Defenses involve proactively identifying and removing *landmines* and *roadblocks*. The *mentor* will (1) recognize all *landmines* and *roadblocks* identified, (2) recognize and encourage efforts to eliminate *landmines* and *roadblocks*, (3) recognize and encourage efforts to bolster *defenses*, and (4) provide any assistance that is necessary/appropriate to help the worker be successful in his/her removal efforts.

The Zero Events Formula and Principle-Based Mentoring™

In conclusion

As I previously indicated, the concept of *observation* and *"coaching"* is rising onto the radar in many industries. Please do not make the mistakes so many others have made in the past. You do not need to learn from your own missteps in this area, nor do you need to 'recreate the wheel'. The Principle-Based Mentoring™ approach works. Once your Leadership Team members are properly trained, the approach is fast, simple, and easy to implement. There is no database required, and man-o-man is it effective. If you'd like more information on how to get started, go here: http://ppiweb.com/human-performance-academy/pbm/

Key Insights from Chapter Nine

1. You must identify, develop, and communicate your *Core Principles*. It is to these that everything must *align*.

2. Running your organization based upon *Principles* allow people with different values to work together effectively.

3. The 'linchpin' to your success is the Frontline Supervisor (FLS). It is the FLS who has (by far) the greatest impact on how work actually gets done on a

day-to-day basis. The influence of the FLS is the single largest contributing factor to the potential for an accident/event to occur.

4. Your organization consists of 'A Players', 'B Players', and 'C Players'. 'B Players' and 'C Players" can be found in management ranks every bit as much as on the 'frontline'. If you are to achieve and sustain next-level performance, you must get rid of your 'C Players'.

5. The true value in any effort to *observe* and *coach* is in the interaction between the observer and the observed. It is NOT in data, metrics, or trends.

6. Requiring a minimum number of observations per unit time (e.g., per month) is stupid. Set your requirements based upon 'time in the field / on the floor', NOT upon number of observations.

7. There are three 'forces' that will drag performance down and increase the potential for accidents/events to occur (unless directly and overtly counteracted): *drift, accumulation, and organizational entropy*

8. The transaction of *observation* and subsequent *engagement* has three distinct steps: FOCUS, ENGAGE, and FOLLOW-THROUGH

9. There are three *vital behaviors* for each of the elements of the HU Factor®. Role modeling, recognizing, and promoting these behaviors will naturally and organically help you achieve and sustain next-level performance.

10. There are three 'hats' of influence: the *boss* hat, the *coach* hat, and the *mentor* hat. In next-level organizations, the *mentor* hat is worn most of the time.

11. The Zero Events Formula defines the relationships between *drift* and *accumulation*, and the behaviors associated with reducing human error and managing defenses, and how these fit together to either increase or decrease the potential for an *event* to occur.

What can you do with what you just learned?

A. Recognize that you do NOT need an expensive database in order to implement and maintain a robust and extremely impactful *Observation & Mentoring* process. What's needed is proper insight on behalf of your observers, and a simple consistent method for engagement and interaction.

B. If you already have an *Observation & Coaching* program that is software/database oriented, conduct a sober and thorough assessment of your return on investment. If you do, you'll likely decide to reorient your focus. I recommend eliminating the database.

C. Get rid of your 'C Players'. This is NOT a 'witch hunt'. The best way to get rid of a 'C Player' is to help them transform into either an 'A Player' or a "B Player". Remember that most workers you might be considering as 'C Players' (based primarily on their [negative] attitudes) are likely not actually 'C Players'. They are likely highly intelligent / highly frustrated workers (who can become tremendous assets if you help them get out of *Suckers' Swamp*).

D. For 'C Players' that absolutely will not transform, you must have the courage to 'help them out the gate'. Your performance improvement efforts will be stifled if you don't. In addition, you're doing a tremendous disservice to the other ~98% of your team members when you allow 'C Players' to remain.

E. Look for (and recognize) people doing things right.

F. Adopt the Core Four™ method of interaction following your observations.

G. Remember to FOLLOW-THROUGH.

H. Take the time to study and fully understand the meaning and relationships within the Zero Events Formula

[1] Merriam Webster's Collegiate Dictionary, Eleventh Edition

[2] Merriam Webster's Collegiate Dictionary, Eleventh Edition

[3] *Linchpin: Are You Indispensable?*; Seth Godin; Penguin Group; 2010

[4] *Beyond Observation and Feedback: Integrating Behavioral Safety Principles into Other Safety Management Systems*; Sherry R. Perdue; 2001

[5] *A cross-validation of a structural equation model of accidents: organizational and psychological variables as predictors of work safety*; Work and Stress; 1999; Vol. 13, No. 1, pgs 49-58

[6] *Top Grading: The Proven Hiring and Promoting Method that Turbocharges Company Performance*; Bradford D. Smart, Ph.D.; The Penguin Group; Third Edition; 2012

[7] *Results That Last: Hardwiring Behaviors That Will Take Your Company to the Top*; Quint Studer; John Wiley & Sons; Studer Group, LLC; 2008

[8] Merriam Webster's Collegiate Dictionary, Eleventh Edition

[9] Merriam Webster's Collegiate Dictionary, Eleventh Edition

Chapter Ten: Your Blueprint for Next-Level Performance

"All progress begins by telling the truth."
-Dan Sullivan

In April of 2012, I had the opportunity to participate as a presenter in the first-ever North American Electric Reliability Corporation (NERC) conference on human performance. NERC is the international regulatory authority whose mission is to assure the reliability of the bulk power system in North America.

When the 'regulator' begins to focus attention in a specific area, in this case, human performance, it tends to get the attention of senior leaders and decision-makers. As such, I saw this as a grand opportunity to help the industry develop a more holistic approach to *human performance* than the rote implementation of prescriptive rules and requirements promoted, taught, and practiced by many.

NERC invited a substantial cast of presenters, each having expertise in an area associated with human performance. The intent was to educate participants in *how* to improve *human performance* within their organizations. The audience was filled with company representatives anxious to grasp information, take home lessons learned, and begin implementation. What I discovered during my evening conversations with those who had come to learn, conversations typically involving an adult beverage or two, was that most were overwhelmed with content. They were now more confused about *what* to do and *how* to do it than they were before they arrived. As one participant put it, "I've been doing my best to 'drink from the fire hydrant'. What am I actually supposed to *do* with all of this when I go back to work?"

There was clearly a need to 'put the pieces together'- a simple roadmap of *what* to do to achieve and sustain next-level human performance. Because of this, I put together the *HU Blueprint™*, a simple 'map' of the basic steps that have been tremendously successful in transforming human performance (and ultimately organizational culture) in a sane, simple, and sustainable manner.

In the previous chapters of this book, I've given you detailed information on the context and content of each of these 'steps'. It's now time to put the pieces together. While there is no 'one size fits all' recipe, there are vital elements involved and, from our experience, a most effective approach to their sequencing. By providing you with a 'blueprint', a sequence of *flow* of these vital elements and their intended outcomes, my intent is to help you conceive and develop a plan of action- your own fast, simple, and easy plan for achieving and sustaining next-level performance.

To Train or not to Train

> *"If you need a thing and don't buy it, then you will ultimately find that you have paid for it and don't have it."* -Henry Ford

Training is an investment. It incurs costs in the short term. The accrued benefits are typically long term. As such, many organizations are horrendously short-sighted when it comes to training frontline workers. They simply cannot justify the 'cost'. Further, when economic cycles or industry shifts cause a bit of a 'pinch' to the bottom line, rather than figuring out how to add more value, most organizations look for where they can lower 'costs'. Training (and travel for training) is typically one of the first things cut from the budget.

Following a presentation with the senior leaders of one of the largest chemical manufacturing facilities in the world, the General Manager was amazed at our proposal to provide "two full days" in the classroom for all workers. "We have provided such training many times to our leadership team," he said. "But for frontline workers, it's typically an hour here or an hour there." Fortunately, this GM is what I call an enlightened leader and is actively seeking new paradigms and a next-level approach. Interestingly, he had never before considered providing such a level of training to frontline workers.

The reality is, if you are going to transform your culture, you must help your workforce members expand their context. This can only be achieved through learning experiences designed to do so. And while it may not require a "full two days" in the classroom (remember- there is no 'one size fits all'), it will take time, and it will incur cost. The reality is, when it comes to safety, quality, and efficiency, you and your organization are 'paying' whether you realize it or not. One significant accident or event typically incurs costs far beyond the investment in training that would likely have prevented it. In addition, the benefits from an increased sense of worker ownership, lower turnover, and higher morale add substantially to the ROI for effective training of employees. Interestingly, the most successful organizations of modern times have figured this out. Organizations such as Southwest Airlines, UPS, The Container Store, Starbucks, and IDEO invest far more in employee training than most companies[1].

When putting your 'plan' together, you simply must provide proper 'training' to all members of the organization. This being said, recognize that 'training' alone will not provide the desired outcome. If you want organization members to honestly think different and do different, you must provide training that is not just 'training', but rather, a learning experience. Such experiences must expand context, reach inside and 'grab' people, and get them to want to do the right thing. While this may sound complex, I've given you all of the insight you need on what to do. All that is now needed is skilled facilitation, and the willingness to commit worker time to lead them through the process. And while this will probably sound like a shameless 'plug', we teach people precisely how to do this in our PPC Certification Course. You can find the details here: http://ppiweb.com/human-performance-academy/ppc-2/

Finally, it is also important for you to realize that while proper learning experiences are essential, they are only part of the implementation process. These should be coincident with and reinforced by the processes and systems outlined in the Blueprint.

Putting it All Together

As we previously discussed, your goal should be for your organization to achieve *Viral Accountability*®. Doing so will transform your entire organization. As you should recall, the elements of Viral Accountability® include Proactive Accountability®, Peer Leadership, and Viral Change. The following sections show you precisely *what* to do, and in *what order*, to maximize your effectiveness and minimize your cost in pursuit of next-level performance.

The "System" Revisited

At the end of Chapter Three, I described the 'system' for achieving and sustaining next-level human performance- the HU Factor®. Since the HU Factor® identifies the four major areas that must be addressed, I thought it appropriate to do a brief recap before we dive into the step-by-step.

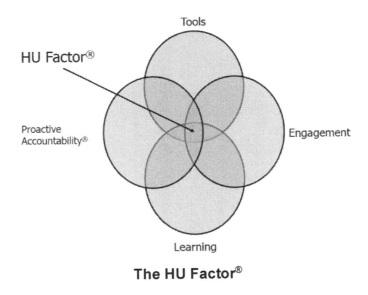

The HU Factor®

As I hope you remember, the HU Factor® has four major elements: Proactive Accountability®, Tools, Engagement, and Learning. When put together in the right proportions under the right conditions, the resulting organizational performance can be magnificent. The region where these four elements intersect is the HU Factor®. This is where maximum potential, power, and synergy for next-level performance manifest.

When you put 'feet' to this four-element system through Viral Accountability®, you will achieve a 'magical upward spiral' of sustainable performance improvement. Keep these elements in mind as we now work through the Human Performance Blueprint.

The Human Performance Blueprint

> **NOTE:** Due to the limitations on graphic size, the Human Performance Blueprint diagrams provided in this book are modified and simplified. You may access and download (free of charge) colored detailed versions of the Blueprint by going here: http://www.6hoursafetyculture.com/resources/hpbp/
>
> I highly recommend that you download the blueprints and study them coincident with reading this chapter. Doing so will deepen your understanding and will help you design the best possible implementation plan for your organization.

The Blueprint is laid out in three separate diagrams:

- A Level I overview that illustrates the flow from *Pre-implementation*, to *Learning*, to *Processes & Systems*

- A Level II *Learning* diagram that illustrates the Vital Elements to be included in your *Leadership* and '*Everyone*'

Learning Experiences (including specifically what to *do,* as well as your desired *outcomes*)

- A Level II *Process/System* diagram detailing the Vital Elements for ongoing growth, sustainability, and measurement of your performance improvement (including specifically what to *do,* as well as your desired *outcomes*)

GET REAL (Pre-Implementation)

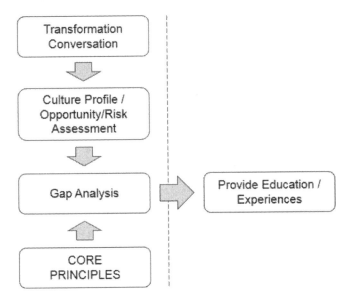

Human Performance Blueprint
Level I- Pre-implementation

Transformation Conversation

The first thing you must do, which is often overlooked, is to identify your *why. Why* are you doing this in the first place? In Chapter Two, I provided you with a process/worksheet to help you determine your true *why.* Referred to as the *Transformation Conversation,* it guides you through four simple questions that will provide proper context for your improvement efforts. If you have not yet watched the short video and downloaded your worksheet, do so now: http://ppiweb.com/future-performance-improvement/pursuing-excellence/

When answering the first question on the worksheet, it is important that you get to the feeling place. This may take a few layers of digging. Do not simply cite metrics or outcomes. Consider the behaviors and benefits underlying those outcomes. Keep digging until you feel passionate about what you have come up with. Your passion will be key to the success of your efforts.

<u>Culture Profile</u>

Hopefully you now understand that *if you don't manage your culture, your culture will manage you.* You should also now be aware that the majority of time human error occurs, whether the consequences impact safety, quality, and/or reliability, some 'thing' (or 'things') helped set the stage for the individual(s) involved to make the mistake (remember Precept #2?).

Things that set people up to make mistakes (*landmines*) are essentially products of your culture. Behaviors are greatly influenced by your culture. The way in which people communicate and interact are a direct result of...your culture.

Wouldn't it be great if there was an instrument/process that could evaluate the 'error likeliness' of the *culture* of your organization so that you might know what to focus upon? There is. PPI has developed the Practicing Perfection® Culture Profile to do exactly that. And again, this may sound like a 'plug', but honestly, it's the only instrument/process that I am aware of that does this. Far beyond a 'satisfaction' survey or an 'employee engagement survey', this process identifies the error-likeliness of your organization in five key areas:

- Systems and Structures
- Ownership
- Openness and Awareness
- Error-likely Environment
- Readiness/Willingness to Learn

Having the information provided by the *Culture Profile* enables you and your organization to strategically target specific areas during implementation of your efforts to improve performance.

For more information on the PPI Culture Profile process, go here: http://ppiweb.com/?p=48

TOROID™ Assessment

Another mechanism for better understanding 'where you are' is to conduct an assessment that looks at culture, structures, and processes from a human performance perspective. Rather than simply looking for 'areas for improvement', such an assessment should also identify organizational strengths, risks, and opportunities.

Again, PPI has devised the only such assessment process I am aware of. It is called the *TOROID™ Assessment*. *"TOROID"* is short for "Targeted Organizational Risk and Opportunity IDentification". It is designed to identify organizational strengths, risks, and opportunities specifically from the human performance perspective. It documents opportunities to improve performance and prevent human performance related events.

Of short duration and high intensity, the assessment provides a 'quick look' at everything from the behaviors of individuals to the processes and programs of the organization. It is driven by the fact that a significant percentage of human error events (84 to 94 percent), can be directly related to process, programmatic, and/or organizational issues.

By using expert investigators with decades of experience and a 'fresh set of eyes', the TOROID™ Assessment offers an insightful and constructive evaluation, resulting in recommendations that will directly mitigate negative consequences and operational events.

The TOROID™ Assessment is, by design, a broad look at many areas of organizational activity, and consequently does not reach deeply into causes or effectiveness. The intent is solution-focused, rather than delving into detail about "how things got that way".

If you would like more information about the TOROID™ process, go here: http://ppiweb.com/?p=6461

Core Principles

In Chapter Seven, I discussed how your *Core Principles* provide you with the opportunity to most effectively and efficiently steer your course from where you are to where you want to be. Knowing your Core Principles, and having them clearly defined, role modeled, and well communicated is essential.

An organization without a clearly defined set of Core Principles is like a ship without a rudder- left to be battered about by any challenge or conflict that arises. A clearly defined set of Core Principles, on the other hand, affords you the opportunity to point in a specific direction, and to stay your course, despite any shifting winds or squalls that may develop along the way.

If you need to, go back a re-read the section on Core Principles. Then, put forth the effort to define and refine yours until you truly understand your *core*. Your Core Principles will be an integral part of all of your efforts to achieve and sustain next-level performance.

Gap Analysis

Using your *Transformation Conversation*, you have now identified *why* you are taking these efforts, and should know culturally/behaviorally *where* you are headed (your 'next level'). Whether you use the PPI profile and assessment instruments indicated above, or other method(s), it is essential that you identify your current challenges and strengths relative to human performance. By analyzing the 'gap' between where you are and where you want to be, you can effectively focus your efforts to deliver the quickest most cost-effective results. Your *Core Principles* provide the underlying base for maintaining a steady course along the way.

Unless you are in a critical situation requiring some sort of triage to stem the tide of unacceptable performance, I implore you to take the time to do this *Pre-implementation* work *before* you take any further action. One of the reasons we're all so familiar with the concept of 'program of the day' is that organizations have tended to latch onto something that seems like a good idea without taking the time beforehand to figure out how it fits into the 'bigger picture'. Such efforts typically only then last until (1) they don't produce the desired results and are abandoned, and/or (2) something else comes along that looks/sounds better to someone with decision-making power.

LEARN

PPI has now been involved in helping organizations achieve and sustain next-level performance for over ten years. We have worked with tens of thousands of workers and leaders around the globe. In addition to the satisfaction of having helped our clients achieve amazing results, our clients and their employees have also been our 'laboratory'. Since the original 'experiment' at the Vermont Yankee nuclear generation facility, we have learned a great deal about what works (and what doesn't), as well as about what is essential (as compared to the 'nice-to-have') for achieving and sustaining next-level performance.

Our goal has always been simple- to provide maximum sustainable impact and maximum return on investment for our clients. My intent of writing this book has been to cut through the hype, to winnow the chaff, and to get straight to the 'meat' of what works relative to influencing and sustaining next-level behaviors. In today's arena of exponential change, there is no standing still- you're either learning, and growing…or you're dying. As such, we are continuing to learn every step of the way as we help to implement and monitor the success of our clients.

What we have learned to this point is that in order to achieve and sustain next-level performance, there are vital elements to your implementation plan that must not be missed nor minimized. In order to *do different*, you must begin by *thinking different*. Providing robust *learning experiences* for your team members that serve to achieve specific outcomes is essential. Following is a '10,000 foot' diagram and brief description of what you must include and achieve at the outset of your implementation plan. Again, for your detailed downloadable Blueprint, go here: http://www.6hoursafetyculture.com/resources/hpbp/

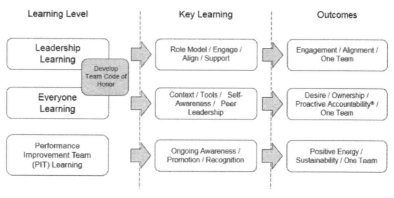

Human Performance Blueprint
Level II- Learning

The first thing to notice about the Blueprint is that "learning" is used in place of "training". This is done to distinguish your next-level approach from 'old school' training, where 'rules' tend to be put forward in lecture format and participants are expected to comply. To be effective, your investment of time and energy in *training* must provide *learning experiences* that generate *behavior change*. It must get beyond the cognitive filtering that takes place in the *lizard brain* and reach inside to *inspire* participants. Again, this has nothing to do with being 'touchy feely'. This is simply the science of influencing behaviors.

As you can see, the Learning Blueprint is sectioned into three distinct segments:

- *Learning Level* (who the training is for, and in the detailed Blueprint, the key areas/topics to be covered)
- *Key Learning* (the key insights to be gained by participants during the associated learning experience)
- *Outcomes* (the changes in perspectives and overall behaviors that will result when the learning experiences are properly conducted)

The *learning experiences* are conducted in three sequenced levels:

- *Leadership*- these are the first sessions to be conducted. Participants include all team members from the FLS (frontline supervisor) and above. Key influencers (such as Union Stewards) should be invited to attend.
- *Everyone*- to be conducted once the *Leadership* sessions are completed. All organization members should attend these sessions, including those who attended the *Leadership* sessions.
- *Performance Improvement Team (PIT)*- once the *Everyone* sessions are completed, those who have volunteered to help 'keep things alive' are provided with additional learning on how to sustain/promote next-level performance on an ongoing basis

Leadership Learning

This is the first level of learning that must take place. If true behavior change is to occur on the frontline, especially behavior change aligned with the Core Principles of the organization, defined leaders (FLS and above) must (1) know and internalize your Core Principles, (2) role model, support, and recognize desired behaviors, and (3) understand how to properly engage with workers in order to align behaviors with your Core Principles and promote the *one team* approach.

The *Outcomes* of doing this properly will include ongoing proactive engagement (both vertically and horizontally through the organization), behaviors and interactions that align with and actively promote organizational Core Principles, and an ever-growing sense of *one team*, which promotes ownership, efficiency, and reliability.

During the *Leadership Learning* session(s), the Leadership Team(s) will develop and implement their Code(s) of Honor. This serves to 'cement' the learnings into leadership team member behaviors, wherein each team member agrees to be accountable to the Code. If you need to review the concepts behind the Code of Honor, see Chapter Six.

Everyone Learning

Upon completion of the *Leadership Learning*, the *Everyone Learning* sessions commence. This sequencing is important. The worst possible thing you could do (which unfortunately happens frequently in the 'old school' methodology) is to provide frontline workers with new perspectives while the leadership team carries on 'business as usual'.

It is critical that <u>everyone</u> attend this level of learning. This is why it's called *Everyone Learning*. This includes senior leadership (and everyone else who attended the *Leadership Learning* sessions). By doing this, your leadership team members gain a whole new appreciation and respect for frontline perspectives. In addition, when workers see that leaders are participating in these sessions, it will reinforce that this is *real*, and that it is *important*. This goes a long way toward promoting rapid initial behavior change. It also promotes the sense of *one team*, which is vital to achieving and sustaining next-level performance.

A primary purpose of the *Everyone Learning* sessions is to expand the *context* of the members of your organization, and to develop Third-Dimension Thinking (see Chapter Two). Participants come to better understand themselves and their co-workers, which leads to more productive and effective interaction and cooperation. During these sessions, the Error Elimination Tools™ are presented, including the expectations for their use while doing work. The concept of Peer Leadership is also developed and experienced.

Members of natural work teams should attend the *Everyone Learning* session together. Doing so will have a tremendous impact upon the sense of purpose and camaraderie of the team members. During these sessions, each natural work team develops its own Code of Honor. The Code of Honor (as detailed in Chapter Six) directly promotes ownership, Peer Leadership, and Proactive

Accountability®. Team members will agree to be accountable to their Code, which (following the learning that has taken place) will directly align with and promote organizational Core Principles.

Our experience has shown that when implemented properly, the *Outcomes* of the *Everyone Learning* sessions can be close to miraculous. Natural work teams transform their working culture essentially 'on the spot'. A culture of *desire* (versus *compliance)* is initiated. Team members begin doing the 'right' things because they *want* to, including use of the Error Elimination Tools™ while performing tasks. The sense of *ownership* that develops greatly enhances commitment and morale. Peer Leadership and Proactive Accountability® become the predominate behaviors. Since each natural work team Code of Honor essentially contains a set of *natural principles*, behaviors are aligned across the organization. This serves to grow a sense of *one team* on an ongoing basis, and directly reinforces the Core Principles of the organization.

Performance Improvement Team (PIT) Learning

Human Performance proves as well as anything I have ever seen that…gravity works. This is seen through the forces of *drift, accumulation, and organizational entropy*, as discussed in Chapter Nine. No matter how brilliant your initial implementation, some amount of positive energy must continually be 'pumped into' your performance improvement efforts in order to sustain an upward momentum. Enter the *Performance Improvement Team (PIT)*.

In the Practicing Perfection® approach, what we have done is to discuss the concept of the PIT during each of the learning sessions. We ask those for whom the next-level approach truly resonates to volunteer to become part of the team to 'keep it alive'. A list of volunteers is accumulated throughout the learning sessions. We typically see 15-25% of the participants volunteer. Once the final *Everyone Learning* session is completed, the volunteers are notified, and a *Performance Improvement Team (PIT) Learning* session is conducted.

During the *PIT Learning* session, the volunteers are provided with additional understanding, insights, and tools for promoting ongoing awareness. They learn how to conduct promotion and recognition campaigns (such as on-the-spot awards). In addition, they brainstorm their initial project(s) (maximum of three), including who will lead each effort and initial target dates and deliverables.

The ongoing efforts of the volunteer PIT members generate *Outcomes* of positive energy to directly overcome *organizational entropy*. While typically focused on specific issues or opportunities of their choosing, the 'projects' implemented by your PIT directly bolster the *sustainability* of performance improvement. And of course, since all PIT efforts align with the individual Codes of Honor and support/reinforce organizational Core Principles, a sense of *one team* continues to grow.

The PIT must be kept to a reasonable size in order for it to be effective. In many organizations, we have seen many more volunteers than can be effectively assembled into one team. For a large organization at one geographical location, you may elect to have more than one PIT (based upon building, etc.). Another option is to rotate volunteers for periods of service (for example, twelve months), after which a portion of new volunteers are given the opportunity to serve. Such rotation can provide an injection of new energy and insight to the process. Another important point to note is that the PIT cannot be too far removed from the frontline. In other words, a large organization having multiple facilities should have a separate PIT at each facility, rather than a 'corporate' PIT that 'serves all'. Keeping it close to home promotes ownership, and will be much more effective at addressing local issues and maximizing local opportunities.

IMPLEMENT & SUSTAIN

All the learning in the world is useless without correspondent action. The *Leadership* and *Everyone Learning* experiences will shift context and attitudes; however, certain processes and systems will greatly support and reinforce desired behaviors, as well as provide the means to monitor progress. These processes and systems are shown in the following figure.

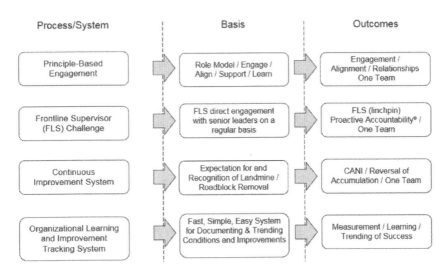

**Human Performance Blueprint
Level II- Processes & Systems**

As can be seen in the figure, the Blueprint for Processes and Systems is also divided into three segments, much like that for the Learning Blueprint. In this case, the three segments are:

- *Process/System* (the ongoing processes and systems that directly support the context and insights gained in the *Learning* sessions, including each of the four elements of the HU Factor®)
- *Basis* (why each process/system exists)
- *Outcomes* (the impact upon / input to organizational success provided by each process/system)

There are two processes and two systems used to ideally support next-level performance:

- *Principle-Based Engagement-* this term relates to ongoing on-purpose engagement between defined leaders and workers that is based upon organizational Core Principles. A defined approach for doing so, Principle-Based Mentoring™ is detailed in Chapter Nine.
- *Frontline Supervisor (FLS) Challenge-* this process places a tremendous amount of Proactive Accountability® directly on the shoulders of the organizational performance linchpin, the FLS. It is a regular opportunity for frontline supervisors to present to / interact with organization senior leadership.
- *Continuous Improvement System-* a defined system for both expecting and recognizing worker involvement in making things better
- *Organizational Learning and Improvement Tracking System-* a fast, simple, and easy-to-use system for documenting, tracking, and trending 'conditions'/issues, as well as proactive actions taken to make things better, such as digging up *landmines* and removing *roadblocks* (reversal of *accumulation*).

Principle-Based Engagement

This is a process of actively engaging team members in a manner that directly role models, reinforces, and supports organizational Core Principles. Once learning sessions are completed and Codes of Honor are in place, this will be a natural element of *doing* what has been *learned.*

In addition to ongoing interaction and engagement during the normal course of business, the defined process of Principle-Based Mentoring™ provides the next-level alternative to the old-school 'observation and coaching' methodology. The Principle-Based Mentoring™ process is detailed in Chapter Nine.

Collectively, Principle-Based Engagement and Principle-Based Mentoring™ promote organizational alignment, directly oppose the forces of *drift*, *accumulation*, and *organizational entropy*, and offer the most powerful method through which to grow relationships and the sense of *one team*. These are the next-level mechanisms through which you address the third element of the HU Factor®- Engagement.

Frontline Supervisor (FLS) Challenge

Patterned after the Work-out Sessions utilized by Jack Welch at General Electric,[2] the FLS Challenge Process is a structured approach for regularly challenging and formally communicating with the linchpins of your organizational performance- your frontline supervisors. It is designed to be a Proactive Accountability® session, where the FLS has the opportunity to present the performance of his/her team, and to demonstrate efforts to continuously improve. The presentation is made to a board of organization senior leaders.

The process should be set up such that each FLS periodically (recommended twice per year), uses a standardized format to present the human performance of his/her team to a "board" of (3) senior organization leaders. It is an opportunity for the FLS to showcase the proactive measures taken by the team to improve human performance, as well as to address actions taken in response to errors, etc. It serves to keep human performance in the forefront of the supervisor's priorities on an ongoing basis. It also promotes organizational alignment, and offers a great opportunity to recognize the organization's next-level priorities while reinforcing the *one team* approach.

When it comes time for him/her to present, the FLS will prepare a standard six-slide PowerPoint presentation, which he/she will present to the board. When scheduling, a 30-minute window should be allotted for each presentation, which breaks down as follows:

- <u>Ten minutes</u> for the FLS to present (during which board members take notes and do NOT interrupt)

- Ten minutes for Q&A between the board members and the FLS
- Ten minutes to close out and prepare for the subsequent presentation

During a given FLS presentation, his/her manager(s) are to be present. This provides for vertical accountability, while the "reporting" is coming from the leadership level closest to the actual work. The other supervisors reporting on that day should be present for all scheduled presentations. This provides an excellent opportunity for cross-functional learning and awareness.

A primary benefit of the FLS Challenge process is that it provides an opportunity for regular dialogue between senior leadership and the frontline supervisors. This promotes common awareness and understanding, helping to align the organization and promote *one team*.

Once the Q&A portion of each presentation comes to conclusion, a final question is asked of the FLS by the senior leader of the board: "*What can we do for you to help make your job easier?*" Upon completion of a FLS Challenge session being conducted at a nuclear power facility a few years ago, an electrical supervisor was asked this question by the Site VP. The supervisor replied, "As supervisors, we have a lot of paperwork to do. We've been provided with small desks on which to work, and in the middle of these desks are large computer monitors. Quite honestly, there is no desk space left upon which to do our paperwork. I've been back and forth with IT for months, asking them to replace our old monitors with flat screens so that we can have space to do our paperwork." Within two weeks of that FLS Challenge session, all maintenance department supervisors had flat screen monitors on their desks. Cost to the company? Minimal. Benefit to the relationship between that VP and the supervisors (not to mention the advancement of *one team*)? Priceless.

If you would like an overview of the PPI FLS Challenge process, including a downloadable set of PowerPoint presentation template slides, go here: http://www.6hoursafetyculture.com/fls/

Continuous Improvement System

While the concept is great, the term *continuous improvement* has unfortunately been overused and abused by many. It's also been around so long that it sounds like 'old news'. In 1996, while I was doing consulting work at the Vermont Yankee Nuclear Plant (VY), the organization adopted a *continuous improvement* system dubbed "CPI" (Continuous Process Improvement). As I came to understand it, I realized that it was simple to manage and extremely effective. It directly taps into and leverages Precept #3 (*People come to work wanting to do a good job*), and Precept #4 (*The people who do the work are the ones who have the answers*).

The company who designed and helped implement the process was Conway Management, founded by Bill Conway in Nashua, New Hampshire in 1983[3]. The way it was implemented at VY was brilliant. All organization members (including bargaining unit employees) were required (per employee expectations and appraisals) to participate. In addition, each time an employee did participate, he/she received an on-the-spot award. The process was so effective that when VY was purchased by Entergy a few years later, Entergy decided to implement the approach fleet-wide, calling it "ECI" (Entergy Continuous Improvement). When we put the Practicing Perfection® approach together, we included a very similar process as part of the implementation, calling it "PPCI" (Practicing Perfection® Continuous Improvement).

Your organization likely has some initiative/program in place to promote and recognize efforts to continuously improve. Rather than describe "CPI" or "PPCI", I simply want to provide you with some things to think about relative to your own efforts in this regard. Things to consider for a next-level *continuous improvement* process include:

- Do not solicit nor reward mere ideas. Reward only documented actions and results.
- Workers at all levels should be empowered to make changes using appropriate channels

- All changes made should be documented as appropriate for your organization (proceduralized, properly referenced, etc.)
- The cost savings, safety improvement, quality/efficiency improvement, human error reduction, etc. should be calculated and included in the presentation for award
- While controls are necessary to ensure appropriate successes, the process for acquiring approval should be simple and expeditious
- The format for presentation for approval should also be simple, consisting of four or five standard PowerPoint slides
- The process should allow for biasing of 'points' based upon significance. For example, a success involving cost savings might be worth one point, while a success that removes a legitimate *landmine* (safety / human error issue) might be worth three points. This allows you to bias the system to increase employee focus in a given area. Biasing of points should reviewed annually to account for any shifts in priorities.
- Every worker should be required to participate in at least one success per year (via the performance appraisal process or whatever means is in place within your organization)
- Points should roll up through the organization. For example, a team of eight people might be responsible for 12 points in a given year, with the team supervisor accountable for her team's 12 points. The department to which the team belongs, with 4 teams and 36 people, might be responsible for 50 points, for which the department head is personally accountable. This should roll all the way to the top of the organization, and should be included in annual goals and associated targets and bonus calculations.
- The individual on-the-spot award should have tangible value, but more as a token of appreciation and recognition than of financial significance. As an example, a $25 gift card has been used by many for this purpose.
- Points should be sharable between departments/disciplines. For example, a specific effort might require both Operations and Engineering expertise. If the success was worth 3 points,

and involved an Operator and an Engineer, the award of points should be split between the associated Operations Crew/Department, and the participating Engineer's team/department. If the effort of each was equal, each team/department would be awarded 1.5 points.
- Points acquired by each department should be reported out regularly at weekly/monthly leadership meetings

Organizational Learning and Improvement Tracking System

As I previously indicated, my last 'job' had the title of *Corrective Action Manager*. While my role included a variety of responsibilities, a large percentage of our department's resources were devoted to managing and administering the site's *Corrective Action Program*. This was an extensive database used for the entry, tracking, trending, and documentation of resolution of *conditions* (actions, occurrences, or 'things' that did not have the desired outcome or did not meet expectations). In US nuclear power plants, such a system is required by the Nuclear Regulatory Commission (NRC).

An entire book could be written on this topic alone. Based upon my experience, here are a few things to consider if you have such a system or are considering purchasing/implementing one:

- The system should be fast, simple and easy to use, including entry of information and generation of reports
- All employees should have access to enter information
- All employees should be able to run reports
- A consistent and effective coding methodology must be used to provide for reporting, tracking and trending. Specific codes must be narrow enough to provide specific appropriate insight, yet broad enough such that there will be enough data in each 'bin' to alert to trends.
- Remember- the system is a tool. The focus should never become about the system itself. If you're confused about this, re-read the sections on the *Shiny Box Syndrome* and *Analoculitis* in Chapter Two.

In addition to a system meeting the above requirements, in order for any reporting system to be effective, an open, trusting, non-punitive *culture* must exist. If you have questions on this, review the section on *Just Culture* in Chapter Seven.

Key Insights from Chapter Ten

1. All progress begins by telling the truth- before you begin any efforts to improve performance, first identify *why* you're doing so, and then identify specific gaps between where you are and where you want to be.

2. If you are to transform your culture, you must be willing to invest in a requisite amount of worker training/learning at *all* levels

3. There is no 'cookie cutter' recipe; however, there are vital elements that must be included in a specific sequence in order to maximize your success. These elements are detailed in the Human Performance Blueprint, which can be downloaded here: http://www.6hoursafetyculture.com/resources/hpbp/

4. *Thinking Different* is not enough. You also must *Do Different.* Two processes and two systems (yep, only two and two) should be implemented to help promote, sustain, and measure your successes.

5. Ensure that you do not succumb to either the *Shiny Box Syndrome* or *Analoculitis* when choosing, implementing, or using your systems for performance improvement.

What can you do with what you just learned?

A. Download and study the detailed Human Performance Blueprint: http://www.6hoursafetyculture.com/resources/hpbp/

B. Watch the video, download the worksheet, and complete your Transformation Conversation to determine your *why* prior to going any further with your implementation. (http://ppiweb.com/future-performance-improvement/pursuing-excellence/)

C. Clearly identify your *Core Principles* (see Chapter Nine)

D. Use the detailed Blueprint acquired in Step A as a guide to plot your course of action

---

[1] *Firms of Endearment: How World-Class Companies Profit from Passion and Purpose*; Raj Sisodia, Jag Sheth, David B. Wolfe; Second Edition; Pearson Education; 2014

[2] *Implementation of a Work-Out program using the General Electric approach*; https://sta.uwi.edu/eng/ie/documents/P02_Andre_GEWork-Out-Nov921.pdf

[3] *About Us*; Conway Management; http://www.conwaymanagement.com/

Epilogue:

> *"I now have a very simple metric I use: are you working on something that can change the world? Yes or no? The answer for 99.99999 percent of people is 'no'. I think we need to be training people on how to change the world."*
> -Larry Page (co-founder of Google)

Whether you realize it or not, you are, at this very moment, standing on the edge of future- your personal future, the future of your organization, ultimately the future of the planet.

As I hope you have recognized, the information provided in *6-Hour Safety Culture* is about far more than *safety culture*, *quality*, *reliability*, minimizing *risk*, or the simple *reduction of human error*. The insights, strategies, and tactics provided are ultimately about transforming context, perspectives, lives, and organizational culture. They're about leveraging the most precious resources on planet earth- the persistent and passionate human mind, and the positive intrinsic aspects of Human Nature.

Larry Page's quote at the beginning of this section was part of an impromptu speech he delivered to approximately 150 people at the founding event for Singularity University at the NASA Ames Research Center in September, 2008. My ultimate intent in writing this book has been to help you better understand how you can help change the world through a focus on *human performance*. Are you open and willing to being part of the '.00001 percent'?

If your answer is *yes*, take heed. Strong forces remain at play in many organizations. New ideas, ideas that can indeed transform culture and ultimately 'change the world', are often acknowledged, met with initial enthusiasm, and then die in the pit of corporate bureaucracy. I've personally witnessed *enlightened leaders* whose forward long-term thinking has been swiftly shut down by the corporate egg-head bean-counters who reduce everything to [short-term] numbers. The 'experts' get involved. Intentions become mired in the 'need' for data, in-depth analysis, and phrases that only those with an MBA and an IQ of 180 can understand. Everything gets bounced against the 3-month bottom line quarterly report. Perhaps…later. After all, we've got day-to-day business to run. Fires to fight. New regulations to deal with. We simply can't justify the cost. Business as usual. Nothing substantially changes.

The short-term and long-term consequences of the choices you make (and actions you take) are typically different and often opposite. There are still those whose prominent focus is upon the 'bottom line', who believe the primary purpose of business is to make as much money as possible (on a quarterly basis). While profits are essential, this is like saying that since we need red blood cells to live, the purpose of life is to make red blood cells. And those so-called 'experts'? In the corporate world, it's been my experience that most 'experts' are those who can best articulate why something *can't* be done. Ten years from now, more than 40 percent of today's 'top' companies will no longer exist.[1] Any ideas why that might be?

It will take guts. You'll likely find yourself swimming against strong currents of bureaucratic resolve and stagnated thinking. Be bold. As Ambrose Redmond put it, *"Courage is not the absence of fear, but rather the judgment that something else is more important than fear."* Leaders such as you who have the courage to stand up to the 'bean counters' and corporate 'experts' can (and will) move their organizations rapidly and sustainably to qualities of outcome and levels of work satisfaction never before imagined. The 'number crunchers' will [ultimately] be happy. The 'experts' will [reluctantly] revise their thinking. And as this occurs in organization upon organization, the 'world', over time, will indeed become a better place.

Standing on the shoulders of many of the greatest minds in leadership, psychology, neuroscience, and human error, I have provided you with the 'recipe' for achieving your 'magical upward spiral' of performance improvement. When properly implemented, this recipe for achieving and sustaining next-level human performance saves lives, keeps people from getting hurt, prevents physical and environmental catastrophe, improves efficiency, reliability, and quality. All of these ultimately serve you, the employees of your organization, your customers, and your shareholders.

The day before something is recognized as a *breakthrough*, it is often cast off as a 'crazy idea'. Indeed you will discover that, in addition to all of the qualitative benefits mentioned above, *human performance* and *profitability* do indeed go hand in hand.

The world is yearning for *leadership*- those who have the courage to defend and act decisively on their convictions. Thanks for having the guts to move forward, to recognize your higher purpose, for doing your part to help make the world a better and safer place.

Please let us know how we may serve in helping you do so.

http://www.6hoursafetyculture.com

http://www.hpaweb.org

http://www.ppiweb.com

---

[1] Babson Olin School of Business, *Fast Company*, April, 2011 (pg 121)

Made in the USA
Lexington, KY
18 July 2017